JIM CROW'S LAST STAND

JIM CROW'S LAST STAND

NONUNANIMOUS CRIMINAL JURY VERDICTS IN LOUISIANA

THOMAS AIELLO

UPDATED EDITION

LOUISIANA STATE UNIVERSITY PRESS

BATON ROUGE

Published by Louisiana State University Press
Copyright © 2015 by Louisiana State University Press
New material © copyright 2019 by Louisiana State University Press
All rights reserved
Manufactured in the United States of America
Louisiana Paperback Edition, 2019

DESIGNER: *Mandy McDonald Scallan*
TYPEFACE: *Whitman*
PRINTER AND BINDER: *LSI*

Library of Congress Cataloging-in-Publication Data

Names: Aiello, Thomas, 1977– author.
Title: Jim Crow's last stand : nonunanimous criminal jury verdicts in
 Louisiana / Thomas Aiello.
Description: Updated edition. | Louisiana paperback edition. | Baton Rouge :
 Louisiana State University Press, 2019. | Includes bibliographical
 references and index.
Identifiers: LCCN 2019005202| ISBN 978-0-8071-7237-7 (pbk. : alk. paper) | ISBN
 978-0-8071-7252-0 (pdf) | ISBN 978-0-8071-7253-7 (epub)
Subjects: LCSH: Jury—Louisiana—History—20th century. | Discrimination in
 criminal justice administration—Louisiana—History—20th century.
Classification: LCC KFL581 .A945 2019 | DDC 345.763/056—dc23

The paper in this book meets the guidelines for permanence and durability of the
Committee on Production Guidelines for Book Longevity of the Council on Library
Resources. ∞

Pearl Harbor put Jim Crow on the Run.
That Crow can't fight for Democracy
And be the same old Crow he used to be—
Although right now, even yet today,
He tries to act the same old way.
But India and China and Harlem, too,
Have made up their minds Jim Crow is through.

—LANGSTON HUGHES, "Jim Crow's Last Stand" (1943)

CONTENTS

PREFACE TO THE UPDATED EDITION

The Sabine Parish courthouse has no metal detector. It is the first thing one notices when walking into the quaint but still imposing edifice in tiny Many, Louisiana, itself quaint and imposing in its own way. I traveled there in July 2018 to testify in an appeal of the second-degree murder conviction of Melvin Maxie, a conviction attendant with a variety of procedural inconsistencies, but also attendant with a nonunanimous jury conviction. That was why I was there.

In the days and weeks prior, I had been brushing up on the subject in aid of serving as an expert witness in Maxie's appeal, rereading old files and discovering some of the amazing new work on nonunanimous jury trials produced since the original publication of *Jim Crow's Last Stand* in 2015. I was in regular contact with Richard Bourke, director of the Louisiana Capital Assistance Center, a nonprofit that provides legal defense services to indigent defendants charged with capital crimes. This case, however, was different. Melvin Maxie was not on death row. But Bourke had taken over his appeal and in the process decided, like so many before him, to take on Maxie's nonunanimous jury conviction as part of his argument for a new trial.

The plan was to deal specifically with the opinion in *State v. Hankton* (2013), in which judge Dennis J. Waldron argued that "the revision of a less-than-unanimous jury requirement in the 1974 Constitution was not by routine incorporation of the previous Constitution's provisions." To the contrary, "the new article was the subject of a fair amount of debate. In that debate no mention was made of race. The stated purpose behind the latest iteration of the less-than-unanimous jury verdict provision is judicial efficiency." On top of that, he argued, the 1974 constitution was submitted for a popular vote.[1]

It was an interesting argument but not one particularly difficult to disprove. Waldron reasoned that Louisiana's change from 9–3 majority verdicts to 10–2 majority verdicts in 1974 abrogated the original racist intent of the 1898 constitution that created the nonunanimous standard because the 1973 convention that created the new formula was not overtly proclaiming white supremacy. The problem with such a claim was that it ignored history and context. It ignored the racial realities of early 1970s Louisiana. It ignored that the starting point for all discussions of the nonunanimous jury provision in 1973 began with the original standard as it had been formed in 1898, and re-formed in 1913 and 1921. And it wrongly assumed that the promotion of a provision with original racist intent and clear racialized outcomes by someone along the way who did not happen to be particularly racist could make that provision somehow equitable.

In the course of reviewing materials to help make the case against such reasoning, I discovered a wealth of new information that had been published by legal scholars since the first appearance of *Jim Crow's Last Stand*. It was information that sometimes validated the claims of the book, and other times demonstrated that more needed to be said, that there were holes in my original account. The first edition of this book, for example, virtually ignores the role of Gilded Age black jury service as a motivating factor in the creation of the nonunanimous jury constitutional provision in 1898 and the implications of that role in the context of the nineteenth-century debate. It also ignores some of the racial context of the 1970s that would help respond to Waldron's *Hankton* opinion.

It also could not help but leave out the legal developments since its original publication. In March 2018, state senator J. P. Morrell introduced a bill to amend the Louisiana constitution requiring unanimous juries for all criminal verdicts. It was successful in early June, and the amendment went on the ballot in November. Grassroots organizers canvassed the state. Former Grant Parish district attorney Ed Tarpley campaigned tirelessly for the amendment. The Unanimous Jury Coalition formed chapters in New Orleans, Lafayette, Baton Rouge, and Shreveport. The issue gained bipartisan support across the state and ultimately, seemingly miraculously, passed by a wide margin.

The night before my testimony at the Sabine Parish courthouse, I met with Bourke, legal scholar Thomas Ward Frampton, who was also testifying, and a group of dedicated clerks in a first-floor motel room in Natchitoches. There were files stacked around the room, a printer in front of the television. I sat on the bed closest to window. The air conditioning unit next to me blasted a cool breeze into a room that would have otherwise been heavy with the heat of the Louisiana summer and the apprehension of the next day's events. We rehearsed the history of nonunanimous criminal jury verdicts, the line of questioning, the strategy of testimony. The others in the cramped motel room were used to such plottings, to the intensity of the night before a trial. But it was my first time. I told them all, giddy with anticipation, that I felt like I was in a scene from *A Few Good Men*, the one with Tom Cruise stalking around with a baseball bat as the defense team debated ideas and scribbled on a whiteboard in preparation for the impending trial.

Except that this was not fiction. Melvin Maxie was waiting in jail, a brief respite from the prison cell he normally called home, a grim reality only because his trial had happened in Louisiana. If it had taken place across the state line in Texas, a 10–2 verdict would have given him another opportunity. But this was Louisiana. I walked back out into the hot July night, back to my own motel room, to do more reading before the next day's events.

My wife and I got to the courtroom early, anticipating a longer drive to Many, a small town thirty miles west of Natchitoches. Walking into a courthouse without a metal detector made her nervous, but I liked the more welcoming atmosphere. Where one might normally see signposts of diligence in other courthouses, here there were a few scattered magazines and a plastic bag filled with soda can pull tabs. We sat patiently in the hallway where the bailiff reassured us that the courtroom would open shortly. He smiled and confirmed we were in the right place.

We entered when the courtroom finally opened. There was a sign on the door warning everyone who entered that no food, drink, chewing gum, or cell phones were allowed inside, but everyone was eating, drinking, chewing gum, and staring into cell phones. It was the relaxed atmosphere infused with the tension of a life hanging in the balance that one might expect in a courthouse without a metal detector. We sat and stared at the wood-paneled walls as Maxie's family made its way into the room, sitting in the rows in front of us. Then Maxie himself came in, chained at the wrists and ankles, wearing an orange jumpsuit but smiling at those who came to see him that day.

It was an all-day affair. First was testimony-by-conference-call by a reporter from the *New Orleans Advocate*, who had been part of a massive research project by the paper to analyze the effect of the nonunanimous jury standard in the state, producing a wealth of damning evidence that nonunanimity created significant racial disparities in convictions and jury deliberations. Then it was my turn. Then Frampton's. We answered Bourke's questions, then those of the prosecution. Looming over everyone was the realization that in November, there would be a statewide vote to end the practice that we were all debating.

But there was something else looming as well. Someone in front of us had on a Sabine Parish youth baseball league T-shirt. We could only see the back of it, with all the names of the players dutifully listed in white on a red background. Among the Thompsons and Smiths, it was hard not to notice the name Maxie. This was a family that was embedded in the community, a large clan in a small town, with at least a dozen members willing to take time off work to come to the courthouse for a glimpse of their brother, cousin, uncle, loved one.

"Oh my God," my wife whispered. "Take a closer look at the bailiff when he walks past again."

He had the same open, friendly smile with which he had greeted us in the early morning, his brown uniform neat and imposing, as are all the outfits of law enforcement, his gun threatening but not a threat. Then I saw it. His nametag. MAXIE.

It was to both of us somehow even more troubling than everything else we had seen that day, a grand demonstration of the devastating horror that nonunanimous juries could cause. I walked out of the courtroom that day, drove away from Many and Sabine Parish, knowing that I needed to write this updated edition of *Jim Crow's Last Stand*.

In the fall, I gave a series of speeches at universities in the state in an effort to draw awareness to the issue before the upcoming November vote. Students at McNeese, Louisiana-Lafayette, LSU, Louisiana Tech, and ULM were engaged and interested in the subject, but what was most surprising was that though the bulk of them were from Louisiana, they did not know that nonunanimous criminal juries existed. Why would they? If no one close to them interacted with the criminal justice system, they would have no reason to know. The state never advertised its system publicly and instead allowed generations of unsuspecting Louisianans to discover it only at their most vulnerable moment. Norris Henderson, a former inmate in the Louisiana penal system, wrongly convicted on a 10–2 verdict and later exonerated after serving decades in prison, explained on a Louisiana-Lafayette panel that when he heard the jury's 10–2 decision, relief washed over him. He thought he was free. Then the harsh reality of the next two decades came crashing down.

Future Norris Hendersons, however, will have a better chance at justice. More than 64 percent of voters approved Louisiana's new unanimous jury amendment. Jim Crow's last stand finally fell to defeat. That said, the new amendment is not retroactive, so appeals of criminal convictions prior to January 1, 2019, will still be ongoing. Oregon, the only other state to include nonunanimous criminal juries as part of its justice system, immediately witnessed its lawmakers announce plans for repeal of its own standard, leaders not wanting to be the only state remaining that does not acknowledge unanimity as the bedrock of fairness in criminal justice.

In this updated and expanded edition, I have added a new chapter at the end of the book, building on the amazing research done by Frampton, Kyle R. Satterfield, Angela A. Allen-Bell, the team of reporters at the *New Orleans Advocate*, and others, discussing in particular the role of black jury service as a motivating factor for the 1898 constitutional convention, the problematic racial effects of the nonunanimous jury standard still in effect today, and the amendment process that led to Louisiana's new unanimity standard.

As Melvin Maxie walked from the courtroom that day, he turned and smiled and thanked me for my testimony, then he was led away in chains. I smiled back and tried to nod reassuringly, knowing it was a fool's errand, then I went the other way, out of the courtroom, down the steps, and out the front door, past no metal detector at all, and into the bright sunshine. Neither of us had been convicted of a crime by a unanimous jury of our peers, but I was the one free to leave.

There but for the grace of God go I.

There but for the grace of God go we all.

PREFACE TO THE 2015 EDITION

Louisiana still lives under a Jim Crow law. This is not a statement about the evolution of racism in the wake of civil rights and Black Power. It isn't a statement about the more esoteric problems of race-related realty abuses and housing prices; nor is it a statement about drug laws or the state of Louisiana prisons. There is no doubt that, even after the Civil Rights Act of 1964 and the Voting Rights Act of 1965 eliminated the racist mistakes of southern legislatures by ending state-sanctioned segregation and voting restrictions, racism still exists. School segregation suits still litter the courts, fueled by a residential segregation much harder to attack. And though all citizens can now vote without fear of reprisal, legislators still gerrymander electoral districts to devalue the votes of minorities. Still, though they depend indirectly on a legacy granted them by the post-Reconstruction era, those are the modern problems of the modern South.

There is a modern law that has a far more direct connection to the late-nineteenth century period of Redemption. Beginning in 1880, Louisiana allowed criminal defendants to be convicted by nine of twelve jurors. Today it allows them to be convicted by ten. It was a law designed to increase convictions to feed the state's burgeoning convict lease system and remained in the first half of the segregationist twentieth century even after convict lease had run its course. As rights advocates of the 1950s and 1960s successfully challenged the ingrained racism of southern laws first conceived in the crucible of turn-of-the-century reactionary politics, they left nonunanimous criminal jury verdicts alone. The law is, among southern states, unique to Louisiana. Many never realized the law existed. Those who did were unaware of the law's genesis, its original purpose, or its modern consequences. And so it remained. It still remains. It is the last active law of racist Redeemer politics in Louisiana.

The 1972 U.S. Supreme Court decision *Johnson v. Louisiana* (1972), which narrowly validated the state's criminal conviction policy, was born in Bourbon Louisiana. Its staying power has been demonstrated through constant legal challenge in the early twentieth century, its success in the Supreme Court, and its evolving role in modern criminal convictions in the late twentieth and early twenty-first centuries.

That said, this is not the stuff of law reviews and legal journals. Nonunanimous criminal jury verdicts have been gamely defended by Michael H. Glasser in the *Florida State University Law Review* and expertly criticized by Kate Riordan in the *Journal of Criminal Law and Criminology*. While those articles parse the various constitutional questions posed by nonunanimous criminal jury verdicts, they make no attempt to understand such laws in historical context and how that context bears on the function of those laws in practice over time. Certainly such constitutional questions are evaluated in the pages that follow, but that evaluation is situated against the backdrop of Louisiana's racial legacy and the evolution of its criminal jury laws over the course of the state's existence.

This is a work of history, not a political treatise. In every history of civil rights, however, no matter the claims of objectivity, there are inherent moral judgments that make themselves clear. No historian, for example, pretends that segregated bus depots were the result of neutral and understandable laws in the context of their time. No historian pretends that the assaults on Freedom Riders who entered those bus depots were battles between equals, each of whom had their own legitimate vested interests in the outcomes. Rather, in the course of an objective explanation of events, historians tease out a subjective argument about right and wrong, better and worse. Tactics are evaluated, strategies are critiqued, but everyone leaves the reading with the same impression of whom the good guys and the bad guys are.

The fallacy of early twentieth-century segregation laws was that, in service to racist assumptions, southern legislatures limited white development as much as they did black development because, as so many sociological studies have demonstrated, interracial contact tends to benefit everyone. Likewise, nonunanimous criminal jury verdicts were passed in service to those same racist assumptions. And they still have significant racial implications both for criminal defendants and for jurors. But they affect everyone. Anyone charged with a crime in Louisiana is more likely to be convicted than in any other state, save Oregon (which also has a nonunanimous criminal jury standard), by a factor of one in six. If someone is charged with a crime on the western bank of the Mississippi River, he or she has a 17 percent better chance of being convicted than if charged on the eastern bank, because the state of Mississippi requires jury unanimity. If a white man is charged with the murder of a black man in Louisiana, he has a 17 percent better chance of being convicted than if he had been charged with a hate crime under federal law, because the federal government requires jury unanimity. When it actually benefits Louisiana criminal defendants to be charged with hate crimes, the system is fundamentally flawed.

The history of nonunanimous criminal jury verdicts acts as its own advocate for ending the practice. What is most surprising about the Louisiana jury standard is that very few people outside of the legal profession seem to know that it exists. We live in a world of John Grisham novels and *Law and Order* episodes, where plots hinge on creating reasonable doubt in the mind of one juror, and so that standard becomes the common and reasonable assumption. But if a Louisiana defense attorney can't create reasonable doubt in the mind of *three* jurors, then the defendant will be convicted. Louisiana doesn't obey the rules of *Law and Order*, and that reality has fundamentally shaped its ability to maintain law and order.

I would like to thank Michael Martin, Shannon Frystak, Mary Farmer-Kaiser, and the students who came to hear us speak at the University of Louisiana at Lafayette for helping to clarify some of my thoughts on this project. Likewise, the members of the Louisiana Historical Association, Mary Howell, Gregory Richard, and Natalie J. Ring also provided valuable commentary. Thank you also to Hill Memorial Library at Louisiana State University, and, as always, to Madison French, Carol Fuller, and Pete Aiello for being who you are.

JIM CROW'S LAST STAND

CHAPTER 1

The Plight of Frank Johnson

It was a clear, sunny day on December 26, 1967. It was cool, but the temperature stayed in the high fifties for most of the day, making work that much more comfortable for Eugene Frischertz, who was frustrated but resigned to be working the day after Christmas. He watched the day prior as local headlines were dominated by the undefeated Wyoming Cowboys arriving in New Orleans for the Sugar Bowl, where they would take on the locals from LSU.[1]

Frischertz lived in Metairie, but came into the city every morning to drive a Coca Cola Bottling Company delivery truck. He was on edge that day after Christmas. His morning rounds had gone as planned, but he was aware, like all of the city's delivery drivers were aware, that there had been a spate of truck robberies in 1967, and worried that his might be next.[2]

The Sugar Bowl saturated the time and energy of the local media through much of December—and it permeated the thinking of Eugene Frischertz, as well—but buried in the back pages of the newspaper for much of the year were the robberies, a seeming epidemic that affected the drivers of local trucks and public buses. The Robbery Division of the New Orleans Police Department's Detective Bureau had been engaged in a broad investigation of a problem that plagued the city for most of 1967 and would continue to plague it for much of 1968.

It was in March 1967 when two black men robbed an Imperial Trading Company truck, kidnapping the driver and taking six hundred dollars "and an undetermined amount of cigarettes." The driver escaped, but the robbery was an early incident in a growing spree across New Orleans. Robberies in April more than doubled over the same month in 1966, from 75 to 163. And the trend showed no signs of abating. On May 22, for example, two bus drivers and a truck driver were robbed at knifepoint, the three separate incidents among many by "Negro thugs" who seemed to be perpetually patrolling the streets. Most of the time, the robbers were after the cash drivers kept on them following product deliveries. Sometimes they just wanted products. In August, a black gunman robbed a New Orleans Beverage Agency truck for "$104 in whiskey." Whatever the individual choices of the city's truck thieves, they were still robbing truck drivers after summer's end. The crime spree would continue throughout the rest of the year and into 1968.[3]

Around 3:30 in the afternoon on December 26, Frischertz finished a delivery to Brown's Grocery on Third Street in New Orleans and returned to his Coca-Cola Bottling Company delivery truck. He wasn't nervous, but he was certainly vigilant. He knew the horror stories from his fellow drivers. It had been a difficult year.

He saw the man coming. He was still in front of Brown's when he noticed him in the driver's side mirror. Frischertz had never had a gun in his face before. "We had just finished making this stop at Brown's Grocery and we were getting in our truck," he explained, referring to himself and a coworker, "and we were getting ready to pull away from the curb, I saw this fellow come up, in the rear view mirror of the truck, and it looked— I didn't know his intentions at first—but as he came up to the door of the truck, he brandished this revolver and he asked for all my money." He handed the robber between five hundred and six hundred dollars that belonged to Coca-Cola, and he gave him the thirty-one dollars in his pocket. After the man fled, Frischertz ran back into Brown's and called the police.

The Detective Bureau's Robbery Division had varying degrees of luck on individual robbery cases, but had nothing specifically on the Frischertz case until January 18, 1968, when a confidential informant told his police contact that a black man named Frank Johnson and an accomplice, Harold Hayes, had been robbing truck drivers. Acting on the tip, the police showed photos of Johnson and Hayes to Marion Catalano, a driver for Brown's Velvet Ice Cream. Catalano had been the victim of three armed robberies, beginning in October 1967. The third happened two days prior, on January 16, when "two Negro men walked up" brandishing a gun and demanding his money. The rattled Catalano identified Johnson, and his positive identification was all the police needed.[4]

Just after five o'clock a.m., on January 20, 1968, Frank Thomas Johnson was asleep in his Philip Street home. His wife was asleep beside him, their youngest son and his cousin asleep in the next room. His friend Harold Hayes was sleeping in the living room and was the first to wake when the banging started. "It was a lot of knocking on the door and I got up and I went to the door and I opened the door and they said, 'This is the police.' And so I let them in." The Detective Bureau had finally arrived.[5]

"They went in the first room and turned the mattress up on the bed and into the second room and that is when they woke my wife up and the kids started crying and they went into the third room, which was the room where two smaller kids were and my oldest son," said Johnson. "And my oldest son was sleeping in the front room. He is about eighteen months old. And they all woke up and started crying." Johnson was incredulous. "They questioned me concerning this supposed armed robbery that I allegedly committed and they questioned me at length about various other individuals whose pictures they brought to me to see, and I told them I didn't know anything about any of that."[6] They arrested him anyway.

Three days later, Eugene Frischertz stood in a cold police station behind reflective glass. He watched as seven men walked into the room on the other side of the glass and immediately identified the one in the middle, number four, as the man who had robbed his truck. It was Frank Johnson.[7]

Johnson was tried and convicted not for the Catalano robbery, but for the Frischertz robbery, and his appeal attacked the conviction on several fronts. His arrest, for example, was, Johnson argued, the result of a warrantless search, in violation of the Fourth Amendment. It was also problematic that he was tried for a crime other than that for which he had originally been arrested. But the principal reason for Johnson's appeal was rooted in the Sixth and Fourteenth amendments. The Sixth Amendment ensured defendants a speedy and public trial by an impartial jury. It promised that they would be informed about the accusation, that witnesses against them would confront them, that they could compel witnesses to testify on their behalf, and that they had a right to legal counsel. Section One of the Fourteenth Amendment prohibited states from making laws "which shall abridge the privileges or immunities of the citizens of the United States." No state could deprive a citizen of "life, liberty, or property without due process of law," nor could it deny "the equal protection of the laws."[8]

The twelve trial jurors convicted the defendant with a tally of nine votes to three, depriving Johnson of his liberty with what Louisiana maintained was "due process of law." Article VII, Section 41, of the Louisiana State Constitution of 1921 validated nonunanimous jury verdicts in noncapital criminal proceedings, and the mandate was upheld in congressional legislation and judicial review for the previous nine decades, but the concept seemed inherently problematic. Only Louisiana and Oregon allowed such decisions. Every other state, as well as the federal government, required unanimous verdicts in noncapital criminal proceedings. Even as Johnson waited in lockup, the Louisiana Supreme Court validated the practice yet again—as it had since 1899—until it received "a clear exposition of this point by the Federal Supreme Court."[9]

Johnson v. Louisiana (1972) would make it to the U.S. Supreme Court, tried in conjunction with a similar Oregon appeal, and the outcome validated the legality of nonunanimous criminal jury verdicts.[10] But it didn't end the controversy about the approximate justice they provided for criminal defendants. In the century prior to *Johnson*, appellants had argued that nine-to-three verdicts made it that much easier to convict. The state countered that they also made it that much easier to acquit. Appellants argued that nine-to-three verdicts in noncapital criminal cases overly complicated a system that often tried defendants on multiple counts, including misdemeanors and capital offenses. The state countered that they reduced the number of hung juries, thereby streamlining the system and saving the state money. The Supreme Court was less concerned with such arguments, instead arguing that consistency provided fairness, and fairness was the fundamental bedrock of due process.

In so doing, however, the court did validate the state's arguments about the inherent justice of nonunanimous verdicts, even though the argument that nine-to-three verdicts made it easier to acquit ignored the reality that criminal defense attorneys in other states needed to create reasonable doubt in the mind of only one juror to be successful. That being the case, the controversy over nonunanimous verdicts would remain after the *Johnson* decision. There is, after all, no necessary equivalency between consistency and fairness. Consistency provides process. Fairness provides people their due. However, the assumption that consistency breeds fairness, and thus a reasonable due process, is a mistake of logic that would confuse even as it clarified.

The principle of nonunanimous jury verdicts in noncapital criminal cases was not a unique Louisiana holdover from the Napoleonic Code. It was not a legacy handed down from France or Spain or the Holy See, as were so many of Louisiana's other governmental idiosyncrasies. It was a conservative measure fired in the crucible of the Bourbon restoration following Reconstruction, when white Democrats sought to return their state to some sense of normalcy following federal occupation. The law validating nonunanimous jury verdicts first passed in 1880 and was codified in the Louisiana State Constitution of 1898. It was the era of the Redeemers. It was the era of Jim Crow. And the same leaders reimposing white southern rule and formulating the convict lease system fundamentally changed a process that had been in place since American transfer following the Louisiana Purchase and used it to create more convicts.

CHAPTER 2

The Politics of Transfer

The dominant assumption that Louisiana's criminal jury requirements were holdovers not from Bourbon restoration but instead from its French ancestry falls at the water's edge of American transfer following the Louisiana Purchase. The process of that transfer was complicated. France signed over Louisiana to the United States on October 1, 1800, even though Napoleon didn't actually own Louisiana at the time (he would sign the Treaty of San Ildefonso with Spain the following day, October 2, even though as a component of the treaty he falsely promised not to give the territory to a country that might prove a threat to Spain). On October 20, ten days before the imposed deadline, the U.S. Senate ratified the deal, and a month after that, on November 30, Spain finally transferred Louisiana to France in a New Orleans ceremony. Finally, on December 20, 1803, the French transferred the territory to United States representatives, William C. C. Claiborne and James Wilkinson. Sparked by the deal, Americans rushed to claim land in the new area, but those who had lived under Spanish and French rule were horrified by the transfer. Trading with Protestants was one thing. Answering to them was another. And so the American Congress moved quickly to develop a system of governance for a people who were skeptical at best about being governed.

In March, Congress divided the territory into two sections, Louisiana and Orleans (the territory that would ultimately become the state of Louisiana) and provided a temporary governmental structure for them. "In all criminal prosecutions which are capital," the law stipulated, "the trial shall be by a jury of twelve good and lawful men of the vicinage; and in all cases, criminal and civil, in the superior court, the trial shall be by a jury, if either of the parties require it." Such was the common assumption of American jurisprudence. When a more permanent governmental structure arrived the following March, Congress refined its edict by formalizing a system by which all criminal trials were determined by a twelve-man jury. When the territory became a state in 1812, the locals produced a constitution in line with its territorial forebear. All criminal prosecutions "by indictment or information" required "a speedy public trial by an impartial jury of the vicinage."[1] The twelve-man edict was gone, replaced by an emphasis on the public nature of criminal trials, but the implication of the territorial legislation was still in place: criminal decisions require unanimity.

Such was a valiant start, but broad constitutional provisions were always seen as nothing more than a start. To that end, the Louisiana legislature tapped one of its most accomplished lawyers, a former U.S. attorney and mayor of New York named Edward Livingston.[2] By 1821, Livingston was a member of the state legislature tasked with developing a comprehensive system of penal law. He had a draft in 1824, another in 1826, but his finished product was finally published in its entirety in 1833. Livingston's text described a traditional criminal jury procedure, in which twelve men decide unanimously on the guilt or innocence of the accused. More than ten of the articles in the author's five chapters detailing the role of juries in criminal cases emphasized the necessity of twelve-man unanimity, and "if the court or either of the parties think that all the jurors have not agreed to the verdict that may have been given by the foreman, they shall severally be asked whether they agree, and if any one answers in the negative, the whole jury shall be sent out for further deliberation."[3] Though Livingston's code was never officially adopted by the state, it was clearly influential, earning its author national and international acclaim and forming a clear basis for an official penal law code for Louisiana eight years later in 1841.

The official code included specifications with which Livingston had not troubled himself. "Free negroes, mulattoes, or mustees" would have a right to a jury trial, but slaves couldn't be witnesses in the trial of a white person. Nor could they be witnesses in the trial of "a free person of color," unless that free person of color was accused of inciting a slave rebellion. Jurors would receive a dollar and fifty cents every day of their service, and six and a quarter cents for every mile traveled to arrive and return. There was, however, a remarkable consistency as to the number of jurors and the need for unanimity in convictions or acquittals. "The method of trial, the rules of evidence, and all other proceedings whatsoever in the prosecution of the said crimes, offences, and misdemeanors, changing what ought to be changed, shall be, except as is otherwise provided for, according to the common law of [England]." Among the 1841 revisions were provisions to ensure that "criminals definitively sentenced to death are incapable, until pardoned, of entering into the marriage contract," and that "persons sentenced to imprisonment, pillory, or other infamous punishment, are not able to contract matrimony, until such punishment has been inflicted, or the offender pardoned." The largest difference between Louisiana's 1841 penal code and Livingston's earlier draft is that the state relegated itself to such individualistic pittances while leaving "the method of trial, the rules of evidence, and all other proceedings" to the general dictates of English common law. But it did leave them to common law, and that meant a unanimous twelve-man jury.[4]

In the two decades between 1841 and the Civil War, Louisiana created two new constitutions, both reiterating the necessity that criminal defendants have "a speedy public trial by an impartial jury of the vicinage."[5] But, as the war came to a close, constitutional overhaul had less to do with congressional whim and more with American requirements for reentering the union. Jury trials, however, were not a core component of state reentry. Thus, while the language of the provision changed, the law stayed the same. The Constitution of 1864 ensured criminal defendants "a speedy public trial by an impartial jury of the parish in which the offence shall have been committed," and the Constitution of 1868 ensured the same, with the exception of allowing for the possibility of venue change. The 1868 constitution mandated a new code of judicial practice, and the 1870 result of that mandate again emphasized a twelve-man jury that could convict or acquit only "if it appear that all the jurors have agreed to the verdict." The 1870 legislation was the clearest example of Livingston's influence in the nineteenth century, even mimicking the congressman's original phrasing.[6]

Every piece of legislation passed during Reconstruction, however, was at least to some degree created under duress. Louisiana was one of the last two states to witness the full removal of federal troops, and the end of occupation brought by the Compromise of 1877 seemed to many to be a catalyst for rebirth. After southern Democrats acceded to the presidency of Republican Rutherford Hayes in exchange for economic favoritism and a final end to Reconstruction, the Louisiana state legislature ordered another in a long line of constitutions, hoping to rid itself of postwar federal mandates it found to be odious in the extreme. None of those mandates involved trial by jury, but in their new document, state officials further refined the jury trial mandate anyway. "In all criminal prosecutions the accused shall enjoy the right to a speedy public trial by an impartial jury," noted the Constitution of 1879, "except that, in cases where the penalty is not necessarily imprisonment at hard labor or death, the General Assembly may provide for the trial thereof by a jury, less than twelve in number." There were misdemeanor cases where jury trials could consist of less than twelve, but with that exception, jury unanimity was still a requirement. The real force for change in the Constitution of 1879, however, wasn't the new wording of jury trial mandates. It was the constitution's requirement that those mandates be subject to the legislature's discretion. Article 116 stated, "The General Assembly at its first session under this constitution shall provide by general law for the selection of competent and intelligent jurors, who shall have capacity to serve as grand jurors and try and determine both civil and criminal cases, and may provide, in civil cases, that a verdict be rendered by the concurrence of a less number than the whole." When discussing the divisions of district courts and grand jury terms, Article 117 noted that the assembly could also "provide for special juries, when necessary for the trial of criminal cases."[7]

Still, the mandate of Article 116 was clear. The legislature was tasked with creating the rules by which jury members would be selected. If it wanted valid civil verdicts that were less than unanimous, that was fine, as well. There was no specific constitutional provision authorizing the state Senate to extend the possibility of binding nonunanimous jury verdicts to criminal cases. But that is precisely what the Senate would do.

CHAPTER 3

The Creation of Convict Lease

The first state penitentiary in Louisiana opened in Baton Rouge in 1835, built on the Auburn model, which would dominate national nineteenth-century corrections. Prisoners slept in solitary cells and marched in military formation to meals and workshops. They were not allowed to speak to each other—silence encouraged discipline and contemplation. Prisoners made products, which prisons then sold to communities to raise money for running them. The prison population was predominantly white and did largely industrial work.[1]

Then came the Civil War. The abolition of slavery changed the penitentiary from a predominantly white institution to one that was majority black. It changed the direction of prison work from industrial to agricultural labor, as white politicians sought to reinstitute a form of control over its newly freed workforce. The state had experimented with leasing convict labor as early as 1844, but the genesis of the late-nineteenth-century system came in 1868 when Governor Joshua Baker privatized the industry by leasing the Baton Rouge penitentiary to entrepreneurs Charles Jones and John Huger. When the practice was ratified by the legislature in 1869, the newly elected Henry Clay Warmoth vetoed it, arguing that there was no government oversight involved in the practice. "Where the lessees have absolute power over the prisoners the tendency is to work them too much and feed them too little and give no attention to their comforts and instruction." The legislature responded by modifying the bill to provide a measure of oversight by the state Board of Control. Even though Warmoth begrudgingly signed it, power still rested in the hands of Jones and Huger, setting a precedent that would continue through the remainder of the century.[2]

Even though the pair signed a five-year lease with the state, they decided in 1870 to close up shop, allowing a corporation headed by Samuel

Lawrence James to lobby for a new contract. A civil engineer who moved to New Orleans from his native Tennessee in 1854, James served in the Confederate Army during the Civil War before resigning his post in late 1861. His rise to power was swift, and his wealth and influence allowed him and a group of business partners to win the bid for convict lease. And it was an endeavor that required plenty of wealth and influence. The "James Gang," as they would eventually be called, managed a contract that quadrupled the tenure of Jones and Huger. The twenty-one-year deal was originally designed for an annual rental of $35,000, but instead settled at an escalating rate beginning at $5,000 the first year, to rise by $1,000 each year until the corporation paid a $25,000 rate in the final year of the contract.[3]

It was a controversial proposition in 1870. Many rightly suspected James of having an undue influence on certain legislators. But many also worried about the role of private contractors in protecting people from those who were supposed to be locked away. An angry James sent a letter denying the report of a local newspaper that doubted the efficacy of private leasing after "the noted burglars Jack Levy and John Schnapper" escaped. "With no one to guard them, an escape is easy and in this way some of the worse characters that ever infested any community have found their way back to their old haunts. A practice so reprehensible as this, and fraught with such peril to the community, should be discontinued. Indeed, it is criminal in itself, and the lessees should be held to a strict accountability for all the prisoners who escape." James, of course, denied the claim, "all of which," he argued, "is false."[4] Still, it was in his best interest to ensure that such an outcry was muted. The best attention his system could receive was no attention at all.

To facilitate profit and to provide a place for the prisoners to work away from the fears (and prying eyes) of the public, James leased a large plantation on the Mississippi River from the widow of Colonel Joseph A. S. Acklen, owner of several Louisiana plantations. The plantation, known as Angola, served as both an active farm worked by convict labor and a staging ground for James to lease prisoners to other plantations and business interests. It was a profit-based system that provided additional revenue to the state, but it was also a racial system that provided something resembling slavery for a crop of prisoners who were overwhelmingly black. That being the case, Louisiana freely divested itself of Warmoth's prodding oversight, allowing James to acquire cheap labor that he could treat as brutally as he liked. It was a system that perpetuated white supremacy, and it was a beast that needed continual feeding. Unlike a slave system that kept workers with an owner for life, and therefore made them a long-term investment, James had custody of his "slaves" only for the duration of their sentence. So what economic incentives existed in the convict lease system worked against those who were leased and made the potential for illness and death that much greater.

Supply had to meet demand. And so the Louisiana legislature created a new law in 1880 that removed the unanimity requirement from criminal trials. Beginning that year, criminal defendants could be convicted when only nine of twelve jurors agreed as to their guilt. The law created a larger criminal population, provided James with more labor, and reenslaved more and more of the state's black population. With the law firmly in place and a greater stream of convicts sure to come, James responded late that year by finally purchasing Angola for $100,000 on December 22, 1880. And with a virtually unlimited supply of convicts, made all the more available by the 1880 jury legislation, James could feel free to exacerbate his brutality. In 1881, the year following the original nonunanimous jury law, 14 percent of leased convicts died. The next year, more than 20 percent died.[5]

And more than three-fourths of Louisiana's leased convicts after 1870 were black. William Ivy Hair used an example of Theophile Chevalier to demonstrate the clear racism of the system, the former slave sentenced to five years in prison for stealing five dollars. On the same day, a white woman was sentenced to one hour in prison for manslaughter, while a black man was sentenced to one year in prison for killing a hog. In light of the racial motivation of such punishments and the overwhelming need of the state for more prisoners to lease to the "James Gang's" growing political machine, the state's change to nonunanimous criminal jury verdicts became almost a fait accompli.[6]

It also only enhanced James's political influence in the state. That influence allowed him to run roughshod over Louisiana, paying his fees in depreciated back warrants rather than actual money. Since James had cheap, available labor, the legislature continued to cater to him by providing his corporation a levee construction monopoly. Such was not rare in Louisiana politics, but it helped make any substantive reforms to the system that much more difficult. Eventually, Angola would cover approximately thirteen square miles, including black sharecroppers on the land to accompany the prison labor. As the plantation grew, so too did James's power. The president of New Orleans's Pickwick Club was ubiquitous in Louisiana politics, which allowed him to become, as historian Mark T. Carleton has described him, "the man who initiated and personally maintained for twenty-five years the most cynical, profit-oriented, and brutal regime in Louisiana history."[7]

And profit was the real motive for James. In 1886, for example, James was leasing slaves to other businesses for overnight work at the rate of one dollar per night. This, of course, after they did their traditional work during the day. He paid individual contractors around thirty dollars for the capture of escaped convicts. And when prisoners left the plantation after serving their sentence, they received five dollars for their trouble, whether they served a sentence of six months or two years. With overhead that was so low and the ability to lease employees during their down time, the "James Gang" was assured of the massive profits that would allow them to remain influential.[8]

James signed a new ten-year convict lease contract in 1891, but he wouldn't live to see its conclusion. He died in 1894, but the system he created continued unabated. Between James's death and the end of 1900, the last full year of privately owned convict lease in Louisiana, 732 prisoners died, well over 100 every year.[9]

When that contract ended on January 1, 1901, however, the state didn't seize the opportunity to reform the system. Instead, it made Angola and the penal system in general a state-run business without the middleman. Louisiana purchased Angola from the James family. It retained most of the "James Gang's" employees. As Burk Foster has demonstrated, "It is doubtful that a Louisiana convict of 1884 or 1894 could have told a whole lot of difference in the Angola of 1904, and even in the Angola of 1914 the only major differences were in sugar cane replacing cotton as the main crop and in the introduction of formal parole as a possibility for early release." The same, he argues, could be said for the intervening period between 1914 and 1969.[10] That being the case, there was no real impetus to get rid of nonunanimous criminal jury verdicts, even after the convict lease system formally ended in 1901, because that "formal" end was only an end in name. The state made even more money from the prison lease system after private corporate contracts were eliminated from the paradigm.

It was a system—even after the end of formal privatized convict lease—of profit-based plantation agriculture using a prison population that was more than three-fourths black. There was no accountability for deaths during incarceration, nor any real attempt at rehabilitating prisoners. It was a system designed to consume human beings in service to the state. Indeed, as Mark Carleton has argued, "Prior to 1952 the system was essentially a business enterprise, administered either by politicians or by lessees, with both forms of management seeking to extract as much money as possible from the labor of thousands of semi-skilled 'state slaves.'" It was an enterprise aided in large measure by public apathy, and with prison reform out of the public eye, the state was allowed to run roughshod over prisoners' rights and use Angola to create a virtual apartheid system on the Mississippi River.[11]

And if the public wasn't paying attention to the problems at Angola, they were even less likely to pay attention to how the plantation was acquiring its convicts. In the nineteenth century, the racist motivations for establishing both the prison lease system and the method of getting more prisoners would have met with general approval by most of white Louisiana. By the time those assumptions changed, the use of nonunanimous criminal jury verdicts was just an understood fact of Louisiana life.

CHAPTER 4

The Triumph of the Redeemers

John D. Watkins was a Kentucky native who came to Louisiana following college to become a teacher and principal at Minden Male Academy.
He studied law in his spare time, however, and passed the bar in 1852.
He became district attorney the same year, abandoning his teaching career for one of law and public service. The following decade, he entered
politics. He had been a Minden delegate to the Louisiana constitutional
convention in 1879, but he was also one of the Twenty-first District's
two state senators, the chair of the Senate's Judiciary Committee.[1] He
was there in the Senate chamber on January 14, 1880, when a message
from Governor Louis A. Wiltz arrived at both houses of the legislature,
encouraging the assembly to remember the new constitution and respond
accordingly to its legislative mandates. To that end, the Senate created a
Committee on Constitutional Legislation, tasked with apportioning the
new constitution's directives to individual committees. Article 116 was
sent unsurprisingly to Judiciary, and on February 23, 1880, Watkins and
his committee submitted Senate Bill No. 100, "An act to carry into effect
article 116 of the constitution; to provide the qualifications and for the
selection of competent and intelligent jurors throughout the State." It
made its way again through Judiciary and back to the floor, where it was
approved without controversy and passed unanimously. The same pattern
held when the bill moved to the House. It was signed on April 1, 1880.[2]

   At the same time, however, Watkins and the Louisiana legislature
were thinking about a much larger, much more radical restructuring of
the state's jury system. The April 1 law set unsurprising rules for select-
ing jurors, but as the Senate debated the intricacies of how to get potential jurors to the courthouse, spurred by that constitutional mandate to
reformulate jury structure, the House of Representatives was debating

methods for getting them to a verdict. Article 527 of the 1870 Code of Practice stated that all jurors had to agree to render a valid verdict: "If it appear that all the jurors have agreed to the verdict, the same shall be recorded," but if jury selection could be modified by mandate, so too could other elements of the system.[3]

On Thursday, February 5, 1880, Henry Heidenhain, a representative from the Fourth District of New Orleans, introduced a bill to modify Article 527. Heidenhain was a lawyer by trade and would follow his stint in the legislature with a New Orleans judgeship. He was a Confederate veteran devoted to the fraternal Grand Army of the Republic, designed to venerate service in the war. His racial sympathies fit the prevailing attitude of white southern Redeemers, as made evident by his reaction to attempts of black Louisiana Civil War veterans to join the Grand Army. "The Confederate organizations and other kind friends have joined us with true friendship every Decoration day," he argued. "Now then, is it reasonable to expect—and, indeed we don't,—that our former friends will join with the Grand Army of the Republic again when they are compelled by virtue of their friendship to us to march with those whom neither they nor the majority of us consider our social equals?"[4]

Heidenhain's bill did a service to both his prosecutorial experience and his inveterate racism. Judges, as always, were required to ask the jury foreman if his group had agreed on a verdict under the dictates of Heidenhain's law, but that agreement no longer required unanimity. If either the plaintiff or defendant were dissatisfied with the verdict and asked that the jury be polled, only nine of the jurors had to agree to make the decision binding. The proposed legislation, known as House Bill 101, would thereby make criminal convictions easier for prosecutors, and it would ensure that more and more black convicts would be available for "re-enslavement."[5]

The bill soon made its way to the Judiciary Committee, chaired by Lafourche's John S. Billiu, who reported back to the House that the committee had no problem with the legislation and recommended its passage. Billiu, a Thibodeaux lawyer and career Democratic politician, seemed to see no fundamental conflict with eliminating jury unanimity in criminal verdicts. Billiu, too, was a Confederate veteran who was principally responsible for crushing the local black Republican Thibodeaux militia following the end of Reconstruction.[6]

The lawyers and ex-Confederates, it seemed, were all on board. And why not? The bill gave them both easier convictions and a way to reenslave the black population. Not all in the House, however, were Rebel attorneys. On the bill's first reading after clearing the Judiciary Committee, Zachary Taylor Young moved that the bill be indefinitely postponed. After being stymied by J. H. Cosgrove of Natchitoches, he tried again. Though shouted down at every turn, Young would be the principal leader of the opposition to House Bill 101. Unlike Heidenhain and Billiu, Young wasn't a former Confederate. Born in 1849 to descendants of Acadian exiles, Young was only thirty-one years old upon taking up his congressional post to serve his native St. Landry Parish. He was too young to have fought in the Civil War, and he had studied medicine, not law, at the University of Louisiana. Though the young Acadian doctor was a Democrat, his perspective was fundamentally different than that of his peers, and the prospect of making it easier for the state to incarcerate its own people seemed a dangerous precedent.[7]

Young, however, was in the minority. On February 19, Billiu moved to engross the bill and bring it to a vote on final passage. This time, opposition was taken up by Theophile T. Allain, a mixed-race Republican born in 1846 to white plantation-owner Sosthène Allain and one of his slaves. While in the state Senate the previous term, Allain had been instrumental in the creation of Southern University and was, to the extent that anyone could be, a champion of black rights. It was obvious to Allain that white Louisiana Democrats were trying to make criminal convictions of freedmen that much easier—aiding the state's criminal conviction rate and its fodder for convict lease. It was obvious to others, too. He was joined in his attempt to stop the engrossment by Democrat Thomas Devereaux, who also served as New Orleans's chief of detectives. Were the legislation simply a method of creating a streamlined trial system, of course, Devereaux would seem a strange bedfellow for Allain. As the city's chief of detectives, he could only benefit from such a law. But the legislation wasn't designed to streamline the trial system. It was designed to create de facto slaves. As an officer, Devereaux was concerned more than anything else with vice and organized crime, and as a part of the New Orleans political machine, he had little to gain from convict lease. He and Allain were unsuccessful in stopping the engrossment, however, and it moved to final passage.[8]

The writing, it seemed, was on the wall. The fifty-to-thirty vote in favor of House Bill 101 mimicked the procedural votes that happened throughout its journey through the House. Young, Allain, and Devereaux were joined by the remaining House Republicans and sympathetic Democrats from either Acadiana or New Orleans, but all who voted against the bill understood that they were outmanned by the Redeemers. Representatives like Wash Lyons, Enos Williams, and Bivien Gardner were used to being outvoted. They were, like Allain, part of the Negro delegation that would survive until the Constitution of 1898 would fully eliminate the black right to vote in Louisiana.[9]

When the bill reached the Senate in late February, it was clear that Watkins and Judiciary were uncomfortable with the change. The committee reported the bill unfavorably, but Natchitoches Democrat M. J. Cunningham postponed consideration of the bill in early March until he was able to lobby his fellow senators. When the body took the legislation back up in early April, everyone's doubts had been allayed—or almost everyone's. There were only two votes against the new jury mandate in the Senate, one by Henry Demas and the other by Murphy J. Foster. The two were strange bedfellows, to say the least. Demas was a black Republican from St. John the Baptist Parish. Foster was a Franklin, Louisiana, lawyer just starting a political career that would take him to the governor's chair in the following decade, leveraging as he did both populist politics and white supremacy for advancement in the state hierarchy. It was Foster's leadership that would steward the Jim Crow Constitution of 1898, which would officially protect the new jury mandate from legal challenge. But in 1880, Foster was new to the legislature, making his name on advocacy for farm relief in the wake of Reconstruction. He would, even in his most prescient moments of white supremacy, still maintain that populist bent, even relying in the early 1890s on Farmer's Alliance support to earn the governor's chair. He consistently demonstrated an opposition to machine politics and, as governor, would bully railroad monopolies for gouging

Louisiana sugar farmers. He was also opposed to the Louisiana State Lottery Company, which was instrumental in the creation of the Constitution of 1879, which mandated the new congress of 1880. It is possible that, because railroads were among the chief purchasers of convict labor, the original bill left a bad taste in Foster's mouth. Or perhaps he resented Cunningham's strong-arm tactics. His distaste for the Lottery might have swung his vote, or his populist tendencies may have convinced him to vote against a bill that would have disproportionately affected the poor. Regardless, Foster's curious alliance with a black Republican at the onset of his political career in a vote that was nothing more than a political statement in an obviously lost cause would be quickly forgotten in his charge for white supremacy in the next decade. And, just as it was in the House, the vote for House Bill 101 was a foregone conclusion anyway.[10]

Signed on April 10, 1880, the law in its final form fundamentally changed the formula for criminal conviction: "After the reading of the verdict [the judge] shall ask the jury if the verdict has been agreed to; and if the foreman answers in the affirmative, he shall enter the verdict upon the records of the court, unless one of the parties require that the jury shall be called and each of them asked if he has agreed to the verdict, and if it appears that nine or more of the jurors have agreed to the verdict, the same shall be recorded."[11] The bill evoked little fanfare or controversy, buried as it was by budget battles, arguments over the role of the Lottery, and the general tumult attending the creation of a new government. But over the next two decades it would become ingrained in the assumptions of the Louisiana legal community.[12] It came as no surprise, then, that when a new constitutional convention was called in 1898, nonunanimous criminal juries would become part of the judiciary debate.

And why not? Momentum seemed to be on the side of the state legislature. Minnesota and Virginia passed laws governing trials for minor offenses clearly influenced by the Louisiana plan. Minnesota allowed five-sixths of a jury to render a misdemeanor verdict after deliberating for more than twelve hours. Virginia allowed misdemeanors to be tried by a jury of seven. Spurred by such practices, Senator George Clement Perkins of California proposed an 1894 federal law that required three-fourths jury agreement in civil actions and five-sixths in federal criminal trials.

It was an odd turn for the former Republican governor of California, known during his 1880–83 administration for actively pardoning many of the state's convicts after personal interviews with inmates. Perkins was a Reconstruction-era Republican who generally supported racial equality. The turn to supermajority verdicts in places like Louisiana, however, seemed to change his mind about the relative ease of criminal convictions. But it hadn't changed many other minds. The proposal never escaped committee and was never debated in the Senate, but Louisiana certainly noticed its growing influence. "For years past the evils of 'hung juries' have vastly increased," proclaimed an unsigned editorial in the *Times-Picayune*, applauding Perkins for a valiant effort in the U.S. Senate. "The necessity for the unanimous agreement of the twelve men of a jury in bringing in a verdict in criminal cases has enormously contributed to defraud justice as well as to increase the costs of judicial administration." And cost, the article claimed, was the real motive. "One man bought up in the interest of the accused will prevent the rendering of a verdict and will entail upon the taxpayers the expenses of a futile and fruitless trial." The *Picayune* proudly lauded Louisiana as a leader in the jury debate, but more needed to be done. "It is in capital cases that the danger of mistrial is greatest, and for that reason some further modification of the jury law is necessary."[13] It was a particularly bloodthirsty screed, and the Louisiana legislature would see no need to act on it. Lowering the prosecutorial bar in capital cases would provide little aid to the state's convict lease program, and with death as the stake, such legislation would surely draw the attention of the U.S. Supreme Court.

Despite the plaudits, however, none of Louisiana's former Confederate counterparts adopted a nonunanimous criminal jury provision. Every southern state developed convict leasing in the second half of the nineteenth century, but Louisiana was the only state among them to change its criminal jury standard. Laws against vagrancy, public drunkenness, and other "crimes" helped feed the systems of every Redeemer state. While historians have described the southern convict lease system for decades, the most popular recent account is Douglas Blackmon's *Slavery by Another Name*, which emphasizes Alabama as its principal example. Blackmon describes a system where convict leasing happened at both the county and state level. At the county level, justices of the peace were given carte blanche to make arrests as they saw fit. Alabama, like its fellow Confederate states, remained paranoid about the creeping hoard of large government. To that end, it kept its legal system to a minimum, eliminating bureaucracy, but replacing it with a pay-per-case system that only encouraged more graft than could ever exist in a normal, functioning bureaucracy. Trial fees not only lined the pockets of those who adjudicated offenders, but they also ensured that indigent defendants would have length added to their sentences to compensate for their inability to pay. Meanwhile, a lack of prisons—again because of small-government thinking—gave white southerners the ability to argue that convict lease was a fait accompli.[14]

Various southern states started and ended their systems at different times. Georgia began leasing former slaves in 1868. Texas didn't begin until 1883. Tennessee's system was finished by 1894, while versions of Alabama's system stayed until 1928. Still, all of those systems remained relatively similar. Arrests at the county level and local fines fed sentences that allowed the states to feed free labor to the industries developing in their states. Alabama had iron mines. Florida had lumber and turpentine industries. Many states had coal. They all had railroads. And then there were the plantations. No state, however, changed its criminal jury standard except Louisiana.[15]

The principal difference between Louisiana's system and those of its former Confederate counterparts was the centralized Samuel James monopoly on convict labor. Instead of working from the county level up (as, for example, in Alabama), Louisiana had a top-down system that dictated prisoner totals for a private prison system with inordinate influence within the state legislature. In Alabama, the state was leasing prisoners to iron-mining corporations in and around Birmingham. In Louisiana, every company that leased prisoners did so from a private company with a sweetheart contract from the state, and most of those prisoners just worked for James at his massive Angola prison farm. That kind of singular corporate lobby from a group that controlled all of the state's prisoners— one that didn't exist in any other southern state—created the impetus for a state-level criminal jury standard to encourage the growth of a corporate monopoly.

So, though the standard didn't develop in other southern states, white public sentiment in Louisiana clearly seemed to be on the side of lawmakers, allowing the confidence of the Bourbon Redeemers to grow in the intervening years between 1880 and 1898. In 1891, the state renewed the convict lease contract of Samuel L. James. The year prior to that, the legislature first experimented with segregation laws, passing the Separate Car Act of 1890, which mandated "equal, but separate," train cars for black and white passengers. That law—and the reaction to it by a group of black New Orleans business leaders—would ultimately lead to the U.S. Supreme Court's *Plessy v. Ferguson* (1896) decision, validating the "separate but equal" doctrine and opening the floodgates of Jim Crow laws throughout Louisiana and the South. In 1894, the state would make miscegenation illegal. It would also take railroad segregation further by segregating train depots. In 1898, the same year as the constitutional convention, the legislature would segregate public education.

The Reconstruction-era code the Redeemers still hadn't cracked as of the mid-1890s was the federal protection of black voting rights. The Fifteenth Amendment barred voting restrictions based on "race, color, or previous condition of servitude," and Louisiana continued to have a substantial tally of black registered voters. In 1880, 88,024 black men were registered (to 85,451 whites). By 1888, it was 128,150 blacks, 124,407 whites. While white Democrats were able to maneuver around such discrepancies with fraud, violence, and intimidation, legal means of disfranchisement seemed far more propitious. The constitutional convention of 1898 was called, in part, to create that disfranchisement.

CHAPTER 5

The Whisper in the Crowd

And so the convention of 1898 would codify Jim Crow and black voting restrictions and would be dominated by celebrations of white supremacy. Convention president E. B. Kruttschnitt opened the proceedings by reminding delegates that "this convention has been called together by the people of the State to eliminate from the electorate the mass of corrupt and illiterate voters who have during the last quarter of a century degraded a politics." In closing the convention, he praised delegates for perpetuating "the supremacy of the Anglo-Saxon race in Louisiana."[1] The new constitution would include a literacy test, a three-hundred-dollar property requirement, a poll tax, and proof of two years' paid taxes as requirements for the franchise. It also included a grandfather clause to cover poor, illiterate whites who couldn't meet the new constitutional standard. In 1897, a year before the new constitution took effect, there were 130,344 registered black voters. By 1900, there were 5,320. By 1922, there were only 598.[2]

The Constitution of 1898 was the culmination of the full turn from the principles of Reconstruction in Louisiana, but lost among the voting-rights restrictions and segregation mandates was the convention's move to codify one of the state's original attempts at reenslaving its freed population. On the third day of the convention, February 10, a Covington judge and Democratic Party leader named J. M. Thompson gave notice of ordinances for allowing misdemeanors to be tried by a judge and felony trials to be decided by a nine-to-three majority. Those ordinances, however, would be folded into a larger judiciary package submitted as Ordinance 365 by Thomas J. Semmes, a New Orleans lawyer and head of the convention's Judiciary Committee. The jury provisions became Article 36 of that ordinance.[3]

Chief opposition to the nonunanimous jury article came from Jared

Young Sanders, who, like Murphy Foster, was from Franklin. And like the young Foster, the Tulane-trained lawyer found a fundamental unfairness in the concept of nonunanimous criminal decisions. In the amendment phase of the legislation, Sanders offered an amendment that stipulated that "cases shall be tried by a jury, the number of same and manner of arriving at a verdict to be fixed by law." Or, to wit, juries should be required to be unanimous. A decade later, Sanders would become governor on a reform platform of bringing better roads to Louisiana, but the constitutional convention of 1898 was in no mood for southern progressivism. His amendment would be voted down fifty-one to twenty-four.[4]

The vote was significant because it mirrored the final passage of the full judiciary ordinance. There were twenty-seven votes against the final measure, and while not all of them made their choice because of Article 36, it was clear that many of them did. Sanders again led the charge against passage, arguing, "I can never give my consent to vote for any measure that in any manner abrogates the right of trial by jury—the very bulwark of our liberties." And lawyers, he seemed to intimate, should know better.[5]

The non-lawyers agreed. Martin Behrman was an Algiers tax assessor and aspiring New Orleans politician in 1898. In the following decade, he would become one of the city's longest-tenured mayors and leader of the local political machine. Of course, machine politics was never known as a bastion of democracy, but prior to his early twentieth-century rise, Behrman was still speaking in the language of populism. "I cannot by my vote help to place in the organic law of our State any measure that will deprive the rights to my people of a trial by jury." Robert Ewing agreed. The man who would help create the Choctaw Club and the modern machine politics that would so benefit Behrman, Ewing had yet to become the newspaper magnate who would wield control over much of the state's politics in the next century's first three decades. He was just an editor in 1898, but he still had the progressive streak he would demonstrate throughout his life. Ewing acknowledged that he had little to do with the debate over Ordinance 365. "The Judiciary bill is a measure," said Ewing, "I have been willing to leave to the lawyers in this body to frame, but when they go so far as to abolish the right of trial by jury I am compelled to dissent."[6]

That dissent, however, was a whisper in the crowd. Thompson and Semmes and Kruttschnitt were far more influential, and the seventy-two to twenty-seven vote made it clear that the vast majority of Redeemer Democrats were perfectly willing to deprive people of the right to a trial by jury. They had already demonstrated a willingness to deprive black Louisiana of the right to vote, and of the right to ride on certain train cars, to marry certain people, to go to white schools. The measure passed. Nonunanimous criminal jury verdicts were now part of the Louisiana constitution.

And they seemed to be receiving, at least indirectly, federal backing. In 1916, for example, the U.S. Supreme Court would uphold the misdemeanor jury laws in Minnesota and Virginia. Even though there had been several challenges to Louisiana's criminal jury laws by 1916, not one was folded into the Minnesota and Virginia decisions because Louisiana's statute dealt with criminal trials and went much farther than either of the other two states. Getting the Supreme Court to validate nonunanimous juries in any context, however, was a victory for state lawmakers.[7]

To that end, the state's subsequent constitutions of 1913 and 1921 would mimic the 1898 jury language. In 1913, the constitutional convention lasted only two weeks, and delegates quickly adopted the 1898 language. The 1921 convention was more comprehensive. Marksville lawyer J. W. Joffrion introduced an ordinance that mimicked the 1898 language, but it was soon folded into a broader judiciary bill. This time there was no opposition, no leaders defending unanimous criminal jury verdicts. While there was a minor debate about language, there was no substantive opposition to the section's intent. Though Martin Behrman was a delegate to this convention, as well, his vote had changed. He, along with 105 others, supported the judiciary ordinance, while only eleven opposed it. And none of those eleven cited the jury mandate as a reason for their opposition. There was little reason for them to do so. Though convict lease had ended, the James Gang come and gone, the principle of nonunanimous criminal jury verdicts had been in place for forty-one years, the vast majority of every delegate's adult life. By that time, the formula was almost assumed. Loyola University's St. Clair Adams, writing on necessary reforms in criminal procedure in 1920, didn't even mention nonunanimous jury verdicts. Where such a law came from was never discussed at the convention and wouldn't have mattered anyway to a group still mired in the assumptions of Jim Crow.[8]

Those assumptions weren't going anywhere. In 1926, the state legislature again empanelled a commission to create a new criminal code that would act as an amendment to the 1921 constitution, but its criminal jury verdict provisions would remain unchanged. They would remain unchanged in 1950 when the legislature did it again.[9] A final code of criminal procedure became law in 1966. Article 782 remained firm in the precedent established over the preceding eighty-six years: "Cases in which the punishment may be capital shall be tried by a jury of twelve jurors, all of whom must concur to render a verdict. Cases in which the punishment is necessarily at hard labor shall be tried by a jury composed of twelve jurors, nine of whom must concur to render a verdict. Cases in which the punishment may be imprisonment at hard labor, shall be tried by a jury composed of five jurors, all of whom must concur to render a verdict."[10]

The civil rights movement had been working for decades by 1966 to overturn Jim Crow. It had succeeded in having state-sanctioned legal segregation in public accommodations outlawed. It succeeded in securing federal oversight of elections that would protect black southerners' right to vote. But the Civil Rights Act of 1964 and the Voting Rights Act of 1965 ignored the more curious and less prominent holdover from Redemption-era Louisiana. The 1966 Code of Criminal Procedure's jury mandate passed without contest.

The change in Louisiana's criminal jury statutes was not a slow evolution of judicial thinking from 1803 to 1966. It was instead two clearly different, if not completely antithetical, methods of determining guilt or innocence in criminal cases, bent on the axis of 1880's legislative session. After the Constitution of 1879, the common legal assumptions stemming from English common law gave way to a revolutionary change in thinking that favored prosecutors and made criminal convictions that much easier. By the time that change had been codified in the Constitution of 1898, it was then the new common assumption, consistently repeated in every new legislative mandate that followed. And so the evolution of judicial thinking on the role of jury unanimity came not from the legislature and the various constitutional conventions it empanelled, but from those most affected by easier, nonunanimous criminal convictions—defendants themselves. Judicial appeals began immediately.

CHAPTER 6

The Burden of Precedent

When Theodule Ardoin burned down a St. Landry Parish house in 1898, the new constitution had yet to be ratified. His conviction, however, fell under the auspices of the new document, and his conviction was by a vote of nine to three. And so he appealed, arguing that his conviction constituted a violation of Article One, Section Nine, of the U.S. Constitution, which prohibited "ex post facto legislation by the state."[1] Ardoin was aided by the Supreme Court's *Thompson v. Utah* (1898) decision the previous year. In that case, two men were originally convicted of stealing a calf by a jury of twelve under the territory of Utah's laws. But they were granted a new trial that didn't take place until the territory became a state, wherein it had changed the law to mandate an eight-man jury. Convicted again, the calf thief appealed, arguing that the decision was the result of an ex post facto law. The Supreme Court agreed, and its decision left the Louisiana Supreme Court with little choice but to begrudgingly allow Ardoin a new trial under the "laws in force when the offense is charged to have been committed." But Ardoin had also appealed on the grounds that a conviction by only nine jurors was inherently unfair. On that point, the court held firm. A decision by nine of twelve jurors meant the possibility of conviction, but it also meant the possibility of acquittal. The deck, the court argued, was not stacked one way or another. If prosecuting crimes was somehow easier because of the nine-man requirement, so too was defending the innocent.[2]

The court's decision ignored the fact that nonunanimous jury verdicts had been signed into law in 1880. While not specifically allowed by the 1879 constitution, they hadn't been specifically banned, either, and state law had provided specificity well before Ardoin committed arson. The Louisiana Supreme Court, however, was concerned with the state constitution, and when combined with the recent *Thompson* ruling, its hands seemed to be tied. But the situation remained no less murky when crimes were committed on the other side of the 1898 constitution.

Maurice Biagas, for example, was tried for a St. Landry Parish murder in 1901, but was convicted instead (by eleven of twelve jurors) of manslaughter. A murder trial, however, carried the possibility of capital punishment, and under the 1898 constitution, "cases in which the punishment may be capital" had to be tried by a twelve-member jury, "all of whom must concur to render a verdict." And so, Biagas argued, even if he was convicted of a lesser crime, the decision had to be unanimous. The state disagreed, arguing that "a trial for murder is a dual trial, it being also a trial for manslaughter, and that, in so far or inasmuch as the trial is for manslaughter, 9 jurors, concurring, may render a verdict." The Louisiana Supreme Court sided with Biagas, emphasizing that the potential punishment for the crime "may be capital," and that therefore any verdict in the case had to be unanimous. Associate Justice Newton Blanchard, however, dissented. Blanchard had been a member of the constitutional convention of 1879 before moving on to the U.S. House and Senate. After his service on the Louisiana Supreme Court, he would become governor, and then president of the constitutional convention of 1913. He agreed with the state that every murder trial inherently includes a potential charge of manslaughter, for which the punishment could never be capital. "It is as though two 'cases' against the accused are being tried at the same time, of one or the other of which (not both) he may be convicted." Ruling as the court did, argued Blanchard, would create a situation where people charged with manslaughter could be convicted by nine jurors, while people charged with murder could only be convicted of the same charge of manslaughter by twelve jurors, setting up a situation whereby there were two different standards of conviction for the same crime. "Any construction of the language of the organic law which leads to so illogical, so inconsistent, so incompatible a result must, I submit, be avoided." It was a question of fairness to be sure, Blanchard reasoned, but also one of pragmatism. "Suppose it should happen (and it will frequently, no doubt) that the jury stands 9 for manslaughter and 3 for acquittal outright; what then? Could the accused be again tried for murder on that indictment? Would not that conviction of manslaughter be a legal one?"[3] These were good questions, and they demonstrated the inherent problems associated with assigning different jury standards in different criminal trials. Overlap was inevitable. Significantly, however, neither those concurring nor those dissenting demonstrated any qualms about the validity of nonunanimous verdicts in noncapital criminal cases. Their qualms were only with the consistency of the application.

And Blanchard was right: the consistency problem wasn't going away. In *State v. Wooten* (1915), another manslaughter conviction came into question. This time, Maud Wooten was indicted for murder but found by the jury to have committed only manslaughter. He was granted a new trial on that charge and convicted by less than twelve jurors. But because Wooten had a second, separate manslaughter trial, the court's previous dilemma was absent. Five years later, in *State v. Trull* (1920), a Richland Parish bigamist named J. M. Trull appealed his conviction on that charge, in part, because his conviction by a ten-to-two jury verdict demonstrated that there were two members of the jury who had a reasonable doubt about Trull's guilt. Reasonable doubt was the standard by which most American states gauged guilt or innocence, but the state constitution was clear: in cases where the penalty was "imprisonment at hard labor," defendants were required to create a reasonable doubt in four of the jurors, not one. This method of framing the argument against nonunanimous criminal verdicts seemed to have weight. If reasonable doubt was the equalizer rather than jury size or unanimity, the standards for successful criminal defenses in Louisiana seemed herculean in relation to any other American standard. That argument wouldn't go away either, but in *Trull*, the court did not meditate on the issue. The state constitution allowed ten of twelve jurors to render a verdict, and that was that.[4]

When Emile Vial appealed his manslaughter conviction three years after *Trull*, none of his thirty-one bills of exception dealt with reasonable doubt. Tried for murder and convicted of manslaughter, his appeal focused instead on the same questions posed by *Biagas*. The state Supreme Court, however, had changed its mind, emphasizing instead Newton Blanchard's dissent in *Biagas* and the 1915 *Wooten* decision. Wooten had received a new trial for manslaughter. Vial hadn't received a new trial, but when the jury returned an untenable nine-to-three murder verdict, the trial judge then told them that the defendant "was then on trial for manslaughter, and that nine jurors could acquit or convict on this charge." That was enough for the court. *Wooten* provided a bridge to Blanchard's original two-trial dissent, allowing the court to "conclude that, as the prosecution for murder was abandoned in this case, nine of the jurors concurring could legally return a verdict of manslaughter under the original indictment."[5]

It was all so unpredictable, or so the legislature thought. When the body created its new Code of Criminal Procedure in 1928, it sought to limit the confusion. Drawing heavily upon the criminal codes of California and Michigan, Article 218 of the new document provided that, "when two or more crimes result from a single act, or from one continuous unlawful transaction, only one indictment will lie." Article 337 stated, "Whenever the indictment charges any capital offense, whether there be or be not counts charging offenses not capital, the trial shall be by a jury of twelve, all of whom must concur for the finding of a verdict."[6] The directives were clear enough, but neither seemed to jibe with the constitution's mandate that noncapital criminal offenses allowed a jury verdict of nine votes to three.

The early Depression period was the age of the bank robber, and Louisiana certainly felt its share of the sting. Bonnie and Clyde would spend time in the state, and would ultimately die there. In 1930, a far less accomplished criminal, Ito Jacques, robbed the Rocheblave Market Branch of the Canal Bank and Trust Company in New Orleans with several accomplices and murdered a customer in the process. Complying with Article 218 of the criminal code, the indictment against Jacques included all of the several counts that resulted from the robbery, including the capital offense. Because of the different standards for each count, Jacques successfully moved to quash the indictment. The state responded by appealing to the Louisiana Supreme Court in 1931. The court was not impressed with the criminal code. It argued that, if the constitution required five-member juries for some trials, twelve-member juries for others, and if it required unanimous jury verdicts for capital crimes and nonunanimous jury verdicts for others, then there was no way that combining various crimes committed in "one continuous unlawful transaction" could possibly meet standards of fairness. Both articles, ruled the court, were unconstitutional.[7]

But in cases like *Biagas, Wooten,* and *Jacques,* the combination of crimes was inherent in the crime itself—murder that could be considered manslaughter by the jury. Such cases were far more thorny, and they remained so when the combination was at the lower end of the criminal scale, when (as opposed to capital murder) the punishment did not necessarily require imprisonment at hard labor. Four months after *Jacques,* the court attempted to clarify its thinking on such inherent combinations in *State v. Flattmann* (1931). Charles Flattmann was a New Orleans drunk driver who killed a pedestrian. He was charged with manslaughter but convicted only of involuntary homicide. Flattmann was convicted by a less-than-unanimous twelve-man jury, but involuntary homicide did not necessarily carry a verdict of imprisonment at hard labor, so Flattmann appealed on the grounds that he could only be convicted of involuntary homicide by a unanimous five-man jury. The court's response was to shift the burden of what "may" constitute a sentence of imprisonment at hard labor to the jury's discretion, not the judge's. The judge in such cases was bound by the most stringent charge brought by the indictment. "It is only when the jury sees fit to lessen the maximum term of imprisonment, and to let it be without hard labor, that the penalty may be imprisonment with or without hard labor, for a term not exceeding five years, in the discretion of the judge." Be thankful, the court seemed to be saying, that the jury lessened your sentence. "The crime of involuntary manslaughter, for the killing of a person by the grossly negligent use or operation of a vehicle, is not a crime for which the penalty is imprisonment with or without hard labor, in the discretion of the judge," the court argued, "because the penalty is necessarily imprisonment at hard labor if the jury so decides."[8] It was a slippery slope, to be sure, allowing jury decision-making to determine the constitutional definitions of "may" and "necessarily," but the result was ultimately the same as it had been in *Biagas, Wooten,* and *Jacques.* When either the maximum or minimum charge did not fall under the auspices of the nonunanimous twelve-man jury requirement, the sentence could stand as long as the convicting charge fell under those auspices.

That made the court's decision in *State v. Doucet* (1933) almost a foregone conclusion. The state charged Desire Doucet with murder, but dropped the charge to manslaughter preceding the trial. When the trial judge instructed the jury that nine had to agree to render a verdict, Doucet's attorney objected, arguing that the charge was illegal. The trial judge was unfazed, and so was the Louisiana Supreme Court. "It is only in capital cases that all twelve of the jurors must concur to render a verdict," and when the state dropped the murder charge, the case ceased to be capital.[9]

The flurry of unsuccessful early twentieth-century challenges to the nonunanimous criminal jury verdict made it clear that the court deemed the process inviolable. So, too, did much of the broader legal community. In 1957, for example, Tulane's Ralph Slovenko wrote an exhaustive treatise on Louisiana's criminal jury system and didn't even feel the need to elaborate at all on the nonunanimous verdict. Such was the assumed a priori place of the jury system in Louisiana criminal law.[10]

Of course, by the time of Slovenko's treatise, the U.S. Supreme Court had already decided *Brown*. The Montgomery bus boycott had run its course, demonstrating the power of organized civil rights protest and elevating local minister Martin Luther King Jr. to national prominence. Over the next decade, the civil rights movement would win a stunning series of victories, forcing the federal government to respond to racial policy in the South, dismantling the edifice of Jim Crow laws passed by late-nineteenth-century Redeemer governments, and fundamentally changing the legal relationship between black and white throughout the country. Nonunanimous criminal verdicts in Louisiana, however, remained, even as the rest of the Jim Crow edifice fell. They were localized to one southern state, and their assaults on minorities and the poor were more indirect than laws that specifically barred black customers from lunch counters. They were assumed to be simply another anomaly in the state with so many countless anomalies.

And so it was more than thirty years after *Doucet* before another serious appeal made its way to the Louisiana Supreme Court. In *State v. Schoonover* (1968), however, the court was worried less about the delegation of multiple charges under one jury trial and more about the constitutional status of nonunanimous verdicts in light of new U.S. Supreme Court decisions. Just two weeks prior to the state court's *Schoonover* decision, the federal court ruled in *Duncan v. Louisiana* (1968) "that the right to jury trial in serious criminal cases is a fundamental right and hence must be recognized by the States as part of their obligation to extend due process of law to all persons within their jurisdiction." The federal court applied the Due Process Clause of the Fourteenth Amendment and the right to a jury trial enumerated in the Sixth Amendment to overturn a battery conviction tried in front of a judge instead of a jury.[11]

Duncan, like so many other facets of Louisiana law, also had racial overtones. Gary Duncan was a black teenager who stopped his car to pick up two of his cousins, who were standing with a group of white youths. There had been a series of racial incidents following the desegregation of a local school, and he wanted to get his cousins out of the situation. One of the white teenagers claimed that Duncan slapped him. It became a contest of white word against black, a contest in 1960s Louisiana that Duncan was destined to lose. But, since simple battery was a misdemeanor, he was only awarded a trial by a judge, not by a jury. That denial sparked his appeal.[12]

Duncan determined that denial of a jury trial was denial of due process, and the Louisiana Supreme Court acknowledged the distinction, but that didn't mean, it argued, that a conviction by a nonunanimous jury—and Gilbert Lee Schoonover had been convicted by a nonunanimous jury for armed robbery—was also a denial of due process. Schoonover's conviction was upheld. Still, the court acknowledged that such verdicts were constitutional only for the moment. "We must await a clear exposition of this point by the Federal Supreme Court before we can decide whether a unanimous verdict is a requirement of the Sixth Amendment of the Federal Constitution which is obligatory on the States."[13] It quoted itself the following year in *State v. White* (1969), upholding a nine-to-three jury verdict on a drug charge but emphasizing that its decision "at the present time" could be altered if the U.S. Supreme Court ruled on the Fourteenth and Sixth Amendment merits of nonunanimous jury verdicts.[14]

It wouldn't have to wait long.

CHAPTER 7

The Vagaries of Due Process

Even as the Louisiana Supreme Court was making its plea in *Schoonover*, Frank Johnson was waiting in lockup following his arrest for the armed robbery of a Coca Cola Bottling Company truck in New Orleans. He was eventually convicted in June 1968, but his appeal would be complicated because, early the following January, Johnson and twenty other felons attempted a prison break. While some of his fellow inmates were able to escape, Johnson's recapture only slowed the process of appeal.[1]

That appeal finally reached the Louisiana Supreme Court in January 1970, one year after Johnson's thwarted escape, and the principal bills of exception dealt with several issues. When detectives arrested Johnson, for example, they brandished shotguns. They didn't have a warrant. They didn't apprise him of the charge for hours. The detectives, Johnson's lawyers argued, did not have the probable cause necessary for a warrantless search, and could easily have obtained one before arriving at Johnson's house because there was no immediacy requirement in the capture. The court dismissed such exceptions, arguing that the rash of armed robberies of trucks in the city provided the justification for the warrantless arrest. Detectives didn't break into the home. They knocked and were allowed inside.[2]

And if the arrest was legal, the lineup was constitutional, as well. Johnson's lawyers had argued that a lineup involving a suspect who was illegally detained should have been suppressed at trial, but, argued Associate Justice Walter Hamlin, writing for a unanimous court, "when the line-up occurred, defendant was in legal custody and under no arrest."[3]

Johnson's other bill of exception had nothing to do with his arrest. It instead involved his conviction, decided by nine of twelve jurors.[4] Sentenced to thirty-five years at the Louisiana State Penitentiary at Angola—founded as it was by the James Gang's convict labor operation—

Johnson believed like so many before him that the provision allowing nonunanimous jury verdicts denied him due process. The Louisiana Supreme Court, however, had remained consistent throughout the century: until the U.S. Supreme Court overturns the provision, the validity of the Louisiana Constitution would remain sacrosanct. The previous year, in *State v. Brumfield* (1969), the court swiftly ruled that a similar challenge was without merit. "Neither the United States Supreme Court nor this Court has ruled the above statute unconstitutional. No further discussion is necessary."[5] Hamlin's opinion in *Johnson* would determine the same, though his ruling would be far less dismissive. The justice quoted the Sixth Amendment provisions for a speedy and public trial by an impartial jury, but noted that each of those mandates could be reasonably carried out without jury unanimity. Each of twelve jurors could be entirely impartial without necessarily being in agreement with one another. The trial could be both quick and public under the same conditions. As it had in *Schoonover*, the state Supreme Court goaded its federal counterpart, ruling that Johnson's nine-to-three verdict was constitutional because, "thus far, the United States Supreme court has not ruled that the Sixth Amendment compels the States under the Fourteenth Amendment to the United States Constitution to require that the verdict of the jury be unanimous in a criminal prosecution."[6] But this time the U.S. Supreme Court would take the bait.

Before it did, however, the Louisiana Supreme Court would clarify its position further. In *State v. Fink* (1970), decided the same day as *Johnson*, January 20, 1970, the court ruled similarly that a conviction for selling marijuana did not require a unanimous jury verdict. It did so again months later in June when validating the nine-to-three armed robbery conviction of Willie Caston Jr. "We are of the opinion," the court ruled in *State v. Caston* (1970), "that our State Constitution and the codal article under attack here, specifying in certain cases for trial by a jury of twelve but providing for conviction or acquittal by nine of the jurors, neither violates the Sixth Amendment to the Federal Constitution nor the Fourteenth Amendment as the concurrence of that number of jurors guarantees the accused a fair trial and due process of law."[7]

The *Johnson* case was first argued before the U.S. Supreme Court the following year in early 1971, and the justices were clearly divided on the issue of jury verdicts. "Unanimity was not required at common law," Chief Justice Warren Burger argued to his colleagues in their original conference, "no one really knows its origins. Majority verdicts were common prior to the Constitution. Madison's failure to get a unanimous verdict is relevant, and suggests that the standard was left to the states. The British system uses majority verdicts." That being the case, he argued, there was no choice but to affirm the Louisiana system.[8]

Burger was right. And he was wrong. Unanimous jury verdicts under English common law became standard in the fourteenth century, though there is no certainty as to why. Medieval criminal punishments were particularly harsh, and medieval epistemology didn't allow for multiple versions of truth. Unanimity could have served to protect defendants, or it could have served to protect an acute worldview that didn't trump dissent. Even more likely, medieval jurists came to twelve-man jury unanimity by way of the earlier system of compurgation, in which judges continued to add jurors until they could find twelve who agreed. When the addition method ended, the principle of an agreement of twelve remained.[9]

However it began, American colonists escaping the vagaries of all things British were not necessarily inclined to adopt the unanimity requirement. In the seventeenth century, Pennsylvania, Connecticut, and the Carolinas all allowed majority verdicts in criminal cases. As the colonies moved closer and closer to self-rule in the eighteenth century, however, American legal scholars—almost all of them educated in England—clearly supported unanimity, and that became the standard prior to the American Revolution. Though James Madison was from Virginia, a state that always required jury unanimity in criminal cases, he omitted that requirement from the Constitution, leading to Burger's assumption "that the standard was left to the states."[10]

Additionally, though the British system had historically required unanimity, a series of jury bribery scandals in the mid-1960s led England to pass a 1967 law allowing ten-to-two criminal verdicts as long as the jury deliberated for a minimum of two hours. The decision would only change a few verdicts, argued Roy Jenkins, England's secretary of state for the Home Office, "but those few cases may well be crucial from the point of view of law enforcement and the breaking-up of big criminal conspiracies." Disagreements among jurors didn't occur on fine points of law. They occurred because "one or two jurors have been persuaded, by bribery or intimidation, to hold out against the evidence."[11] By framing the law as one specifically designed to combat corruption, Jenkins established a false choice but mollified some of the debate about the validity of the law.

Still, "states can do this if they want to do so," Burger affirmed. So, too, did Hugo Black. And Thurgood Marshall. But William Douglas and William Brennan stumped for reversal, arguing that unanimity provided the baseline standard for reasonable doubt that ultimately provided for fair trials. Potter Stewart was also inclined to reverse. "Under the Fourteenth Amendment," he told his colleagues, "I would affirm. If the Sixth Amendment is incorporated by the Fourteenth and applies across the board, I would have to reverse. And since *Duncan* is not retroactive, I am more confused than ever. I am inclined to reverse on the ground that the Sixth Amendment requires a unanimous jury." *Duncan*, decided in December 1968, had incorporated the Sixth Amendment right to a jury trial into the Fourteenth Amendment's due process charge to the states, but was not made retroactive because of the thousands of criminal convictions it would have affected. However, that lack of retroactivity didn't mean, Stewart reasoned, that the principle of incorporation didn't apply. His understanding of the Sixth Amendment as requiring unanimity was enough.[12]

But not for Byron White. "You won't get around the retroactivity issue," he told Stewart. "*Duncan* is not retroactive, so I say that the Sixth Amendment does not apply in this case. Therefore, I would affirm." White never specifically disagreed with Stewart's interpretation of the Sixth Amendment's protection of unanimity, or even his interpretation of the Sixth's incorporation into the Fourteenth. He was, after all, the author of the majority opinion in *Duncan*. But *Duncan* appeared months after Johnson's trial and therefore couldn't apply. Hugo Black had argued in a concurring opinion in *Duncan* that all of the amendments in the Bill of Rights—including the Sixth—were applicable to the states under the Fourteenth Amendment, but White hadn't gone that far. For him, the right to trial by jury in criminal cases was inherent in the Fourteenth, and therefore applicable to the states.[13] "This is not an easy case," concluded Harry Blackmun, summing up the confusion of his colleagues. "Louisiana grades offenses, requiring unanimous verdicts in death cases. I am inclined to affirm, with a question mark."[14]

The question marks remained until the next term, when the case was reargued on January 10, 1972, this time with two new justices. John Marshall Harlan hadn't been around for the first conference, suffering the effects of cancer. He retired on September 23, 1971. That day, Hugo Black had a massive stroke that would eventually kill him two days later. Harlan and Black were contrasting figures. Black's tenure on the court began in 1937, and he built a career on reading the Fourteenth Amendment as imposing the guarantees of liberty provided in the Bill of Rights to the states. Harlan, nominated by Eisenhower in 1955, was known largely as the conservative stalwart on the otherwise progressive Warren Court. Still, Harlan took an expansive view of the Fourteenth Amendment's Due Process Clause, applying it beyond mere procedural guarantees. Despite their differences, both Black and Harlan seemed at least open to the possibility of rejecting Louisiana's claims.[15]

Richard Nixon replaced the two justices with Lewis Powell and William Rehnquist. Powell was a judicial moderate with a penchant for building consensus on the court, while Rehnquist was an unabashed conservative constructionist. The case they heard was much the same as that from the previous year, and, as Burger told his colleagues, "this was not a well-argued case." His opinion hadn't changed. Neither had that of Douglas, Brennan, or White. Blackmun was more confident in his affirmation, Stewart more confident in his reversal. Thurgood Marshall, however, changed his mind, emphasizing the reasonable doubt standard as needing unanimity to give the best possible chance for acquittal. "The jury was out twenty minutes," he said in conference. "It must be a unanimous jury. I reverse." In the first conference, Marshall affirmed, arguing "the only qualification of the Sixth Amendment's guarantee of a jury trial is 'impartial,' not unanimous. The state can cut the number from twelve to nine, but not to one. There is no difference between twelve and five or six or nine." The short deliberation period, however, was enough to convince him the second time around that "impartiality" was somehow compromised by a lack of unanimity. After Marshall's turn, Rehnquist had no trouble affirming, leaving Lewis Powell to break the tie. He wasn't quite ready. "I would like to reserve my vote for a week," he announced. He noted the Virginia state constitution's unanimity rule, but questioned its applicability in the *Johnson* case. "The federal standard requires unanimity, but the Fourteenth Amendment does not. I have not been able to sort out all of my views."[16]

The same day the court reheard the *Johnson* case, it also reheard a similar case from Oregon. Three defendants, who committed three separate crimes, were all convicted by jury decisions of ten to two in the only other state to allow majority verdicts.[17] Oregon, like Louisiana, hadn't entered statehood with such a mandate, but in the early 1930s amended its constitution to allow "that in the circuit court ten members of the jury may render a verdict of guilty or not guilty, save and except a verdict of guilty of first degree murder, which shall be found only by a unanimous verdict." Pamphlets distributed to Oregon voters in hopes of ratifying the 1934 amendment argued that it would make convictions easier.[18]

The Oregon law developed out of a confluence of factors. Nationally, there was a federal push for a "war on crime," prompted by the popularity of criminals like John Dillinger, folk heroes to many in the hard days of the Great Depression. At the same time, despite the recent death of Prohibition, the restriction of alcohol throughout the 1920s and early 1930s had given rise to gangsterism and organized crime. That national push to strengthen criminal statutes, however, was also matched in Oregon by state concerns. First, there were the Okie migrants made famous by John Steinbeck's *The Grapes of Wrath*, mistrusted as outcasts and criminals by locals on the West Coast. That bigotry towards outsiders was also pushed by a notorious Ku Klux Klan movement. The Klan first appeared in Oregon in 1921, brought by Louisiana's Luther Powell. The following year, with over fourteen thousand members, it was powerful enough to help pass an anti-Catholic school bill through the Oregon legislature. Of course, the Klan was also exceedingly anti-Semitic, opposing everyone who was neither white nor Protestant.[19]

That broader concern about the growing menace of organized crime and the bigotry and fear of minority groups ultimately coalesced in the case that would spur Oregon's jury amendment. James Walker had killed the former boyfriend of his lover, Edith McClain, in a Portland speakeasy. Seeking retribution for the death of his friend, Jacob Silverman, his brother Maurice, and the speakeasy's bartender, Abe Levine, went looking for the couple. Jacob Silverman found both Walker and McClain in a local motel, drove them out of town, and shot them in retribution. The Silverman case captured the imagination of Oregon citizens, combining a murder that had the flavor of a gangland execution with defendants, witnesses, and accomplices who were part of a hated minority. Oregon had a Jewish population since the 1880s, but they, like Catholics, had been targets of groups like the Klan for a long time. They would become even more vulnerable as the Nazi rise in Germany would find sympathetic ears in Oregon, where white Protestants associated Jewishness with labor unions and communism (the same labels applied to Steinbeck's Okies). The public infamy of the Silverman case came to a boil when the murder charge against him was reduced because one juror held out for a verdict of manslaughter. The Jewish defendant was sentenced to three years and a one-thousand-dollar fine for the murder of two white Protestants, and the outrage provoked in the Oregon public pushed the creation of the new constitutional amendment.[20]

As voters were debating the merits of the law in the weeks before the May 1934 election, there was a massive dockworker strike on the Portland waterfront, stoking fears about poverty, crime, and labor unions. Things became violent when strikebreakers were brought to the waterfront. Ultimately, six died, dozens were wounded, and hundreds found themselves in jail. It had nothing to do with the legislation itself, but it surely swayed votes in favor of the law. When the election took place on May 18, 1934, the amendment passed by a margin of thirty-four thousand votes.[21] And so Oregon, like Louisiana, made it easier to convict the next Jewish offender of murder.

Also like Louisiana, Oregon's conditional majority verdict decree had survived several challenges over the course of the century, even though its detractors found nothing compensatory about Oregon requiring the agreement of one more juror than did Louisiana.[22] Though the states and their legislative motives were different, the crimes of the defendants were different, and the number of jurors required to agree to reach a verdict were different, it was understood that the court's decision in one case would necessarily bear on its decision in the other.

Looming just as large over the court's decision in *Johnson* was its own ruling two years prior in *Williams v. Florida* (1970). Florida law required a unanimous six-person jury for noncapital criminal cases, and *Williams* upheld the practice, arguing that twelve-member juries were "accepted at common law" but "historically accidental." The Sixth Amendment required a criminal defendant to be tried by group of his or her peers, but there was nothing in the text to regulate the number required for peer review. Byron White, writing for the majority—as he would in *Johnson* and its counterpart, *Apodaca v. Oregon*—left it up to the states to decide on the number of jurors required for criminal trials, seemingly consistent with what would become his conference position in *Johnson*. Still, the two cases weren't necessarily translatable. "It might be suggested," wrote White in his *Williams* opinion, "that the 12-man jury gives a defendant a greater advantage since he has more 'chances' of finding a juror who will insist on acquittal and thus prevent conviction. But the advantage might just as easily belong to the State, which also needs only one juror out of twelve insisting on guilt to prevent acquittal." Such was the Louisiana Supreme Court's argument that had prevailed since *Ardoin*.[23] But in emphasizing the unanimity of twelve- and six-member juries to marshal a case for the equivalency of justice present with both, White seemed to be out of step with his own thinking about unanimity as a necessary part of criminal jurisprudence.[24] If nothing else, it left a hole to be filled two years later.

CHAPTER 8

The Decision in *Johnson*

After Lewis Powell slowly came around to affirming nonunanimous jury verdicts in the *Johnson* case, Byron White would again write the opinion of the U.S. Supreme Court, this time for a slim five-to-four majority. He opened his opinion by clarifying the reasonable doubt standard as presented by Johnson's attorneys, noting that "the jurors were told to convict only if convinced of guilt beyond a reasonable doubt. Nor is there any claim that, if the verdict in this case had been unanimous, the evidence would have been insufficient to support it." Instead, it was Johnson's claim that nine jurors "will be unable to vote conscientiously in favor of guilt beyond a reasonable doubt when three of their colleagues are arguing for acquittal," and that guilt in general could not be proved beyond a reasonable doubt "when one or more of a jury's members at the conclusion of deliberation still possess such a doubt." To make such claims, White argued, is to assume that the opinions of the three voting to acquit somehow impose themselves on the surety of the nine, that the fact of being in the majority acts as a barrier to reasonable discussion that exhausts all options and leads people to valid conclusions. And those assumptions are tantamount to accusing those in the jury's majority of irresponsibly ignoring the reasonable doubts of their peers, which could never be proved.[1]

More difficult was Johnson's claim that the three dissents in and of themselves constituted a reasonable doubt. Sure, White argued, the agreement of twelve jurors would have been more convincing, as would the agreement of twenty-four or thirty-six. But nine was a "substantial majority" of the jury, and the three opposed were still unable to convince their peers of that opposition. "That rational men disagree is not in itself equivalent to a failure of proof by the State," wrote White, "nor does it indicate infidelity to the reasonable-doubt standard." Furthermore, there were myriad cases where unanimous juries returned guilty verdicts even though the evidence easily could have swayed the jury the other way. By the federal criminal standard, which did require unanimity, the dissent of one juror did not mean acquittal; it meant a new trial. "If the doubt of a minority of jurors indicates the existence of a reasonable doubt, it would appear that a defendant should receive a directed verdict of acquittal" at the federal level. But defendants weren't acquitted in those situations, and the hung jury standard, in White's view, was itself an argument that minority dissent did not meet the reasonable doubt qualification.[2]

How, then, could nonunanimous criminal jury verdicts provide equal protection when other types of trials—capital trials or trials for petty crimes and misdemeanors—required other jury standards? That, argued White, wasn't a problem, either. *Williams* established that juries of less than twelve were constitutional, and "we perceive nothing unconstitutional or invidiously discriminatory" in increasing the number of jurors required for conviction based on the gravity of the crime being tried. Conviction was most difficult in capital cases because of the severity of the punishment possibly imposed. Even though Johnson "might well have been ultimately acquitted had he committed a capital offense," he still received equal protection of the law because he went to trial with lesser stakes.[3] Crime and punishment, in White's rendering, was a scale weighted on one side by the trial, on the other by the severity of the consequence of the outcome. As the consequences lightened, so too did the burden on the state. It was a difficult argument, at best, as maintaining different standards for different people didn't usually end in equality. Such was the lesson of the Warren Court's civil rights decisions the generation prior.

Because Frank Johnson's original trial took place before *Duncan*, and *Duncan* precluded retroactivity, he was limited in his appeal "from raising his due process argument in the classic 'fundamental fairness' language adopted there." Robert Apodaca's original trial, however, took place after *Duncan*, thus allowing the court to expand its thinking in *Johnson* to include the Fourteenth Amendment's relationship to the Sixth, and the relationship of both to nonunanimous jury verdicts at the state level. Apodaca was convicted by ten of twelve jurors for assault with a dangerous weapon after stabbing Ronald Joe Swanson in Salem, Oregon. Decided on the same day as *Johnson*, *Apodaca v. Oregon* allowed the justices to further elaborate their thinking on those relationships, each opinion citing the other liberally throughout. White's majority opinion in *Apodaca*, then, was unsurprisingly consistent with his majority opinion in *Johnson*. While the Fourteenth Amendment did mean that the Sixth Amendment was applicable to the states, there was no necessary demand for unanimity in the Sixth, and therefore states couldn't be required to maintain it. That federal courts required unanimity was incidental. "The reasonable-doubt standard developed separately from both the jury trial and the unanimous verdict," White argued, and so any Sixth Amendment claim that reasonable doubt necessitates unanimity "founders on the fact that the Sixth Amendment does not require proof beyond a reasonable doubt at all."[4]

Lewis Powell concurred with White in both opinions, validating the constitutionality of nonunanimous criminal jury verdicts, but took issue with the idea that the federal standard for jury trials had to apply to the states under the Fourteenth Amendment. "I do not think," he argued, "that all of the elements of jury trial within the meaning of the Sixth Amendment are necessarily embodied in or incorporated into the Due Process Clause of the Fourteenth Amendment." Providing due process and providing fair trials didn't necessarily mean providing unanimous jury verdicts just because federal courts required it. As long as one's peers were determining guilt or innocence, and as long as that determination was fair, then states had met the standard of due process.[5]

Harry Blackmun also concurred separately, evincing the question mark he noted in conference. He joined the court's opinion, with the caveat "that in so doing I do not imply that I regard a State's split-verdict system as a wise one. My vote means only that I cannot conclude that the system is constitutionally offensive. Were I a legislator, I would disfavor it as a matter of policy."[6]

Justices Douglas, Brennan, Stewart, and Marshall disfavored the system as a matter of policy and of constitutionality. "Though unanimous jury decisions are not required in state trials, they are constitutionally required in federal prosecutions," wrote Douglas. "How can that be possible when both decisions stem from the Sixth Amendment?" It was a double standard, and double standards did not augur well for equality. "After today's decisions, a man's property may only be taken away by a unanimous jury vote, yet he can be stripped of his liberty by a lesser standard." The majority decision, Douglas argued, was watering down the civil rights of those at the state level. Civil rights "extend, of course, to everyone, but in cold reality touch mostly the lower castes in our society. I refer, of course, to the blacks, the Chicanos, the one-mule farmers, the agricultural workers, the offbeat students, the victims of the ghetto. Are we giving the States the power to experiment in diluting their civil rights?" The answer was undoubtedly yes. Louisiana and Oregon had substantially higher conviction rates than other states because the nonunanimous jury standard "eliminates the circumstances in which a minority of jurors (a) could have rationally persuaded the entire jury to acquit, or (b) while unable to persuade the majority to acquit, nonetheless could have convinced them to convict only on a lesser-included offense."[7]

Marshall and Stewart's concurring dissents also emphasized the historical legacy of unanimity as a core component of due process and a safeguard of equal justice under the law. "After today," wrote Marshall, "the skeleton of these safeguards remains, but the Court strips them of life and of meaning." William Brennan's dissent placed the blame for the decision squarely on Powell's waffling. It was odd that nonunanimous verdicts survived the day "when a majority of the Court agrees that the Sixth Amendment requires a unanimous verdict in federal criminal jury trials, and a majority also agrees that the right to jury trial guaranteed by the Sixth Amendment is to be enforced against the States according to the same standards that protect that right against federal encroachment." But they did survive the day, because, "while my Brother Powell agrees that a unanimous verdict is required in federal criminal trials, he does not agree that the Sixth Amendment right to a jury trial is to be applied in the same way to State and Federal governments."[8]

The Supreme Court's opinions in both *Johnson* and *Apodaca* were supposed to settle the issue of nonunanimous verdicts once and for all, but such was a difficult task with a five-to-four verdict, particularly when one of the majority, Harry Blackmun, only affirmed while holding his nose. The split decision in *Johnson* did validate the Louisiana practice as constitutional, but by an unofficial five-to-four verdict, declared it to be a bad idea.

Press coverage of the ruling emphasized that it "demonstrated the conservative impact of President Nixon's four nominees." Burger, Blackmun, Powell, and Rehnquist had all been nominated by Nixon, combining with Byron White, "a prosecution-minded holdover from the Warren Court," to produce the slim majority. The Associated Press account, which ran in the local *New Orleans Times-Picayune*, quoted Douglas in describing the ruling as being "in the tradition of the Inquisition." The *Wall Street Journal's* interpretation was similar, though far more celebratory: "President Nixon's determined effort to turn the Supreme Court toward what he has termed 'a conservative judicial philosophy' is beginning to pay off." The *New York Times* worried that the ruling would "prompt other state legislatures to adopt the less than unanimous jury rule." Without Lewis Powell's interpretation that the Fourteenth Amendment didn't require states to meet the federal requirements for jury trials inherent in the Sixth Amendment, the decision could have allowed federal criminal trials to be decided by nonunanimous juries. The *Times* noted the dissenters' emphasis on the need to provide protection for those most vulnerable from "the prosecutorial power of the state," and those most vulnerable were racial minorities and the poor. The *Washington Post* reminded its readers that, "for the first time since the Warren Court constitutional 'revolution' began a decade ago, a provision of the Bill of Rights was applied with less than full force to the states." Hugo Black, replaced by Powell, "often spoke sharply against a 'watered down' application of the Bill of Rights to the states." John Marshall Harlan, replaced by Rehnquist, dissented in *Williams*. Nixon's nominees, however, had turned from judicial liberalism. The "revolution" was over. The conservative backlash had begun.[9]

Of course, that backlash was itself a radical transition, or, as University of Pennsylvania law professor Paul Bender termed it, "the Nixon judicial revolution." As reported by Richard Stout in a scathing *Christian Science Monitor* editorial using the *Johnson* decision as an example of everything wrong with Nixon's appointees, "Mr. Bender says Warren precedents are not being set aside by frontal attack, but by the erosion of refinements and exceptions." The Warren Court sought to protect individual rights at the federal level, then marshaled the Fourteenth Amendment to protect those rights at the state level, as well. "The Nixon justices, on the other hand," argued Bender, "seem to assume that those in high places with power over their fellow men will almost inevitably act correctly and responsibly." The Nixon appointees "tend to see the Warren court's safeguards as unwarranted intrusions into the activities of other branches of government." Just a month after its *Johnson* ruling, for example, the Burger Court ruled that the First Amendment's freedom-of-the-press mandate did not protect reporters when concealing sources in grand jury testimony. The five-to-four vote was identical to the one in *Johnson*.[10]

Nixon's nomination of Warren Burger to replace Earl Warren was one of the first major acts of his presidency, followed later by his nomination of Harry Blackmun. Then came Powell and Rehnquist. All would side against reporters, and all would side against Frank Johnson. Indeed, when Powell and Rehnquist ascended to the court prior to the second hearing of *Johnson v. Louisiana*, it may not have made the outcome a foregone conclusion, but it certainly made it predictable.

Lost in the coverage of the court's new conservatism was the decision's place among other civil rights milestones. Douglas's question about diluting the civil rights of dispossessed groups was a fair one. The Civil Rights Act and Voting Rights Act had removed almost all of the legal vestiges of Jim Crow. The civil rights movement had turned radical in their wake, as activists grappled with the fundamental economic inequalities that remained after their implementation and questioned the efficacy of working so diligently for the right to attend the same schools as people who clearly found them to be inferior. Meanwhile, the U.S. Supreme Court decided *Swann v. Charlotte-Mecklenburg Board of Education* (1971) the same year that it heard initial arguments in the *Johnson* case (and before the retirement of Harlan and the death of Black), ruling that busing was a viable method of enforcing *Brown's* school desegregation mandate. Busing dominated race news in 1971, as controversy over whether *Brown* intended to outlaw segregation or force integration led to popular frustration and a backlash among white parents in many areas. *Johnson's* place in the timeline of civil rights activism was ultimately lost in the broader racial conflicts of the day.[11]

That doesn't mean, however, that it didn't have a place in that time-line. *Johnson* validated a law with Jim Crow intent, but one that had worked against defendants of all races. Such was the reason that Douglas referred to "the blacks, the Chicanos, the one-mule farmers, the agricultural workers, the offbeat students, the victims of the ghetto." The effects of poll taxes and segregation restrictions on race were obvious to the naked eye. The effects of Louisiana's nonunanimous criminal jury verdict law on race required an understanding of the relationship between blackness and poverty in the South and a corresponding understanding of the sociological bearing of those factors on criminality. Because of the less obvious racism of the law and because of its confinement to Louisiana and Oregon, it never received the same treatment from activists that other Jim Crow measures received. It was, however, having similar effects as those other Jim Crow measures, regardless of public notice, prompting Douglas to speculate that the *Johnson* Court was "giving the States the power to experiment in diluting their civil rights."

CHAPTER 9

The Ghost in the Machine

In the intervening time between the *Johnson* opinions of the Louisiana Supreme Court and the U.S. Supreme Court, a flurry of criminal defendants appealed their convictions by Louisiana courts in anticipation of the possible unconstitutionality of the state statute. In 1971 and 1972, no less than eight appeals to the state Supreme Court took exception to a criminal conviction in Louisiana made by a less-than-unanimous jury. In each case, the court validated the constitutionality of the practice—as it had in *Johnson*, as it had since the 1890s.[1]

The same held in 1973 and 1974, when more criminal defendants challenged criminal verdicts rendered by less-than-unanimous juries—in cases of armed robbery, attempted murder, and second-degree murder. The only thorny issue the court faced in those years involved an armed robbery conviction where a nonunanimous jury convicted a defendant even though the judge did not instruct the body on penalty provisions. Penalties were at the discretion of the judge, he argued, not the jury. He was right, of course, but the defendant in *State v. Blackwell* (1973) appealed on the argument that, if the number of jurors required to render a verdict vacillated based on the type of punishment that could come from a verdict of guilty, then such instructions clearly mattered. Even then, however, the Supreme Court's decision was relatively easy. Nine-member criminal jury verdicts were constitutional.[2]

Even as those decisions appeared, however, Louisiana was in the process of writing another constitution. In the Constitution of 1974, legislators moved the criminal punishment provisions to the Declaration of Rights in Article One, but the change was more than one of simple location. Despite press concerns that the Supreme Court's *Johnson* decision would loosen standards for criminal convictions, Louisiana actually responded by tightening them. "A case in which the punishment is necessarily confinement at hard labor," said Section 17, "shall be tried before a jury of twelve persons, ten of whom must concur to render a verdict." The section also increased the number of jurors for trials of relative felonies and misdemeanors from five to six, with only five of the jurors needing to agree to render a verdict. It was an idea that had been floating through the legislature since 1950, when the Louisiana State Law Institute created a projet for a new constitution and included a suggestion that misdemeanors should be tried by a jury of eight with a majority of six concurring for a verdict. Three years later, Louisiana State University law professor Dale Bennett suggested a five-member jury with four needing to concur. Five out of six became the new constitutional standard, however. *Williams* had upheld six-person juries, and since *Johnson* upheld verdicts of nine out of twelve, or 75 percent, then surely, the framers argued, the Court would be fine with a concurrence of five out of six, or 83 percent.[3]

The move from nine to ten concurring jurors seems more strange, coming as it did two years after the U.S. Supreme Court validated Louisiana's original system, one that had been in place since the nineteenth century. Oregon, the other state to allow nonunanimous criminal verdicts—and whose system was the subject of *Apodaca*—required ten of twelve jurors to concur. But the new Louisiana provision was less the result of a desire to get in line with Oregon and more the result of an opposition movement to the status quo. In committee proceedings during the writing process, a group of legislators proposed to require a unanimous twelve-member jury for major felonies that didn't allow parole or probation. "In cases involving a crime necessarily punishable by hard labor," the original draft read, "the jury shall consist of twelve persons, all of whom must concur to render a verdict in capital cases or cases in which no parole or probation is permitted." It wasn't a move for unanimity in all hard-labor felonies, but instead an attempt to treat non-parole sentences such as life in prison with more gravity. There were plenty, however, who liked the old system just fine, and noted that it had been upheld by the Supreme Court just two years prior. Ultimately, the two sides compromised by raising the majority standard by one for all noncapital criminal trials. Thibodeaux judge Walter I. Lanier was joined by dozens of representatives in amending the proposal to read, "Criminal cases in which the punishment may be capital shall be tried before a jury of twelve persons, all of whom must concur to render a verdict; cases in which the punishment is necessarily confinement at hard labor shall be tried before a jury of twelve persons, ten of whom must concur to render a verdict." There were only three dissents, one of them Oberlin, Louisiana, attorney Errol D. Deshotels. Another came from Webster Parish's R. Harmon Drew, a Louisiana judge since the 1940s. The third vote against the measure came from Emmett Asseff, who held a doctorate in government from the University of North Carolina and was seminal in creating the Public Affairs Research Council of Louisiana, an independent state government watchdog organization designed to provide more transparency to executive and legislative actions. His opposition to the law seemed obvious considering his background. The overwhelming sentiment, however, was for passage.[4]

The other major concern of post-*Johnson* commentators concerned the potential for other states to lower their own criminal jury standards to make criminal convictions easier while staying within the bounds of the Burger Court's interpretation of the Sixth and Fourteenth amendments. That, however, wouldn't happen, either. While Louisiana and Oregon maintained their majority verdict provisions, no other state modified its law to allow them. It surely would have been a hard sell to voters, as no public official wants to be associated with making it easier for the state to deprive people of their rights, but certainly it could have been done. Rather, the lack of action by other states probably demonstrates a fundamental disagreement with the controversial and close decision. In 1994, for example, the New York Court of Appeals commissioned a study to evaluate the state's jury system, but did not even address revisions to the unanimity requirement. Unanimity was simply assumed to be a priori, a necessary bedrock of criminal justice. Or, as supermajority advocate Michael Glasser has argued, "perhaps tradition has prompted [states like New York] to ignore the compelling arguments made in favor of abandoning the rule."[5]

Those arguments tracked along several different fronts. Nonunanimous juries make their decisions more quickly and vote sooner in the process than juries required to be unanimous, and studies demonstrate that people rarely change their minds about cases after further deliberation. Harry Kalven and Hans Zeisel's seminal jury study of 1966 went so far as to argue that, in criminal deliberations, "the outcome is pre-determined." Even in cases where the initial minority ultimately wins over its peers, Glasser argues, "there is nothing to suggest that majority-rule juries, which take less time to render a verdict, simply ignore the rational arguments forwarded by jurors in the minority."[6] In addition, larger factions tend to win out more easily over smaller groups in the decision-making process, only validating, according to Glasser, the likely conclusion near-determined at the outset of the deliberation process.[7]

Most influential in such debates, however, is the contention that nonunanimous verdicts reduce the number of hung juries and eliminate the possibility of a lone holdout dominating the outcome of a trial. Glasser made this claim, as did Klaven and Zeisel before him. While hung juries are a significant problem, however, the most complete study of the relationship of such verdicts with hung jury rates argues that "it is misleading to argue that nonunanimous verdicts reduce the hung jury rate." Economists William Neilson and Harold Winter argue that, when the eventual verdict is taken into account, "a unanimous jury rule tends to lead to more accurate verdicts when compared to nonunanimous rules." While nonunanimous verdicts reduced the hung jury rate "when considering the first trial only," argue Neilson and Winter, "it is not true when properly considering the effect of these rules on the *final disposition* of the trial."[8] Harvard business professor Peter Couglan demonstrates that the "unanimity rule maximizes ex ante expected utility for all jurors." Such arguments have tended to dominate the discussion, most commentators being unwilling to impede upon the rights of the accused for a mythical expediency that inordinately favors prosecutors.[9]

Byron White had used hung juries to make his point about the validity of nonunanimous verdicts. "If the doubt of a minority of jurors indicates the existence of a reasonable doubt," he wrote, "it would appear that a defendant should receive a directed verdict of acquittal rather than a retrial." The problem of hung juries had lingered for centuries. For hundreds of years before 1866, British courts forbade judges from discharging juries until they reached a verdict, keeping the jurors locked away without food or drink to expedite the process. Finally, however, in 1866, a hung jury law allowed juries to be discharged if the members were unable to agree in a reasonable amount of time. In that case, the defendant would be tried again in front of a new jury. The problem for England was that those defendants would then appeal on double jeopardy claims.[10]

The young United States would move even more swiftly to the hung jury standard, though it would have its detractors in the late 1700s and early 1800s, and many sued claiming a violation of double jeopardy laws. The issue was finally settled in 1824, when the Supreme Court ruled in *United States v. Perez* (1824) that jurors unable to reach a verdict in federal cases could be dismissed, and that the dismissal did not result in acquittal, but rather a new trial. It was a decision designed to relieve jurors of those British-like pressures to arrive at a unanimous verdict, thereby maintaining the sanctity of that unanimity when it appeared. "Properly understood in historical context," argues legal scholar Anthony Moreno, "*Perez* can only be regarded as having championed, perhaps unwittingly, unanimity–reasonable doubt principles by assuring the reality of their interdependence and integration as a combined standard of proof and persuasion." White's decision in *Johnson* cited *Perez*, but clearly misread the case. *Perez*—and the hung jury standard in general—protected the sanctity of unanimous juries and implicitly argued for their role in the creation of due process.[11]

But the use of nonunanimous juries is even more problematic. In 2010, the U.S. Supreme Court ruled in *McDonald v. City of Chicago* (2010) that Second Amendment gun rights were fully incorporated by the Fourteenth. States were not allowed to limit gun rights following any standard that deviated from that set by the federal government. If the standard as of 2010 is now incorporation, then the notion that the Sixth Amendment is not fully incorporated by the Fourteenth, thus requiring states to adhere to the federal standard of unanimous criminal jury verdicts, seems inherently flawed.[12]

Of course, verdicts after the fact mean less in historical context than verdicts that could have provided precedent for the *Johnson* court. In *Billeci v. United States* (1950), the Supreme Court argued that guilt "must be established beyond a reasonable doubt. All twelve jurors must be convinced beyond that doubt." The bedrock principle of criminal jurisprudence was that "the prosecutor in a criminal case must actually overcome the presumption of innocence, all reasonable doubts as to guilt, and the unanimous verdict requirement." Twenty years later, *In re Winship* (1970) stated, "Although virtually unanimous adherence to the reasonable-doubt standard in common-law jurisdictions may not conclusively establish it as a requirement of due process, such adherence does 'reflect a profound judgment about the way in which law should be enforced and justice administered.'" Justice Brennan argued for the majority that "expressions in many opinions of this Court indicate that it has long been assumed that proof of a criminal charge beyond a reasonable doubt is constitutionally required."[13]

And so, before and after the decision in *Johnson*, the U.S. Supreme Court viewed the Fourteenth Amendment as fully incorporating the Bill of Rights and unanimous jury verdicts as bedrock principles of American due process. But in 1972 that formula fundamentally changed.

CHAPTER 10

The Trial of Derrick Todd Lee

Despite arguments to the contrary, a mythical expediency that inordinately favored prosecutors continued to hold sway in Louisiana, as did the belief that due process was a concept fundamentally segregated from jury unanimity. In the years following the adoption of the state's new constitution in 1974, more appeals before the state Supreme Court sought to overturn convictions on the grounds that nonunanimous juries did the convicting. In *State v. Gilmore* (1976), a district attorney amended an indictment to replace a first-degree capital murder charge with a second-degree noncapital murder charge. With the reduced indictment came a constitutionally valid reduction in the number of jurors required to reach a verdict.[1] The decision seemed to prove, more than any academic argument ever could, that nonunanimous criminal verdicts favored prosecutors. Still, the supermajority standard would stand.

Or, at least, the ten-to-two supermajority standard would stand. As the Louisiana Supreme Court continued to validate nonunanimous criminal jury verdicts, Daniel Burch and his company, Wrestle, Inc., were showing pornographic movies to those willing to slip coins into a private viewing machine in downtown New Orleans. In May 1977, Burch was arrested and tried for the minor crime of obscenity. Burch was tried before a jury of six, with five concurring to convict him, and since the new constitution prescribed it, the state Supreme Court validated the conviction. On appeal to the U.S. Supreme Court, however, the justices who upheld nonunanimous jury verdicts proved that there were limits to the power of the majority. The year after Burch's arrest, the court had ruled in *Ballew v. Georgia* (1978) that five-member criminal juries, even for petty crimes, were unconstitutional. A minimum of six was required. It elaborated on its decision the following year when Burch's case reached Washington. In

Burch v. Louisiana (1979) the U.S. Supreme Court struck down the 1974 state constitution's provision that five of six jurors could concur for minor crimes and misdemeanors. "Lines must be drawn somewhere if the substance of the jury trial right is to be preserved," the court argued, and the line that it drew was at a unanimous six-member jury. However, one of the court's principal reasons for the decision was "the near-uniform judgment of those States utilizing six-member juries in trials of nonpetty offenses that the verdict must be unanimous to convict." It was another hole in the logic of the court, as there was a near-uniform judgment by states as to the unanimity of twelve-member juries, as well. That part of Louisiana's constitution, however, would remain in place.[2]

Nonunanimous twelve-member juries seemed functionally bulletproof in Louisiana, but in the early 1990s, they also began gaining traction outside of the state. Just as George Clement Perkins had proposed less-than-unanimous verdicts in Congress in 1894, one hundred years later another crusading California politician began making the same arguments. Governor Pete Wilson watched as jury deadlocks drew out the Los Angeles murder trial of Lyle and Erik Menendez for three years, beginning in 1993. On June 17, 1994, the world watched as O. J. Simpson's white Bronco drove down a Los Angeles freeway, and by September 1995, the trial was still ongoing. As of summer 1995, Wilson was making a bid for a presidential nomination, and part of his anticrime rhetoric included adopting the Louisiana policy of ten-to-two jury verdicts for the federal government, using the cases of Menendez and Simpson as examples of overblown, lengthy, expensive trials that could be reigned in by the common sense of nonunanimous juries. He was also seeking state legislation that would create a new standard for California. "This," the *New York Times* argued bluntly, "is not a good idea." An unsigned editorial acknowledged the *Johnson* decision, but reminded readers that "not everything that is constitutional is wise." The paper worried that nonunanimous juries would "deliver quickie verdicts" that would come without the sustained deliberation that unanimity required. "Even if the unanimity requirement were flawed, which it is not, it would be better for public confidence in justice to live with this kind of imperfection."[3] The *Times* had little to worry about. Wilson's candidacy petered out, and

California never seriously considered nonunanimous jury verdicts. But the simple appearance of the suggestion in the national public discourse, ten decades after Louisiana's convict lease program spurred the first example of such verdicts, demonstrated both the stability of Louisiana's law and the influence of *Johnson.*

Over the next three decades, the Louisiana Supreme Court would rebuff dozens of appeals attempting to overturn the nonunanimous jury provision codified by *Johnson.* The legislature, buoyed by the continued validation and hungry for a higher conviction rate in noncapital murder cases, passed an August 2007 law allowing ten of twelve jurors to convict in first-degree murder cases, as long as the district attorney did not pursue the death penalty.[4]

Three years before the change in law, Derrick Todd Lee was convicted of cutting the throat of Geralyn DeSoto in her home in Baton Rouge. Lee, known publicly as the Baton Rouge Serial Killer, was linked to the murders of several women in the neighborhoods surrounding Louisiana State University. The particularly violent death of DeSoto first led police to suspect her husband, but DNA evidence turned the investigation. Police captured Lee in Atlanta and brought him back to Baton Rouge for trial in August 2004. In October 2004, Lee would also be tried for the murder of LSU graduate student Charlotte Murray Pace. It was clear that the state had substantial evidence of violent first-degree murder, but the district attorney chose to try Lee for second-degree murder in the case of DeSoto, which would allow a nonunanimous verdict. There was no sexual assault in the DeSoto murder, the state argued, thus the second-degree murder charge, but it was clear that a conviction in the DeSoto case in August would allow the state to demonstrate a record of murder, making a conviction for first-degree murder—and thus the death penalty—easier in the Pace trial.[5]

The second-degree murder charge for the killing of Geralyn DeSoto was rendered by a less-than-unanimous jury, prompting an appeal that almost made it to the Supreme Court. On the petition for a writ of certiorari, the Houston Institute for Race and Justice presented an amicus brief on behalf of Lee, emphasizing the gendered and racial implications of the Louisiana jury standard. Women and minorities were already underrepresented on juries, and "prosecutors disproportionately use peremptory strikes on people of color." The brief reminded the court that the Louisiana Constitution of 1898 was the document that officially adopted Jim Crow segregation and voter restriction provisions that denied African Americans the right to vote. One was not necessarily correlative to the other—the original provision was designed to take rights from defendants, the twenty-first century result was the disfranchisement of minority jurors—and there was certainly no guarantee that racial minorities or women would necessarily vote differently from white men on juries and therefore constitute the minority. Still, it was clear that nonunanimous verdicts took power from defendants, but also from individual jurors, and since minority jurors were already underrepresented and the majority of criminal defendants were members of racial minorities, the race problems on either side of the jury box were exacerbated. In a similar case, *Bowen v. Oregon* (2009), an amicus brief by Harvard's Charles Ogletree argued that "one of the original purposes of the non-unanimous jury was to functionally silence the views of racial and ethnic minorities and women, and suggests that the current operation of nonunanimous juries *de facto* accomplishes that purpose." Ogletree pointed out that nonunanimous juries allowed prosecutors to keep one or two minorities on a jury without having to worry about their effect on the outcome of the trial.[6]

As Kim Taylor-Thompson has discussed, women tend to speak less than men during jury deliberation, and men tend to interrupt them when they do. "Men and women remember evidence and testimony differently," argues legal scholar Kate Riordan, "and in particular, men tend to neglect conduct in the context of relationships and conceptualize moral issues in a rights-oriented—and consequently more abstract—manner." That being the case, the thoroughness bred by unanimity requirements allows all jurors to have adequate input about the trial's outcome. The same is true for racial distinctions. "Unconscious stereotyping" can affect everyone, even those without any tangible racist tendencies, and members of stereotyped groups tend to cognize information differently. Diverse groups bring more perspectives to juries, only benefiting the process, and tend to deliberate longer. Unanimous juries, researchers have argued, only further help to bring such deliberations forward.[7]

Regardless, the court refused to hear the case of Daniel Burch, and it refused to hear the case of Derrick Todd Lee. It didn't hear *Bowen v. Oregon*, and it didn't hear a similar case from Louisiana in 2010.[8] More important than the Supreme Court's continued refusal to rehear cases, however, is that the cases continue to appear. A law forged in post-Reconstruction politics has remained one of the last holdovers from the early Jim Crow era in Louisiana. The original impetus of legislators to make convictions easier for a state hungry for more convicts withstood constant challenges throughout the following century. Its constitutionality was confirmed in *Johnson v. Louisiana* (1972), not because a racist court sought to reinstitute one of the final vestiges of Jim Crow, but because it ruled that equal protection could be granted by nine of twelve jurors. Still, as the twentieth century became the twenty-first, it was clear that race still played a role in the formula created by the nonunanimous standard. It was a subtle racism, to be sure. A racist law became a simple matter of constitutional policy. It didn't have the racist odor of poll taxes or separate train cars, and so it remained, with effects that reached far beyond the bounds of race. It still remains.

Louisiana has never commissioned a study of the role nonunanimous verdicts have played in the outcomes of trials, but Oregon has. The Appellate Division of the Oregon Office of Public Defense Services studied a sample of felony trials between 2007 and 2008 and found that 65.5 percent of trials in which the jury was polled (and thus the final vote of the jury was known) featured a jury vote that was nonunanimous on at least one count.[9] It is a startling number, a frightening number. If the statistic holds for all criminal juries, then more than half of defendants are being convicted when they otherwise wouldn't in any other state— save Louisiana. And there is no reason to assume that such numbers aren't at least relatively correlative to Louisiana. And so the debate about the debits and credits of nonunanimous criminal jury verdicts and the assumption of their inherent place in the system by Louisiana legislators and prosecutors has fundamentally shaped the state's criminal justice policy, for better and for worse. Mostly, however, for worse.

Epilogue

The year after Louisiana passed its Separate Car Act, a group of concerned black business leaders in New Orleans formed a citizens committee and planned a test case to challenge the law's constitutionality. They chose Homer Plessy to be the tester, largely because he was of mixed race. He could "pass" for white. They wanted someone who would by his very presence demonstrate how arbitrary concepts of race really were in practice. On June 7, 1892, Plessy was arrested in a planned breech of the Separate Car Act. The conductor had been warned. There was a private detective there to arrest Plessy. The Louisiana District Court ruled that the state had the right to regulate railroad companies within its borders. If that regulation involved racial segregation, then so be it. That started the process of appeal, and in 1896 Plessy's case finally reached the U.S. Supreme Court.[1]

The Supreme Court, of course, ruled against Plessy in an eight-to-one decision. Henry Billings Brown wrote the majority opinion, which featured two principal arguments. First, he argued, blacks and whites were politically equal (in the sense that they had the same political rights) but socially unequal (blacks were not as socially advanced as whites). "Legislation is powerless to eradicate racial instincts or to abolish distinctions based on physical differences, and the attempt to do so can only result in accentuating the differences of the present situation," he wrote. "If the civil and political rights of both races be equal, one cannot be inferior to the other civilly or politically. If one race be inferior to the other socially, the Constitution of the United States cannot put them on the same plane." Second, Brown argued that separate facilities for blacks were fine as long as they were equal to those of whites. Whites, after all, were "equally" barred from riding on black train cars, just as black riders were barred from white cars. Separation was neither an aid nor a hindrance to equality. It was simply separation.[2]

The lone dissenter in the court's *Plessy* decision was John Marshall Harlan, the grandfather of the second John Marshall Harlan, whose retirement in 1971 would allow Richard Nixon to appoint William Rehnquist to the court. In his dissent, the first Harlan attacked the constitutionality of the Louisiana law, arguing that, while it may appear to treat blacks and whites equally, "every one knows that the statute in question had its origin in the purpose, not so much to exclude white persons from railroad cars occupied by blacks, as to exclude colored people from coaches occupied by or assigned to white persons." Constitutional law is one thing, argued Harlan, but in practice, such things are never equal.[3]

The Supreme Court's *Plessy v. Ferguson* (1896) decision validated Louisiana's segregation laws and would only encourage their proliferation. The state began segregating every aspect of white and black social life. In 1894, Louisiana made interracial marriage illegal. In 1902, the state segregated streetcars in New Orleans—over the objections of the trolley companies, who didn't want to be responsible for turning away customers. The legislature then passed a law that kept white prostitutes from sleeping with black clients, and vice-versa. It made serving alcohol to whites and blacks at the same bar illegal.[4] All of it was made possible by *Plessy*.

It would take more than half a century to overcome the precedent set by *Plessy*, not because a racist court was scheming to destroy the equality of the black population, but instead because the core of Brown's second-argument logic was sound. The Supreme Court was there to balance laws against the hard weight of the Constitution, and if the law mandated equality, the two were effectively balanced. And so it took until the 1954 *Brown v. Board of Education of Topeka* decision to overturn the precedent. *Brown* acknowledged that, no matter what the wording of a law might say, the practice of various laws matters in determining whether those laws are constitutional. South Carolina's public schools were dramatically unequal. In Kansas, financial allotments to schools were equivalent, but black children who lived nearer to the white school still had to travel to the black school. There were differing levels of inequality in segregated systems, but in practice all segregated systems were unequal. So, even though the laws of both South Carolina and Kansas mandated both separation and equality, they were both fundamentally unequal.

Plessy and its removal provide a useful lens through which to view nonunanimous criminal verdicts. The Separate Car Act of 1890 was a state law born in the crucible of Redeemer politics with inherently negative racial implications. It was validated by the U.S. Supreme Court partly because of a racist bent, but also because of a technical reading of the court's mandate in judging state law. That being the case, it took decades for the body to make concessions to the racist context of the law's creation and the functional contemporary problems it caused on the ground. Louisiana's nonunanimous criminal jury legislation, first passed in 1880, was also a state law born in the crucible of Redeemer politics with inherently negative racial implications. It was also validated by the Supreme Court because of a technical reading of its mandate in judging state law. It has been decades, and it is time to make concessions to the racist context of the law's creation and the functional contemporary problems it causes.

Understanding segregation laws as racist in 1954, of course, was far more obvious than a similar understanding of nonunanimous criminal jury verdicts in the twenty-first century. The former was blatantly based on inferiority claims and specifically targeted minorities based solely on their minority status. The latter simply argued for a different standard of conviction equally applicable to any defendant charged with a noncapital state crime. As criminal appeals throughout the twentieth century demonstrated, however, equal applicability was a red herring that distracted from the state's easier ability to put its citizens in prison. It was discriminatory by jurisdiction, as it made prosecution at the state level easier than at the federal level. It was discriminatory by gender, as jury selection and deliberation studies demonstrated. Those studies also demonstrated racial discrimination inherent in Louisiana's framework, but the reality of that discrimination did not stop at the water's edge of the jury box or the Jim Crow era. In 2005, for example, Louisiana incarcerated 523 white people and 2,452 black people per 100,000, a differential of roughly 4.7 to 1. That differential was actually below the national average of 5.6 to 1 because, while Louisiana's rate of incarceration for black prisoners was higher than that of the nation as a whole, so too was its rate of incarceration for white prisoners. The differential between black and white prisoners was highest in Washington, D.C., whose ratio was a staggering 19 to 1. It was lowest in Hawaii at just under 2 to 1.[5] When the best a state can do is to incarcerate twice as many black prisoners as white per 100,000 citizens, the system is obviously weighted racially. When a state creates a mechanism whereby convictions become easier, it only feeds that racial system. The doctrine of nonunanimous criminal jury verdicts in Louisiana began with a clear racist intent, to feed a system that was discriminatory in intent and consequence. It now feeds a system that may or may not be discriminatory in intent, but is undoubtedly discriminatory in consequence.

As the nineteenth century became the twentieth, and that became the twenty-first, legal action eroded most of Redeemer political ideology. Segregation laws fell to legal challenges and civil rights activism. Poll taxes were eliminated in federal elections by the Twenty-fourth Amendment, in state elections by *Harper v. Virginia Board of Elections* (1966). Convict lease, too, fell to good-government reform throughout the South in the early twentieth century.

Louisiana's law allowing nonunanimous verdicts in criminal prosecutions was born as a child of the state's convict lease program. Like segregation laws and poll taxes, it stemmed from the white southern Democratic attempt to "Redeem" the South following the end of Reconstruction. But unlike segregation laws and poll taxes, Louisiana's nonunanimous criminal jury verdict law still exists. It still affects every criminal defendant in the state, every criminal jury in the state. It is today the last of Louisiana's Jim Crow laws, its last Redemption. And it is now time for it to be redeemed.

2019 Update: Success at the Ballot Box and the Evolution of Jim Crow

The 1890s

One additional factor buttressing Louisiana's nonunanimous criminal jury law that the 2015 edition of this book ignored (to its detriment) was the desire by white leaders in the state to mitigate what they saw as the problematic repercussions of black jury service. The work of that valuable research was done by legal scholar Thomas Ward Frampton, a former New Orleans public defender and Climenko Fellow and Lecturer on Law at Harvard.

Racial exclusion for jury service was outlawed by the Civil Rights Act of 1875, one of the final major pieces of Reconstruction legislation before the Compromise of 1877. But after the Bourbon restoration, conservative Democrats known as Redeemers were often able to maneuver around such mandates with discriminatory voting restrictions that limited jury pools and peremptory challenges. In some instances, they patently refused to abide by the 1875 legislation.[1]

Five years after the passage of the Civil Rights Act in 1880, the United States Supreme Court reversed the conviction of Taylor Strauder, a black West Virginia man convicted of murder by an all-white jury. West Virginia specifically barred black jury service, and the Court ruled that such restrictions violated the Fourteenth Amendment's Equal Protection Clause. "The very fact that colored people are singled out and expressly denied by a statute all right to participate in the administration of the law as jurors because of their color, though they are citizens and may be in other respects fully qualified, is practically a brand upon them affixed by the law, an assertion of their inferiority, and a stimulant to that race prejudice which is an impediment to securing to individuals of the race that equal justice which the law aims to secure to all others." At the same time, Justice William Strong, who wrote the majority opinion in *Strauder*, hedged on other elements of jury service equality. "We do not say that, within the limits from which it is not excluded by the amendment, a State may not prescribe the qualifications of its jurors, and, in so doing, make discriminations," he wrote. "It may confine the selection to males, to freeholders, to citizens, to persons within certain ages, or to persons having educational qualifications. We do not believe the Fourteenth Amendment was ever intended to prohibit this." In addition, the Court's only real problem with West Virginia's scheme was the wholesale exclusion of black jurors from service. It did not require black representation on juries that fit the demographic makeup of a community, for example, only categorical denial of the opportunity to serve. Therefore made it illegal for state law to explicitly bar black jury service, but it also gave jurisdictions plenty of ways to do so without state law.[2]

Still, in Louisiana in particular, black jury service would occur with at least an infrequent regularity after Reconstruction. Louisiana had an established, economically stable free black population headquartered in New Orleans from even before its statehood. Thus, it had a population not only qualified for jury service even under racially restrictive metrics, but one that was willing to fight to ensure itself the opportunity to serve. Because that educated, economically stable black middle class existed almost exclusively in and around New Orleans, the city was where the bulk of black jury service took place. But it was not only in New Orleans. In 1885, the *Shreveport Times* complained of black jury service that "we were 'broke in' to it immediately after the war. That the custom has in many instances turned the jury system into a roaring farce is undeniable." One 1890 letter writer to the *Baton Rouge Advocate* complained that on one jury upon which he served, trying a case for battery, "one obstreperous colored juror claimed that the accused had a right to whip his wife and his grandmother-in-law, and held out for acquittal, but on a compromise verdict of assault, yielded." On another during a trespassing case, "half of the jury was talesman taken from right out of the court room, and it is needless to say, were all colored, of this number, several held out for acquittal, not caring to convict anybody, and it was only after they found out it had to be a verdict of not guilty or be locked up perhaps until Monday, and thus miss their game of 'craps,' that a verdict was obtained." It was a frustrating procedure. "Of what avail to raise the standard of the regular venire, and then allow one or more rag-tag negroes (as talesman) to sit on a case. If the law contemplates the selection of good, intelligent men, only, as jurors, why are ignorant negroes selected as talesman?"[3]

Three years later, the *Daily Picayune* came up with a solution. "The failures of courts to mete out punishment to criminals is, in a great majority of cases, due to the juries themselves. It is too often the case that juries do not wish to punish criminals, and in spite of the most conclusive proof will either bring in verdicts of acquittal or secure a mistrial. If a criminal can get one partisan on the jury that tries him he can always accomplish a 'hanging' of that body, and so escape punishment until all the witnesses can be got out of the way or public interest in the case is lost," the New Orleans paper explained. "It has been repeatedly urged that nine jurors should be competent to bring in a verdict, and so overthrow the power of a single person to disappoint or obstruct justice, but it is not easy to accomplish the necessary change in a most ancient usage fortified by so many hoary precedents and appeals to the spirit of liberty." Thus it was that the *Picayune* first suggested to a popular audience enforcing the 1880 legal standard that created the possibility of 9–3 verdicts, responding as it did to the jury mandate of the 1879 constitution.[4]

As Frampton has explained, the suggestion that the 1880 law be enforced came after a particularly brutal lynching in Convent, Louisiana, seat of St. James Parish. The *Times-Picayune* laid the reliance on mob action at the feet of the slow wheels of justice, wherein long trials and the possibility of hung juries only made popular certainty less certain. But just as in civil cases, nine of twelve jurors "should be competent to bring in a verdict, and so overthrow the power of a single person to disappoint or obstruct justice." Louisiana averaged more than a dozen lynchings per year. Northeast Louisiana, and Ouachita Parish in particular, led the nation, and bore the moniker of "lynch law center of Louisiana."[5] The

Picayune's nine-juror suggestion also demonstrates that the 1880 law that changed the jury standard was not uniformly, or even regularly, applied, so much so that whites in the press remained up in arms over potential conviction disruptions based on black jury service.

The *St. Martinville Weekly Messengre* picked up on the thread later that year, tying black jury service to the necessity of lynch mobs. "But what shall we do, then?" the paper asked. "We live in the midst of an alien race who far outnumbers us. A certain portion of them are savages. They have a gloss of civilization, but in all the relations of religion, morality and respect for law they are no better than cannibals." It was a particularly brutal version of racist language. "These, it is true, are few very few—but the decent members of their race shield them and protect them. A law trial of one of them with negro witnesses and negro jurors would be a farce. Must we permit our women and even female children to live in constant peril of outrage?"[6]

Meanwhile, the *Comité de Citoyens*, the Gilded Age black citizens committee that initiated the case against segregated train cars that would become *Plessy v. Ferguson* (1896), was also concerned about black service on juries. In 1894, in Orleans Parish, James Murray—known in the press as "Greasy Jim"—was convicted by an all-white jury of killing a white man. He even made the case at his trial about the racial makeup of the grand jury that indicted him. The trial judge, however, disagreed, admitting that there was discrimination against black jurors, but that it was not because of their race. Instead, it was "because of their lack of intelligence and of moral standing. The jury commissioners are authorized by law to so discriminate, for the purpose of the law is to secure competent jurors, and, therefore, white men are preferred to colored men."[7]

The *Comité* responded at a public meeting, where it proclaimed "THE JIM CROW JURY SHOULD BE FOUGHT TO THE DEATH." It resolved to raise money to aid Murray in his appeal. It was an effort that would make its way to the Supreme Court. His appeal, however, eventually failed in 1896, the same day as the *Comité* lost its *Plessy* case. The Supreme Court noted the evidence that of the total number of voters in Orleans Parish—59,262—there were 9,654 who were black. "This admitted record contained the testimony of several deputy sheriffs, who served jury summons, and which went to show that few persons of color were so summoned; also, the testimony of the three jury commissioners, who testified that colored persons were summoned to appear before the commissioners to qualify as jurors, and that there were names of colored persons in the jury wheel from which this grand jury was drawn." It was little surprise that the *Plessy* court believed white officials. "They testified that in taking names from the registration list, the commissioners selected them with reference to their qualifications as jurors, without regard to color; that a great many colored men were summoned, and there was no discrimination against colored men." While that was certainly untrue, the fact did remain that more than 16 percent of registered voters in Orleans Parish were black, were eligible for jury service, and were part of "the jury wheel." Those realities, combined with the massive public attention garnered by *Plessy* and its consequences for segregation of public accommodations across the South, pushed the "Greasy Jim" case off the front pages and largely out of the historical narrative until Frampton's work reemphasized its significance. After the failure of his final appeal, Murray was executed in New Orleans in 1896.[8]

The following year, a New Orleans federal bank fraud trial witnessed the inclusion of a Creole named Harry Thezan on the jury. It was, however, less a nod to inclusion and more a mistake made in voir dire on the status of a light-skinned juror who often passed for white. It was the white jurors themselves who ultimately realized that "there 'was a nigger in the woodpile.'" It was abhorrent to them that they "would have to sit down at table and sleep in the same room with any negro" as part of their service, and after their protest, Thezan was removed from the jury.[9]

The *Comité* again took up the case, this time petitioning both President William McKinley and other federal legislators. Its protest letter to these leaders argued that those in Louisiana "are here upon the eve of a constitutional convention, the avowed purpose of which is to disfranchise the colored citizens" of the state.[10] Right on the eve of that convention, *Comité* leader Louis Martinet traveled to Washington, D.C., to meet with the Republican administration and the Republican attorney general to call attention to racial discrimination in the selection of federal jurors. He was so persuasive that one of the most powerful Republican senators at the time, William Chandler of New Hampshire, former head of the Republican National Committee, had a resolution passed in the United States Senate calling upon the U.S. attorney general to look into the *Comité*'s allegations that something was amiss in the way that jurors were being impaneled and selected in Louisiana and in New Orleans in particular. The resolution, passed by unanimous consent, asked the attorney general "to inform the Senate whether or not the records of the Department of Justice show that in the State of Louisiana there have been recent violations of the Constitution of the United States by the exclusion from service on juries in the United States court of duly qualified citizens on account of color" and to develop remedies if the violations existed. Perhaps most importantly, the resolution passed on January 26, 1898, two short months before Louisiana's new constitutional convention was to be held, a reality that put the state's white Democrats on edge. "If Mr. Chandler is really anxious to have negroes serve on juries he ought to encourage the importation of negroes to New Hampshire and then nobody here would object if he composed his juries entirely of negroes all the time," wrote the *Baton Rouge Advocate*. "It is unfortunately too true that too many negroes serve on juries in this State and the interests of justice are not subserved thereby. Even intelligent negroes in this State prefer to be tried by white juries as they feel that in such cases the evidence will be properly weighed and the verdict reached will be in accordance with the testimony, while in the majority of instances the negro juryman is governed by his feelings rather than by the law and the evidence."[11]

It was an argument that would be reprised by white supremacists time and time again in the twentieth century, from the use of white umpires at Negro League baseball games to white politicians representing overwhelmingly black southern districts: it was in the best black interest that competent white minds oversee their behavior in official capacities. The argument also worked well with its target audience, subtly dismissing Chandler as someone who could afford to introduce such a resolution because New Hampshire was overwhelmingly white.

New Orleans's newspapers picked up the *Advocate*'s thread, denouncing the senator as a "hater of the Southern people" who wanted "to turn loose the Federal power on the whites of this section." Such was another common trope that would remain popular during the life of Jim Crow: outside agitators were trying to insert federal power into a matter they could never understand, to the detriment of state sovereignty.[12] It was, in a sense, a dress rehearsal for the next seventy years, and it was in this context that Louisiana delegates met in 1898 to rewrite the state's constitution.

Of course, overriding the politics of all such jury and lynching debates was the gubernatorial electoral politics that usually was an unquestioned line of Democratic Party succession following the end of Reconstruction. In 1896, however, in the months following the *Plessy* and *Murray* decisions in the Supreme Court, Democrats would actually draw a viable challenger in the form of John N. Pharr, the preferred candidate of the Republican and Populist parties, which had joined forces in an attempt to break the stranglehold of statewide Democratic rule. The appeal of Populism was real in the north Louisiana cotton farming hubs and in the sugar cane fields of the southwest part of the state. That unique alliance of traditionally Democratic voters led to a comparatively high black voter turnout and thus an even more unique voting coalition to oppose Democrat Murphy J. Foster. Foster would survive the challenge, but the Populist-Republican fusion candidate received 43 percent of the vote, only further convincing state leaders to retrench and refocus on the politics of white supremacy.[13]

The 1898 convention's push for nonunanimous jury verdicts as part of state-sanctioned private convict lease was also clearly a response to white worries about black jury service and black electoral political power. Members of the convention specifically asked the secretary of state for a racial breakdown of voters by parish (and by ward in New Orleans), coming to the conclusion that 14.7 percent of eligible voters were black, and thus 14.7 percent of potential jurors were black. The best method to override that possible percentage of black jurors was to mandate that only nine of the twelve needed to agree to convict, 75 percent of the total.[14]

And so the convention added the new stipulation to the new constitution, and did so as quietly as possible so as not to awake federal authorities who had been roused by Chandler and the *Comité*. The delegates were pushed by the special interest of Samuel Lawrence James and convict lease, to be sure, but also by political worries about black jury service and its potential consequences for white Democratic hegemony.

The 1970s

The 1973 constitutional convention was one similarly dominated by special interest politics. Historian Mark T. Carleton has called the document it created, the 1974 Louisiana constitution, "a temporary haven for special interest provisions from meddling by unpredictable governors and legislators." Like its forbear in 1898, however, it was also a decided creature of its time and place.[15]

This period was one of racial transition in Louisiana. When the civil rights movement found success in the 1960s, it prompted an unsurprising white backlash that took a variety of forms, the most oppressive of which was a new push for mass incarceration. Lyndon Johnson, a white southern Democrat—a classification that for more than a century had been code for states-rights white supremacist—told the nation, "We shall overcome." He signed the Civil Rights Act of 1964 and the Voting Rights Act of 1965. Richard Nixon and the Republican Party capitalized on the white South's sense of betrayal with his infamous 1968 Southern Strategy, which hinged on electoral success in Dixie and a full-throated call for "law and order." This not-so-subtle dog whistle harkened to the language used in the debates around convict lease, the original white response to black success. It was a winning scheme for Nixon, who would only continue to move farther to the right, pushed by third-party candidate George Wallace, for whom Louisiana's electoral college votes actually went in 1968.[16]

But the state's turn was not inevitable. The Louisiana gubernatorial election of 1971, Democrat Edwin Edwards's first victory, "demonstrated, for the first time, the decisive influence of the black vote on the state level." The success of candidates like Nixon and Wallace in national campaigns belied the influence of black voters in the state after the Voting

Rights Act, and Edwards was the first white politician in Louisiana to harness the statewide power of that vote for electoral success. It was a demonstration of real gains by the black population, but precisely because of such gains, there was another inevitable white backlash.[17]

In 1972, racial tension reached a fever pitch in Baton Rouge after police shot into a crowd of thirty-one black militants who were members of the Nation of Islam from California and Illinois. The police claimed that the protestors shot first, but witnesses said they were unarmed. Four deaths, two of them cops, left the city on edge.[18]

At the parish level, heated fights over school desegregation, especially in the river parishes—St. John the Baptist Parish and St. Charles Parish, for example—created a racial powder keg, with communities on edge, waiting for an excuse to demonstrate their rage. The classic case of such racial reckonings was the murder conviction of Gary Tyler after an incident at Destrehan High School in October 1974. There had been ugly racial scenes at the school, pilloried in the local press as "race riots," and in response officials finally closed the school down, sending the students home and boarding them on two buses, one for black students and the other for whites. The bus that Tyler was on, the one filled with black students, was mobbed by white students. In response, someone from that bus fired a gun. A white student in the crowd was killed. The racial temperature in St. Charles Parish, already at a fever pitch, continued rising. David Duke led a Ku Klux Klan march in Destrehan after the killing, laying a wreath at the grave of the boy who was killed. Tyler would be the sacrificial lamb for the resulting white rage, convicted of murder despite no substantial evidence that he was the one who fired the gun.[19]

It was the Redeemer era returned to the 1970s, and Tyler's conviction made it clear that this period of racial retrenchment extended beyond the bounds of public schools and into the state's criminal justice system. White prosecutors, for example, often struck jury members during venire simply because of their race. In 1979, the Louisiana Supreme Court ruled in two cases that white prosecutors were deliberately and systematically striking potential jurors simply because they were black. In one case, the prosecutor had described his system as "exclud[ing] blacks not because they were black, but because they had a history of being black."

While such cases were decided in the state's high court at the end of the decade, they belied a process that was in place throughout the 1970s.[20] Such was the climate into which the 1973 constitutional convention came, made all the more potent by the Supreme Court's *Johnson* decision the year prior, which justified nonunanimous juries and loomed over the delegates much as the threatened federal investigation into black jury service had loomed over their 1898 counterparts.

Convention delegate Chris J. Roy, Sr., of Alexandria, chairman of the Committee on the Bill of Rights and Elections, was the major proponent for expanding the constitutional requirement for unanimous juries. His principal opponent on unanimity and the most vocal advocate for retaining the nine-out-of-twelve standard was delegate I. Jackson Burson, Jr., a Eunice attorney and, at the time, an assistant district attorney in St. Landry Parish. Burson was also part of the all-white St. Landry Parish School Board. The deadlock between them led delegate Walter Lanier, Jr., of Thibodaux, an assistant district attorney in Lafourche Parish, to broker a compromise.[21]

Importantly, the Bill of Rights Committee started with the 1921 constitution's existing Bill of Rights and examined possible changes or additions. When delegate Roy introduced Committee Proposal 25, an original attempt at compromise to increase the jury vote requirement to 10–2, on September 8, 1973, he acknowledged the existing constitutional standard and framed the proposal in terms of the limited amendments it was making to the existing law.[22]

Delegate Burson specifically cited the existing constitutional provision and the fact that it had been upheld by the Supreme Court in *Johnson* the year prior. Roy responded by noting that most people convicted, especially of murder, are minorities and urged the conventioneers to remember that the delegates represented even this 0.0003 of one percent of the population. Put another way, the notion that changing the law to recognize a 10–2 standard to reduce its discriminatory burden on black persons charged with serious crimes is itself an admission that nonunanimous juries (whatever the number of jurors needed for conviction) were themselves discriminatory. Ultimately a compromise was reached rejecting the expansion of unanimous verdicts but moving the voting tally to 10–2. There was no broader philosophical discussion about whether majority verdicts should exist nor any recognition of or attempt to break with the past. The law, introduced with discriminatory intent, was continued in effect and continued to have a discriminatory impact.[23]

The 2010s

This book originally appeared in 2015. The following year, Kyle R. Satterfield published an article in the *Tulane Law Review* trodding much the same ground and arguing that the state's nonunanimous jury policy violated the Equal Protection Clause when read through the lens of the 1977 case *Village of Arlington Heights v. Metropolitan Housing Development Corp.* Southern University law professor Angela A. Allen-Bell provided a similar account in the *Mercer Law Review,* emphasizing the stories legal scholars use to justify practices such as nonunanimity despite the clear racialized historical reality. Two scholars from Lewis and Clark Law School, Aliza B. Kaplan and Amy Saack, made a similar case in the *Oregon Law Review* based on that state's precedent, arguing that "criminal convictions in state courts should be subject to the same unanimity requirements that the Sixth Amendment imposes on federal criminal convictions."[24]

There were also more public discussions of the racial problems inherent in the system, those led primarily by former Grant Parish district attorney Ed Tarpley. Tarpley read Bryan Stevenson's harrowing memoir *Just Mercy: A Story of Justice and Redemption* and the first edition of this book. He then began a tireless effort to raise awareness about nonunanimous criminal jury verdicts, arguing to audiences across Louisiana that the practice was "something that is a stain on the legacy of our state." In June 2016 he convinced the Louisiana Bar Association to go on record in favor of overturning the practice. Even the *New York Times* editorial board printed an editorial in May 2018 condemning the practice and advocating unanimous juries in Louisiana and Oregon.[25]

But by far the most public and damning testimony against the practice came in a devastating and comprehensive series of studies in the

New Orleans Advocate. The *Advocate* was able to collect data from roughly three thousand cases in the state from 2011 to 2016, 993 of which included documentation of individual jury votes. The paper found that 40 percent of convictions came at the hands of a nonunanimous jury. When the defendant was black, the statistic rose to 43 percent, when white, it decreased to 33 percent. The study also examined the jury pools of the state's nine busiest courthouses and found that those pools were substantially whiter than the surrounding population. The actual juries pulled from those pools were whiter still. Only one such jurisdiction adequately reflected the black population on its criminal juries, the rest disproportionately reducing their presence by anywhere from 10 to 42 percent. It was a misrepresentation made all the more significant because, as the study showed, a review of forty-six nonunanimous criminal convictions in East Baton Rouge Parish demonstrated that black jurors were 2.7 times more likely than their white counterparts to vote against the majority. In a state with the highest incarceration rate in the world, with a black population that is roughly one-third of the total but two-thirds of the prison population and three-fourths of those serving life without parole, with far more serving that sentence than in any other state, the consequences of such statistics became all the more stark.[26]

The power of these figures cannot be overstated. Yet the fact that the *Advocate* was able to unearth them at all is just as remarkable. Just as the records of convict lease have remained sparse by legislative intent—much of the leasing record destroyed to cover the sins of its creators—so too are the records of nonunanimous juries not retained at the parish level. Almost as powerful as the data the *Advocate* found was the amount of data reporters were unable to find. The system, so demonstrably racially weighted and so constitutionally problematic, was largely happening in secret.[27]

With the new glut of legal and popular commentary appearing on the subject, however, there seemed to be a new light shone on the practice and legitimate momentum for change, but just as there was in the 1890s and 1970s, a backlash soon developed.

The Louisiana Association of Criminal Defense Lawyers sought an amendment to end nonunanimous juries and recruited a state senator to sponsor the legislation. On March 12, 2018, New Orleans Democrat Jean-Paul Morrell introduced SB 243, "A constitutional amendment to require unanimous juries for felonies." The proposed amendment only changed one word of the 1974 constitution's language: "A criminal case in which the punishment may be capital shall be tried before a jury of twelve persons, all of whom must concur to render a verdict. A case in which the punishment is necessarily confinement at hard labor shall be tried before a jury of twelve persons, *all* of whom must concur to render a verdict. A case in which the punishment may be confinement at hard labor or confinement without hard labor for more than six months shall be tried before a jury of six persons, all of whom must concur to render a verdict."[28]

It was no coincidence that later the same day, Jefferson Parish Republican Joseph A. Stagni introduced his own bill in the state House chamber. Originally, the Stagni bill mandated that no longer did jurors have to affix their name and signature to their individual vote on a jury. By the end of the month, however, the Republican-led Committee on Administration of Criminal Justice had expanded the new bill, adding that not only were jurors exempt from affixing their names to individual votes, but that "the polling slips shall be placed under seal in the court record and shall not be released to the public unless such release is ordered by the court." It was an effort in the face of the potential jury change to ensure that statistics such as those used by the *Advocate* to demonstrate the racialized nature of Louisiana's criminal justice system would be hidden from those attempting to make a similar case in the future. Jefferson Parish judge Glenn Ansardi openly admitted that he lobbied for the bill after the *Advocate* requested to view jurors' polling slips in dozens of cases for the paper's study. Such is the nature of a backlash.[29]

The Stagni House bill would make its way swiftly to the governor's desk, passing unanimously in the lower chamber before heading to the Senate for cosmetic amendment and ultimate passage. It was signed into law on May 15, two months after its original introduction. That day was significant for Morrell's Senate bill as well. As the governor signed into law severe new restrictions on what could be known about the makeup of Louisiana juries, the state Senate finally passed an amended version of the unanimity amendment. The House had passed its version by a vote of 82–15, and the Senate concurred. It was a process not without its detractors but one that was fundamentally bipartisan in its support. Morrell's original effort seemed to be a longshot until Baton Rouge Republican Dan Claitor, a former prosecutor, admitted that "if I had a particularly hard case, and I had the opportunity to have a more difficult felony—I would up-charge them, because it was easier for me to convict them with 10 out of 12, than it is 6 out of 6." Claitor's frank admission, his regret, and his support for the amendment pushed many in opposition to change their minds. The state Republican Party's Central Committee voted 78–17 at a meeting in Lafayette to support jury unanimity. Ultimately twenty-seven senators, one more than the minimum requirement, voted to approve the legislation.[30]

The new constitutional amendment it created would not be retroactive, meaning that all of the victims of the system described in the *Advocate*'s reporting would remain behind bars. It was a compromise necessary for passage, but advocates of the change hoped that the new amendment would aid appeals of those currently incarcerated. It officially became Act 722 on June 7, 2018, and with that, the race was on.[31]

The two new bills meant that Louisiana's November vote would be an all-or-nothing proposition. If the amendment met with approval by the state's voters, jury unanimity would be required in criminal trials, sparing countless defendants the agony that had haunted thousands before them and eliminating Louisiana's last remaining Jim Crow law. If it met with the state's disapproval, however, the nonunanimous standard would be sure to stay in place in perpetuity because the racial crimes it perpetrated could no longer be measured. "For those of us in the unanimous jury fight, all of our eggs are in one basket," said Christie Smith, chairperson of the legislative committee of the Louisiana Association of Criminal Defense Lawyers. "If we can't convince the voting population that jury unanimity is the way to go, we're actually worse off than where we started. It's a great irony."[32] There was much at stake.

Ed Tarpley would be instrumental in moving the amendment from ballot measure to law of the land. "After I read the book," Tarpley explained, referring to the first edition of *Jim Crow's Last Stand*, "I became convinced that this was a law that Louisiana had to repeal, that this was important, and we needed to do something about this. So I just made a commitment, right then, to make it a life goal to get rid of the nonunanimous jury verdict law in Louisiana." After the amendment made it through congress, Tarpley began speaking across the state. The Republican leader knew that in a state dominated by conservative politics, appeals to the historical roots of nineteenth-century Jim Crow realities would not be enough to push the new amendment across the finish line. Instead, Tarpley focused his argument around federalism and individual liberty. If the state could take someone's freedom without a unanimous jury, what else would it be able to take? He consistently quoted John Adams, who stated that it was "the unanimity of the jury that preserves the rights of mankind."[33]

Tarpley also put his message into organized form, creating a new PAC, the Alliance for Constitutional Integrity, but his organization was not alone. Americans For Prosperity, the political PAC founded by the Koch brothers, contributed more than $100,000 to the cause. The Louisiana Family Forum, the state's most influential conservative Christian group, also supported the measure, its leader, Gene Mills, pledging that the organization would work in an "educational capacity" to inform voters about the issue and encourage them to support it. Even Grover Norquist's Americans for Tax Reform pledged its endorsement to end nonunanimous juries. The Louisiana Republican Judiciary PAC, led by Baton Rouge lobbyist Scott Wilfong, even created an advertisement linking the liberty being denied to defendants by nonunanimous juries to the liberty to own guns that was constantly under threat from big government. While such may have been an argumentative stretch, it was the kind of effort that many conservative Louisiana voters could understand and support.[34]

Even the Louisiana District Attorneys Association, the group with the most to lose through the passage of the amendment, did not speak out against it. In a note of supreme irony, the body required unanimity to declare official positions of the organization, and since members could not come to a unanimous consensus against the jury amendment, the association did not make a public case against its passage. In fact, district attorneys for East Baton Rouge, Jefferson, Caddo, and Lafayette parishes, four of the state's six busiest trial dockets, all came out in favor of the new unanimity amendment. Hillar Moore, district attorney for East Baton Rouge Parish, told the press that supporting unanimous juries gave him the "opportunity to be on the right side of history."[35]

Such typically conservative forces were joined by strange bedfellows from the political left, who focused their arguments on racial disparities in sentencing, the need for criminal justice reform, and the historical legacy of Jim Crow. The largest outside contributor to the cause was George Soros's Open Society Foundation. FWD.us, founded largely by Silicon Valley activists including Bill Gates and Mark Zuckerberg, also donated generously, as did San Francisco's Tides Advocacy Fund. Within the state, the Louisiana Legislative Black Caucus and the Southern Poverty Law Center, under the leadership of criminal justice reform field director John Burkhart, worked for the campaign that became known as Yes On 2. (The amendment was the second on Louisiana's November ballot.)[36]

Perhaps most influential was the Unanimous Jury Coalition, founded and led by Norris Henderson. Henderson had been wrongly incarcerated for twenty-seven years after a nonunanimous conviction, and upon his release in 2003 began a career of activism that led him to create Voice of the Experienced (VOTE) and other organizations specifically related to criminal justice reform. Joined by state leaders such as Sister Alison McCrary and Lynda Woolard, and local field directors Kelly Garrett, Jennifer Harding, Alvin Anthony, and Kim Turner, the Unanimous Jury Coalition embarked on a massive statewide campaign to ensure the amendment's passage. The group produced yard signs, mailers, a robust phonebanking effort, and even staged a parade. "We are at a crossroads, with an opportunity to right this long-standing wrong," wrote Henderson in a *Louisiana Weekly* op-ed. "It's time to come together, reject prejudice in all its forms and build a future in which everyone is valued and supported. The 1898 constitutional convention was about denying voice to the expression of all of Louisiana's citizens. This ballot question in November is about giving Louisiana her voice back."[37]

It was, despite different motivations on each side, a truly bipartisan effort. The groups did not stick to their respective corners but instead engaged with one another, united for a common cause. It was a feat made all the more remarkable by the broader national hyperpolarization of the 2018 midterm election climate, and the opposition of the state's attorney general, Jeff Landry. Landry refused to comment on the record about his thinking on nonunanimous juries, but through a spokesperson argued for the judicial efficiency of the practice. Nonunanimous juries also "make the jury selection process easier." It was a guarded admission of racial bias, but then the spokesperson became more candid, professing that the attorney general "is not concerned" about the racial disparities in sentencing caused by the Louisiana standard. There were "safeguards in the legal system to ensure juries don't have a racial bias." It was a complete denial of basic facts, but Landry did not organize his opposition or openly fight against the amendment. Landry was debating a gubernatorial run and understood the consequences of being on the wrong side of such a bipartisan issue.[38]

His silence proved prescient. The effort of groups on both sides of the political aisle paid substantial dividends. The final vote saw 938,126, or 64.35 percent, of Louisianans in favor of the new amendment, and 519,716, or 35.65 percent, against it. Only three parishes, Franklin, LaSalle, and Sabine, home of Melvin Maxie, failed to muster majority support for the measure. Don Burkett, the district attorney in Sabine Parish, was proud of Sabine's rejection of the amendment. "The public here knew I was opposed to it, and I think that was a factor," he said. "I think my people look at things a little differently than the rest of the state." His people, however, will now be held to a unanimous standard. It was a resounding victory, the final nail in the coffin of nineteenth–century Jim Crow policy. After the amendment's passage, several Oregon lawmakers and activists announced their determination to end their own state's nonunanimous jury provision, the domino effect of good government falling all the way to the Pacific Northwest.[39]

And the dominos kept falling. In March 2019 the U.S. Supreme Court agreed to again take up nonunanimous jury verdicts, opening a potential avenue to new trials for thousands still incarcerated in Louisiana and

Oregon. The case considers the conviction of Evangelisto Ramos, an offshore oil worker convicted by a nonunanimous jury of second-degree murder in New Orleans in 2014. The Promise of Justice Initiative took his case and was finally able to convince the high court to reconsider the practice. Then, the following month, the New Orleans *Advocate* won a Pulitzer Prize for its investigative work into nonunanimous juries. That's the thing about dominos: once they start falling, it's hard to make them stop.[40]

The use of criminal justice practices to approximate Gilded Age institutionalized racism, however, is still ongoing. Jim Crow policy is a twentieth- and twenty-first century reality, as well, for many who have moved and still move through the criminal justice system in Louisiana, Oregon, and elsewhere. And so for many, the fight to end the practice of nonunanimous criminal jury verdicts was not simply the conclusion of more than a century of unequal justice; it was the initiation of a new momentum for further criminal justice reform that eliminates structural inequalities from the system.

Unanimous juries aren't an end. They are a beginning.

APPENDIX I

Constitutional Jury Mandates

What follows is a demonstration of the evolution of the thinking of Louisiana lawmakers in relation to juries and their role in criminal prosecutions, beginning with the two principal territorial governing laws of 1804 and 1805 and proceeding through the various incarnations of the state's constitution from 1812 to 1974.

An Act erecting Louisiana into two territories, and providing for the temporary government thereof, 1804

In all criminal prosecutions which are capital, the trial shall be by a jury of twelve good and lawful men of the vicinage; and in all cases, criminal and civil, in the superior court, the trial shall be by a jury, if either of the parties require it. The inhabitants of the said territory shall be entitled to the benefits of the writ of habeas corpus; they shall be bailable, unless for capital offences, where the proof shall be evident or the presumption great; and no cruel and unusual punishments shall be inflicted. (Section 5)

An Act further providing for the government of the district of Louisiana, 1805

That in all criminal prosecutions the trial shall be by a jury of twelve good and lawful men of the vicinage, and in all civil cases of the value of one hundred dollars the trial shall be by jury, if either of the parties require it. (Section 3)

Constitution of 1812

In all criminal prosecutions, the accused have the right of being heard by himself or counsel, of demanding the nature and cause of the accusation against him, of meeting the witnesses face to face, of having compulsory process for obtaining witnesses in his favour, and prosecutions by indictment or information, a speedy public trial by an impartial jury of the vicinage, nor shall he be compelled to give evidence against himself. (Article 6, §18)

Constitution of 1845
Prosecutions shall be by indictment or information. The accused shall have a speedy public trial by an impartial jury of the vicinage; he shall not be compelled to give evidence against himself; he shall have the right of being heard by himself or counsel; he shall have the right, unless he shall have fled from justice, of meeting the witnesses face to face, and shall have compulsory process for obtaining witnesses in his favor. (Article 107)

Constitution of 1852
Prosecutions shall be by indictment or information. The accused shall have a speedy public trial by an impartial jury of the vicinage; he shall not be compelled to give evidence against himself; he shall have the right of being heard by himself or counsel; he shall have the right of meeting the witnesses face to face, and shall have compulsory process for obtaining witnesses in his favor. (Article 103)

Constitution of 1864
Prosecutions shall be by indictment or information. The accused shall have a speedy public trial by an impartial jury of the parish in which the offence shall have been committed. He shall not be compelled to give evidence against himself; he shall have the right of being heard, by himself or counsel; he shall have the right of meeting the witnesses face to face, and shall have compulsory process for obtaining witnesses in his favor. He shall not be twice put in jeopardy for the same offence. (Article 105)

Constitution of 1868
Prosecutions shall be by indictment or information. The accused shall be entitled to a speedy public trial by an impartial jury of the parish in which the offence shall have been committed, unless the venue be changed. He shall not be compelled to give evidence against himself; he

shall have the right of being heard by himself or counsel; he shall have the right of meeting the witnesses face to face, and shall have compulsory process for obtaining witnesses in his favor. He shall not be twice put in jeopardy for the same offence. (Article 6)

Constitution of 1879

In all criminal prosecutions the accused shall enjoy the right to a speedy public trial by an impartial jury, except that, in cases where the penalty is not necessarily imprisonment at hard labor or death, the General Assembly may provide for the trial thereof by a jury, less than twelve in number; *provided*, that the accused in every instance shall be tried in the parish wherein the offense shall have been committed, except in cases of change of venue. (Article 7)

Constitution of 1898

The General Assembly shall provide for the selection of competent and intelligent jurors. All cases in which the punishment may not be at hard labor shall, until otherwise provided by law, which shall not be prior to 1904, be tried by the judge without a jury. Cases in which the punishment may be at hard labor shall be tried by a jury of five, all of whom must concur to render a verdict; cases in which the punishment is necessarily at hard labor, by a jury of twelve, nine of whom concurring may render a verdict; cases in which the punishment may be capital, by a jury of twelve, all of whom must concur to render a verdict. (Article 116)

Constitution of 1913

The General Assembly shall provide for the selection of competent and intelligent jurors. All cases in which the punishment may not be at hard labor shall, until otherwise provided by law, be tried by the judge without a jury. Cases in which the punishment may be at hard labor shall be tried by a jury of five, all of whom must concur to render a verdict; cases in which the punishment is necessarily at hard labor, by a jury of twelve, nine of whom concurring may render a verdict; cases in which the punishment may be capital, by a jury of twelve, all of whom must concur to render a verdict. (Article 116)

Constitution of 1921

The Legislature shall provide for the election and drawing of competent and intelligent jurors for the trial of civil and criminal cases; provided, however, that no woman shall be drawn for jury service unless she shall have previously filed with the clerk of the District Court a written declaration of her desire to be subject to such service. All cases in which the punishment may not be at hard labor shall, until otherwise provided by law, be tried by the judge without a jury. Cases, in which the punishment may be at hard labor, shall be tried by a jury of five, all of whom must concur to render a verdict; cases, in which the punishment is necessarily at hard labor, by a jury of twelve, nine of whom must concur to render a verdict; cases in which the punishment may be capital, by a jury of twelve, all of whom must concur to render a verdict. (Article 7, § 41)

Constitution of 1974

(A) Jury Trial in Criminal Cases. A criminal case in which the punishment may be capital shall be tried before a jury of twelve persons, all of whom must concur to render a verdict. A case in which the punishment is necessarily confinement at hard labor shall be tried before a jury of twelve persons, ten of whom must concur to render a verdict. A case in which the punishment may be confinement at hard labor or confinement without hard labor for more than six months shall be tried before a jury of six persons, all of whom must concur to render a verdict. The accused shall have a right to full voir dire examination of prospective jurors and to challenge jurors peremptorily. The number of challenges shall be fixed by law. Except in capital cases, a defendant may knowingly and intelligently waive his right to a trial by jury but no later than forty-five days prior to the trial date and the waiver shall be irrevocable.

(B) Joinder of Felonies; Mode of Trial. Notwithstanding any provision of law to the contrary, offenses in which punishment is necessarily confinement at hard labor may be charged in the same indictment or information with offenses in which the punishment may be confinement at hard labor; provided, however, that the joined offenses are of the same or similar character or are based on the same act or transaction or on two or more acts or transactions connected together or constituting parts of a common scheme or plan; and provided further, that cases so joined shall be tried by a jury composed of twelve jurors, ten of whom must concur to render a verdict. (Article 1, § 17)

APPENDIX II

The *Johnson* Decisions

What follows are the three substantive decisions that encompass the *Johnson* ruling. The first, *State v. Johnson*, is the Louisiana Supreme Court's ruling in the case. The second, *Johnson v. Louisiana*, is the U.S. Supreme Court's response to that decision. The third, *Apodaca v. Oregon*, was decided in conjunction with the federal Supreme Court's *Johnson* decision and continues and completes its argument.

STATE V. JOHNSON
230 So.2d 825 (1970)
255 La. 314

STATE OF LOUISIANA
v.
FRANK JOHNSON.
No. 49861.

Supreme Court of Louisiana.
January 20, 1970.

Richard A. Buckley, New Orleans, for appellant.

Jack P. F. Gremillion, Atty. Gen., William P. Schuler, Asst. Atty. Gen., Jim Garrison, Dist. Atty., Louise Korns, Asst. Dist. Atty., for appellee.

Hamlin, Justice:

Defendant was charged by bill of information with the crime of armed robbery. He was tried by a jury of twelve, convicted (the verdict was nine to three), and sentenced to serve thirty-five years at hard labor in the Louisiana State Penitentiary. He appeals to this Court from his conviction and sentence and presents for our consideration two specification of errors, which recite:

1. The arrest of appellant was illegal, and the ensuing line-up identification while appellant was still illegally detained should have been suppressed and excluded from evidence.

2. The verdict of guilty in which only nine out of twelve jurors concurred denied appellant due process and equal protection of the laws guaranteed by the Fourteenth Amendment to the United States Constitution.

Twenty-five bills of exceptions were reserved in this matter. However, before argument in this Court, counsel for the defendant stated that all bills taken at trial were without merit. Therefore, contrary to our usual format in writing a criminal case, herein infra we shall only consider the specification of errors urged supra.

The testimony taken on the hearing of the motion to suppress and on trial discloses in substance the following account of defendant's arrest, booking, line-up, the incidents of the crime charged, and the actions of the victim following his being robbed by an armed man:

On December 26, 1967, at approximately 3:30 P.M. (the weather was clear and the sun was shining) Eugene Frischertz, a route salesman for Coca Cola Bottling Company, had just made a delivery at Brown's Grocery, 2139 Third Street, New Orleans, Louisiana, when a man, whom he saw from the mirror of his truck (there was a mirror on the right side and on the left side of the front of the truck), approached the door of the truck, brandished a revolver at him and demanded that he give him all of his money.[1] Frischertz gave the robber between $500.00 and $600.00

of money belonging to Coca Cola Bottling Company and $31.00 of his own money, and the robber fled. Frischertz reentered the grocery store and summoned the police; they arrived within approximately fifteen minutes, and Frischertz related the details of the robbery and gave them a complete description of the robber—weight, hair and clothing. Later, Frischertz went to the Detective Bureau where he was shown mug shots of suspects; he did not identify any of the pictures as being that of the defendant, but he pointed out characteristics—build and facial make-up—of the robber similar to those of the parties appearing in the mug shots. Thereafter, at a line-up, which we shall discuss infra, he identified the defendant as the man who had robbed him.

The robbery of truck drivers was prevalent in the City of New Orleans at the time Frischertz was forcibly robbed. The police were conducting an investigation for the purpose of arrest, and Lieutenant Theodore Feld, New Orleans Police Department, Detective Bureau, Robbery Division, was in charge. On the hearing of the motion to suppress, Lt. Feld testified:

"A. On the 18th of January we received information from a confidential informant—I didn't receive it—my superior, Captain Newman received it from one of his informants that Frank Johnson and Hayes, Harold Hayes—[Colloquy]

"A. Saying that these two subjects were involved in an armed robbery of truck drivers. So I sent one of the men over to the B of I to get photographs on subjects by the name of Harold Hayes and Frank Johnson in a group and have one of the men bring it to one of the victims who was employed by the Brown's Velvet. The man looked at the pictures and identified Frank Johnson and also a photograph of Harold Hayes. He initialed the same with the date and then that gave us probable cause to arrest him. The man positively said that was the man that held him up."

Marion Catalano, an employee of Brown's Velvet Ice Cream Inc., had been the victim of about three armed robberies; he identified defendant's photograph as that of a man who had committed a robbery on him. At Lt.

Feld's instruction, Detective John Lanza secured the photograph identification. This was done shortly after Captain Newman, Assistant Chief of the Detective Bureau, communicated to Lt. Feld the information given to him by an informant, January 18, 1968.

On January 20, 1968, at approximately 6:00 A.M., Lt. Feld and Sgt. Lawrence John Vigurie arrested the defendant at his residence, 2135 Philip Street, New Orleans, Louisiana, for the robbery of Brown's Velvet Ice Cream, Inc. truck driver Catalano, but at the time of arrest Lt. Feld was not specific with the defendant; six officers were involved in the arrest. Lt. Feld testified that he knocked on Johnson's front door and was admitted by Mrs. Johnson and a male other than Johnson; that they were shown the officers' identification and told that the officers were looking for Frank Johnson. Defendant was taken from under his bed by Sgt. Vigurie, who told him that he was being placed under arrest for armed robbery; he was allowed to get dressed and was then handcuffed. Lt. Feld did not have an arrest warrant, but he testified that there was no reason for not securing one.

A search was made of the defendant's house, but we are not herein concerned with any fruits of the search. The issue of search and seizure connected with an arrest is not an issue herein involved.

Defendant was brought to the Detective Bureau at approximately 6:45 A.M., where he was apprised of his constitutional rights[2] and then interrogated. A short time later he accompanied and assisted the officers in the arrest of a suspect. He was returned to the Detective Bureau about mid-morning and then booked with a number of armed robberies.[3] Lt. Feld testified, "Catalano was the original booker and that is what we went out there to arrest him on."

A line-up was held at the Detective Bureau on January 23, 1968, and victims of all truck driver holdups in the location herein involved were requested to attend. Eugene Frischertz, the instant victim, was present and, as stated supra, identified defendant as the man who had robbed him on December 26, 1967. The testimony of Frischertz is in part as follows:

"Q. Now, let's get to the line-up, Mr. Frischertz: What happened at the line-up, tell us about it in your own words?

"A. I identified this man as being the man that held me up.

"Q. Did you identify him by a number?

"A. No.

"Q. If I showed you a picture, would it refresh your recollection: Is that the line-up?

"A. Yes, sir.

"Q. Were there a number at that date?

"A. There were.

"Q. I ask you if: Did you identify them by number?

"A. I did not. I identified him, then picked the number.

"Q. But you did identify by number?

"A. Not by number. I identified his face.

"Q. And then tied a number in with it?

"A. Right.

"Q. But there was always a number around his neck, correct?

"A. Right.

"Q. And that number was four?

"A. Right.

"Q. And did you identify him as to position in the line-up?

"A. No.

"Q. Do you know how many persons were in the line-up: I just showed it to you?

"A. Seven.

"Q. Who was the middle man?

"A. The middle man?

"Q. Yes. Number four—three on one side and three on the other—who was the middle man?

[Colloquy, and objection sustained.]

***

"Q. When you saw him, you immediately recognized him, is that correct?

"A. I did.

"Q. No officer was sitting beside of you prompting you?

"A. No.

"Q. No one had made any suggestions to you at the Detective Bureau?

"A. No."

Rene Belsom, a patrolman employed in the Bureau of Identification, having as one of his primary duties the taking of photographs, testified that he took a line-up picture on January 23, 1968. He identified S-1 offered in evidence as the picture he had taken; it is a line-up pose of seven men with defendant appearing as No. Four.

Byron Legendre, an attorney connected with Legal Aid, was present at the line-up of January 23, 1968. He testified:

"I went over to the Federal Lockup [Orleans] and interviewed a number of people who were booked at that time with the crime of armed robbery. I interviewed them on this premise: Whether or not they had a counsel or a lawyer of their own at that time and for those who said they did not, I told them that I would be available as their attorney for the purpose of the line-up alone to make sure that they got a fair line-up, and Number Two, to be able to report to their attorneys at a later date as to what transpired at that line-up. And to each of these men I gave my card if I had one available and to each of them I promised I would let them know the results of the line-up after it was finished. Mr. Johnson was one of these men who said he did not have counsel."

Mr. Legendre further stated:

"These people are instructed by me, the suspects, are instructed by me to make a choice of the number they wish: They can stand next to whom they please. And the numbers are so chosen and then the rest of the people are handed out the numbers. Only the suspects get a choice of what number they want: They don't get a choice of who they stand next to. Once they have their numbers and the other numbers are given out, they are placed against the wall and then I have an opportunity to let the police know my appreciation of what I see."

Lt. Feld testified that Mr. Legendre represented the defendant at the line-up. On the hearing of the motion to suppress, defendant himself testified that he went to a line-up on January 23, 1968. He said that he had an attorney—he thought that he was Mr. Legendre from Legal Aid.

He stated that the attorney represented him at the line-up and talked with him before same was held, advising him of his rights.

On February 14, 1968, a bill of information was filed against the defendant. He was charged with a violation of LSA-R.S. 14:64, in that "while armed with a dangerous weapon, to wit: a pistol, robbed one EUGENE FRISCHERTZ of Six Hundred and Thirty-One ($631.00) Dollars in United States Currency,***"

SPECIFICATION OF ERRORS NO. 1

In this Court, counsel for the defendant urge:

A. The arrest was illegal because the arresting officer did not himself have the probable cause required of warrantless searches under the Louisiana and United States Constitutions.
B. The arrest of appellant was illegal because the arresting officer intentionally declined to obtain a warrant so that he could search "incidental" to the arrest.
C. The identification of appellant at a line-up after his illegal arrest, and while still illegally detained should have been suppressed and all evidence pertaining to it excluded at trial.

In *Wong Sun v. United States,* 371 U.S. 471, 83 S.Ct. 407, 9 L.Ed.2d 441 (1963) the United States Supreme Court said:

"*** It is basic that an arrest with or without a warrant must stand upon firmer ground than mere suspicion, see *Henry v. United States,* 361 U.S. 98, 101, 80 S.Ct. 168, 170, 4 L.Ed.2d 134, though the arresting officer need not have in hand evidence which would suffice to convict. The quantum of information which constitutes probable cause—evidence which would 'warrant a man of reasonable caution in the belief that a felony has been committed, *Carroll v. United States*, 267 U.S. 132, 162, 45 S.Ct. 280, 288, 69 L.Ed. 543—must be measured by the facts of the particular case.***

"Whether or not the requirements of reliability and particularity of the information on which an officer may act are more stringent where an arrest warrant is absent, they surely cannot be less stringent than where an arrest warrant is obtained.***

"*** We have held that identification of the suspect by a reliable informant may constitute probable cause for arrest where the information given is sufficiently accurate to lead the officers directly to the suspect. *Draper v. United States*, 358 U.S. 307, 79 S.Ct. 329, 3 L.Ed.2d 327.***"

In the *Henry* case mentioned above, 80 S.Ct., at 171 (1959) the United States Supreme Court said:

"Evidence required to establish guilt is not necessary. *** On the other hand, good faith on the part of the arresting officers is not enough. Probable cause exists if the facts and circumstances known to the officer warrant a prudent man in believing that the offense has been committed. *** It is important, we think, that this requirement be strictly enforced, for the standard set by the Constitution protects both the officer and the citizen. If the officer acts with probable cause, he is protected even though it turns out that the citizen is innocent.***"

In *Johnson v. United States*, 333 U.S. 10, 68 S.Ct. 367, 92 L.Ed. 436 (1948) the United States Supreme Court was in essence considering the legality of a search, but with respect to arrest it stated:

"The Government contends, however, that this search without

warrant must be held valid because incident to an arrest. This alleged ground of validity requires examination of the facts to determine whether the arrest itself was lawful. Since it was without warrant, it could be valid only if for a crime committed in the presence of the arresting officer or for a felony of which he had reasonable cause to believe defendant guilty."

"Probable cause has been defined as a reasonable grounds for belief of guilt. It exists where the facts and the circumstances within the officer's knowledge are sufficient in themselves to warrant a man of reasonable caution in the belief that an offense has been or is being committed. *Carroll v. United States*, 267 U.S. 132, 45 S.Ct. 280, 69 L.Ed. 543; *Brinegar v. United States*, 338 U.S. 160, 69 S.Ct. 1302, 93 L.Ed. 1879." *State of Louisiana ex rel. Naylor v. Walker*, 206 F.Supp. 544, Cert. Denied, 371 U.S. 957, 83 S.Ct. 514, 9 L.Ed.2d 504 (1963).

"An arrest is a wholly different kind of intrusion upon individual freedom from a limited search for weapons, and the interests each is designed to serve are likewise quite different. An arrest is the initial stage of a criminal prosecution. It is intended to vindicate society's interest in having its laws obeyed, and it is inevitably accompanied by future interference with the individual's freedom of movement whether or not trial or conviction ultimately follows." *Terry v. State of Ohio*, 392 U.S. 1, 88 S.Ct. 1868, 1882, 20 L.Ed.2d 889 (1968). Cf. *Sibron v. State of New York*, 392 U.S. 40, 88 S.Ct. 1889, 20 L.Ed.2d 917.

"A case of arrest without a warrant necessitates striking a balance as to (a) considerations respecting the rights of the individual citizen taken into custody, and (b) consideration respecting the responsibility of police officers for the safety and security of all members of the community; *i.e.*, the propriety of law enforcement or police action. It is a problem of value judgment. The test, purely and simply, is one of reasonableness, considering the time, the place, and the pertinent circumstances." *Plancich v. Williamson*, 57 Wn.2d 367, 357 P.2d 693, 92 A.L.R.2d 559.

"*** That the officer had time to have obtained a warrant and failed to do so does not make an otherwise legal arrest or legal search and seizure illegal. *Agnello v. United States*, 269 U.S. 20, 46 S.Ct. 4, 70 L.Ed. 145." *State of Louisiana ex rel. Naylor v. Walker*, 206 F.Supp. 544, 546.

In Louisiana an arrest by an officer without a warrant may be made when "the peace officer has reasonable cause to believe that the person to be arrested has committed an offense although not in the presence of the officer." LSA-C.Cr.P., Art. 213(3). "The law has not ordained hard and fast rules for the determination of reasonableness. The facts and circumstances of each case must be judged separately, with wide latitude accorded the trier of facts. That determination should not be overturned unless there is clear error." *State v. McIlvaine*, 247 La. 747, 174 So.2d 515, 520. Cf. *State v. Aias*, 243 La. 945, 149 So.2d 400; *State v. Christiana*, 249 La. 247, 186 So.2d 580; *State v. Pagnotta*, 253 La. 770, 220 So.2d 69; *State v. Devenow*, 253 La. 796, 220 So.2d 78. "*** the Government has the burden of showing probable cause to believe that a crime had been or was being committed both in obtaining a warrant prior to arrest and in sustaining the legality of an arrest without a warrant. ***" *United States v. Rivera*, 2 Cir., 321 F.2d 704. Cf. *Beck v. State of Ohio*, 379 U.S. 89, 85 S.Ct. 223, 13 L.Ed.2d 142; 6 C.J.S. Arrest § 5 a., p. 580.

We find that defendant's arrest was legal. At the time of his arrest armed robberies were widespread in the City of New Orleans. The facts supra disclose that Captain Newman had informants on whom he relied. One confidential informant conveyed reliable information to him, and this information pointed out the defendant as having committed some of the then recent truck driver robberies. The information was immediately relayed to Lt. Feld who trusted and believed his superior officer. The Lieutenant was alert to the tense situation existing among truck drivers handling money receipts. Sgt. Vigurie was a co-worker with Lt. Feld. There was a chain of command, which is usual for all large operations whose procedures are intricate, involving many police officers; six officers were detailed to the instant arrest.

A prudent man of reasonable caution, considering the time, place, and pertinent circumstances,—and having the facts available to him which Lt. Feld had in his personal possession and immediate knowledge (although they might not have been written on papers on his person)— would, in our opinion, have certainly believed that the defendant was guilty of armed robbery. Again, in our opinion, there would have been more than suspicion. Substantiating this conclusion is the fact that Marion Catalano, the Brown's Velvet driver, had identified a mug shot of the defendant as that of the man who had robbed him.

We conclude that Lt. Feld, Sgt. Vigurie, and the other officers—under the totality of the circumstances—acted under more than good faith and suspicion; they had probable cause to arrest the defendant. There was no reason why a warrant of arrest could not have been secured, but the failure to secure the warrant did not invalidate defendant's arrest. State of *Louisiana ex rel. Naylor v. Walker*, supra.

The officers did not break into defendant's home; there was no forceful entry; they were admitted by defendant's wife. Therefore, the entry was legal. Cf. *Sabbath v. United States*, 391 U.S. 585, 88 S.Ct. 1755, 20 L.Ed.2d 828 (1968).

When arrested, defendant was told that he was being arrested for armed robbery. This statement was sufficient to apprise him why his freedom of movement was suffering an interference.

We find that the State bore its burden of proving that defendant's arrest was constitutional and legal, and that there was probable and reasonable cause for such. The sum total of the facts and circumstances of this prosecution more than warrant such a conclusion. *United States v. Elgisser*, 2 Cir., 334 F.2d 103 (1964).

The fact that defendant was booked some four hours after he was arrested does not make his arrest illegal. As stated supra, he was interrogated, but none of his statements were introduced in evidence. Defendant suffered no deprivation of his constitutional rights.

Having found that the defendant was legally arrested, we proceed to a determination of the constitutionality vel non of the instant line-up.

When the line-up occurred, defendant was in legal custody and under no arrest. We find no impairment, Federal or State, to a line-up conducted under constitutional standards. Here, as stated supra, defendant was represented by able counsel at a critical stage of his prosecution; there was no prohibited self incrimination.[4]

> "We have no doubt that compelling the accused merely to exhibit his person for observation by a prosecution witness prior to trial involves no compulsion of the accused to give evidence having testimonial significance. It is compulsion of the accused to exhibit his physical characteristics, not compulsion to disclose any knowledge he might have. It is no different from compelling Schmerber to provide a blood sample or Holt to wear the blouse, and, as in those instances, is not within the cover of the privilege. Similarly, compelling Wade to speak within hearing distance of the witnesses, even to utter words purportedly uttered by the robber, was not compulsion to utter statements of a 'testimonial' nature; he was required to use his voice as an identifying physical characteristic, not to speak his guilt. ***" *United States v. Wade* (1967) 388 U.S. 218, 87 S.Ct. 1926, 1930, 18 L.Ed.2d 1149.

We conclude that the pretrial line-up herein was legal, and that the picture of the line-up (S-1), which includes as No. Four the photograph of the defendant, was properly admitted in evidence. We further find that evidence of the pretrial line-up identification by the victim was properly admitted in evidence. There was no need for suppression.

The record also discloses that there was an in-court identification at trial. The testimony with respect to this identification is as follows:

> "Q. Do you [victim] see this person in Court today?
> "A. I do.
> "Q. Would you point him out, please?
> "A. That gentleman right there (indicating).
> "Q. Is this the same gentleman that held you up on December 26, 1967?
> "A. It is."

Defendant suffered no violation of his constitutional rights by either the pretrial line-up identification or by the incourt identification. The trial judge was correct in admitting such in evidence. Cf. *State v. Allen*, 251 La. 237, 203 So.2d 705; *State v. Miller*, 254 La. 73, 222 So.2d 862; *State v. Lewis*, La., 229 So.2d 726.

Davis v. Mississippi, 394 U.S. 721, 89 S.Ct. 1394, 22 L.Ed.2d 676 (1969), is not apposite to the instant matter. No legal arrest was involved in that case. The United States Supreme Court distinctly said, "The legality of his arrest was not determined by the Mississippi Supreme Court." The Court then held the finger-prints taken during a period of detention unconstitutional evidence which could not be admitted during trial.

Specification of Errors No. 1 is without merit.

SPECIFICATION OF ERRORS NO. 2

We find no merit in Specification of Errors No. 2 which contends that the verdict of guilty in which only nine out of twelve jurors concurred denied appellant due process and equal protection of the laws guaranteed by the Fourteenth Amendment to the United States Constitution.

Article 782 of the Code of Criminal Procedure provides:

> "Cases in which the punishment may be capital shall be tried by a jury of twelve jurors, all of whom must concur to render a verdict. Cases in which the punishment is necessarily at hard labor shall be tried by a jury composed of twelve jurors, nine of whom must concur to render a verdict. Cases in which the punishment may be imprisonment at hard labor, shall be tried by a jury composed of five jurors, all of whom must concur to render a verdict. ***"

The Sixth Amendment to the United States Constitution provides that, "In all criminal prosecutions, the accused shall enjoy the right to a speedy and public trial, by an impartial jury of the State and district wherein the crime shall have been committed, which district shall have been previously ascertained by law, and to be informed of the nature and cause of the accusation; to be confronted with the witnesses against him; to have compulsory process for obtaining Witnesses in his favor, and to have the Assistance of Counsel for his defence."

Thus far, the United States Supreme Court has not ruled that the Sixth Amendment compels the States under the Fourteenth Amendment to the United States Constitution to require that the verdict of the jury be unanimous in a criminal prosecution such as the instant one. Herein, therefore, our ruling in *State v. Schoonover*, 252 La. 311, 211 So.2d 273, which upheld the ruling of the trial judge refusing to charge the jury that, "The verdict of the Jury, either to acquit the defendant or to convict him [armed robbery] must be by the unanimous vote of the entire jury," is applicable. In *Schoonover* we said, "These arguments do not impress us. We are entirely satisfied that the Constitution and laws of our state provide a system for this prosecution in which fundamental fairness and even-handed justice can be and was dispensed. ***" We are still of the same belief.

Specification of Errors No. 2 is without merit.

For the reasons assigned, the conviction and sentence are affirmed.

JOHNSON

V.

LOUISIANA.

No. 69-5035.

Supreme Court of United States.

Argued March 1, 1971.
Reargued January 10, 1972.
Decided May 22, 1972.

APPEAL FROM THE SUPREME COURT OF LOUISIANA.

Richard A. Buckley reargued the cause and filed a brief for appellant.

Louise Korns reargued the cause for appellee. With her on the brief were *Jack P. F. Gremillion*, Attorney General of Louisiana, and *Jim Garrison*.

MR. JUSTICE WHITE delivered the opinion of the Court.

Under both the Louisiana Constitution and Code of Criminal Procedure, criminal cases in which the punishment is necessarily at hard labor are tried to a jury of 12, and the vote of nine jurors is sufficient to return either a guilty or not guilty verdict.[5] The principal question in this case is whether these provisions allowing less-than-unanimous verdicts in certain cases are valid under the Due Process and Equal Protection Clauses of the Fourteenth Amendment.

I

Appellant Johnson was arrested at his home on January 20, 1968. There was no arrest warrant, but the victim of an armed robbery had identified Johnson from photographs as having committed the crime. He was then identified at a lineup, at which he had counsel, by the victim of still another robbery. The latter crime is involved in this case. Johnson pleaded not guilty, was tried on May 14, 1968, by a 12-man jury and was convicted by a nine-to-three verdict. His due process and equal protection challenges to the Louisiana constitutional and statutory provisions were rejected by the Louisiana courts, 255 La. 314, 230 So. 2d 825 (1970), and he appealed here. We noted probable jurisdiction. 400 U.S. 900 (1970). Conceding that under *Duncan v. Louisiana,* 391 U.S. 145 (1968), the Sixth Amendment is not applicable to his case, see *DeStefano v. Woods,* 392 U.S. 631 (1968), appellant presses his equal protection and due process claims, together with a Fourth Amendment claim also rejected by the Louisiana Supreme Court. We affirm.

II

Appellant argues that in order to give substance to the reasonable-doubt standard, which the State, by virtue of the Due Process Clause of the Fourteenth Amendment, must satisfy in criminal cases, see *In re Winship,* 397 U.S. 358, 363–364 (1970), that clause must be construed to require a unanimous-jury verdict in all criminal cases. In so contending, appellant does not challenge the instructions in this case. Concededly, the jurors were told to convict only if convinced of guilt beyond a reasonable doubt. Nor is there any claim that, if the verdict in this case had been unanimous, the evidence would have been insufficient to support it. Appellant focuses instead on the fact that less than all jurors voted to convict and argues that, because three voted to acquit, the reasonable-doubt standard has not been satisfied and his conviction is therefore infirm.

We note at the outset that this Court has never held jury unanimity to be a requisite of due process of law. Indeed, the Court has more than once expressly said that "[i]n criminal cases due process of law is not denied by a state law . . . which dispenses with the necessity of a jury of twelve, or unanimity in the verdict." *Jordan v. Massachusetts,* 225 U.S. 167, 176 (1912) (dictum). Accord, *Maxwell v. Dow,* 176 U.S. 581, 602, 605 (1900) (dictum). These statements, moreover, co-existed with cases indicating that proof of guilt beyond a reasonable doubt is implicit in constitutions recognizing "the fundamental principles that are deemed essential for the protection of life and liberty." *Davis v. United States,* 160

U.S. 469, 488 (1895). See also *Leland* v. *Oregon*, 343 U.S. 790, 802–803 (1952) (dissenting opinion); *Brinegar* v. *United States*, 338 U.S. 160, 174 (1949); *Coffin* v. *United States*, 156 U.S. 432, 453–460 (1895).[6]

Entirely apart from these cases, however, it is our view that the fact of three dissenting votes to acquit raises no question of constitutional substance about either the integrity or the accuracy of the majority verdict of guilt. Appellant's contrary argument breaks down into two parts, each of which we shall consider separately: first, that nine individual jurors will be unable to vote conscientiously in favor of guilt beyond a reasonable doubt when three of their colleagues are arguing for acquittal, and second, that guilt cannot be said to have been proved beyond a reasonable doubt when one or more of a jury's members at the conclusion of deliberation still possess such a doubt. Neither argument is persuasive.

Numerous cases have defined a reasonable doubt as one "'based on reason which arises from the evidence or lack of evidence.'" *United States* v. *Johnson*, 343 F. 2d 5, 6 n. 1 (CA2 1965). Accord, *e.g.*, *Bishop* v. *United States*, 71 App. D. C. 132, 138, 107 F. 2d 297, 303 (1939); *United States* v. *Schneiderman*, 106 F. Supp. 906, 927 (SD Cal. 1952); *United States* v. *Haupt*, 47 F. Supp. 836, 840 (ND Ill. 1942), rev'd on other grounds, 136 F. 2d 661 (CA7 1943). In *Winship*, *supra*, the Court recognized this evidentiary standard as "'impress[ing] on the trier of fact the necessity of reaching a subjective state of certitude of the facts in issue.'" 397 U.S., at 364 (citation omitted). In considering the first branch of appellant's argument, we can find no basis for holding that the nine jurors who voted for his conviction failed to follow their instructions concerning the need for proof beyond such a doubt or that the vote of any one of the nine failed to reflect an honest belief that guilt had been so proved. Appellant, in effect, asks us to assume that, when minority jurors express sincere doubts about guilt, their fellow jurors will nevertheless ignore them and vote to convict even if deliberation has not been exhausted and minority jurors have grounds for acquittal which, if pursued, might persuade members of the majority to acquit. But the mere fact that three jurors voted to acquit does not in itself demonstrate that, had the nine jurors of the majority attended further to reason and the evidence, all or one of them would have developed a reasonable doubt about guilt. We have no grounds for believing that majority jurors, aware of their responsibility and power over the liberty of the defendant, would simply refuse to listen to arguments presented to them in favor of acquittal, terminate discussion, and render a verdict. On the contrary it is far more likely that a juror presenting reasoned argument in favor of acquittal would either have his arguments answered or would carry enough other jurors with him to prevent conviction. A majority will cease discussion and outvote a minority only after reasoned discussion has ceased to have persuasive effect or to serve any other purpose—when a minority, that is, continues to insist upon acquittal without having persuasive reasons in support of its position. At that juncture there is no basis for denigrating the vote of so large a majority of the jury or for refusing to accept their decision as being, at least in their minds, beyond a reasonable doubt. Indeed, at this point, a "dissenting juror should consider whether his doubt was a reasonable one . . . [when it made] no impression upon the minds of so many men, equally honest, equally intelligent with himself." *Allen v. United States*, 164 U.S. 492, 501 (1896). Appellant offers no evidence that majority jurors simply ignore the reasonable doubts of their colleagues or otherwise act irresponsibly in casting their votes in favor of conviction, and before we alter our own longstanding perceptions about jury behavior and overturn a considered legislative judgment that unanimity is not essential to reasoned jury verdicts, we must have some basis for doing so other than unsupported assumptions.

We conclude, therefore, that, as to the nine jurors who voted to convict, the State satisfied its burden of proving guilt beyond any reasonable doubt. The remaining question under the Due Process Clause is whether the vote of three jurors for acquittal can be said to impeach the verdict of the other nine and to demonstrate that guilt was not in fact proved beyond such doubt. We hold that it cannot.

Of course, the State's proof could perhaps be regarded as more certain if it had convinced all 12 jurors instead of only nine; it would have been even more compelling if it had been required to convince and had, in fact, convinced 24 or 36 jurors. But the fact remains that nine jurors—

a substantial majority of the jury—were convinced by the evidence. In our view disagreement of three jurors does not alone establish reasonable doubt, particularly when such a heavy majority of the jury, after having considered the dissenters' views, remains convinced of guilt. That rational men disagree is not in itself equivalent to a failure of proof by the State, nor does it indicate infidelity to the reasonable-doubt standard. Jury verdicts finding guilt beyond a reasonable doubt are regularly sustained even though the evidence was such that the jury would have been justified in having a reasonable doubt, see *United States* v. *Quarles*, 387 F. 2d 551, 554 (CA4 1967); *Bell* v. *United States*, 185 F. 2d 302, 310 (CA4 1950); even though the trial judge might not have reached the same conclusion as the jury, see *Takahashi* v. *United States*, 143 F. 2d 118, 122 (CA9 1944); and even though appellate judges are closely divided on the issue whether there was sufficient evidence to support a conviction. See *United States* v. *Johnson*, 140 U.S. App. D. C. 54, 60, 433 F. 2d 1160, 1166 (1970); *United States* v. *Manuel-Baca*, 421 F. 2d 781, 783 (CA9 1970). That want of jury unanimity is not to be equated with the existence of a reasonable doubt emerges even more clearly from the fact that when a jury in a federal court, which operates under the unanimity rule and is instructed to acquit a defendant if it has a reasonable doubt about his guilt, see *Holt* v. *United States*, 218 U.S. 245, 253 (1910); *Agnew* v. *United States*, 165 U.S. 36, 51 (1897); W. Mathes & E. Devitt, Federal Jury Practice and Instructions § 8.01 (1965), cannot agree unanimously upon a verdict, the defendant is not acquitted, but is merely given a new trial. *Downum* v. *United States*, 372 U.S. 734, 736 (1963); *Dreyer* v. *Illinois*, 187 U.S. 71, 85–86 (1902); *United States* v. *Perez*, 9 Wheat. 579, 580 (1824). If the doubt of a minority of jurors indicates the existence of a reasonable doubt, it would appear that a defendant should receive a directed verdict of acquittal rather than a retrial. We conclude, therefore, that verdicts rendered by nine out of 12 jurors are not automatically invalidated by the disagreement of the dissenting three. Appellant was not deprived of due process of law.

III

Appellant also attacks as violative of the Equal Protection Clause the provisions of Louisiana law requiring unanimous verdicts in capital and five-man jury cases, but permitting less-than-unanimous verdicts in cases such as his. We conclude, however, that the Louisiana statutory scheme serves a rational purpose and is not subject to constitutional challenge.

In order to "facilitate, expedite, and reduce expense in the administration of criminal justice," *State v. Lewis,* 129 La. 800, 804, 56 So. 893, 894 (1911), Louisiana has permitted less serious crimes to be tried by five jurors with unanimous verdicts, more serious crimes have required the assent of nine of 12 jurors, and for the most serious crimes a unanimous verdict of 12 jurors is stipulated. In appellant's case, nine jurors rather than five or 12 were required for a verdict. We discern nothing invidious in this classification. We have held that the States are free under the Federal Constitution to try defendants with juries of less than 12 men. *Williams v. Florida,* 399 U.S. 78 (1970). Three jurors here voted to acquit, but from what we have earlier said, this does not demonstrate that appellant was convicted on a lower standard of proof. To obtain a conviction in any of the categories under Louisiana law, the State must prove guilt beyond reasonable doubt, but the number of jurors who must be so convinced increases with the seriousness of the crime and the severity of the punishment that may be imposed. We perceive nothing unconstitutional or invidiously discriminatory, however, in a State's insisting that its burden of proof be carried with more jurors where more serious crimes or more severe punishments are at issue.

Appellant nevertheless insists that dispensing with unanimity in his case disadvantaged him as compared with those who commit less serious or capital crimes. With respect to the latter, he is correct; the State does make conviction more difficult by requiring the assent of all 12 jurors. Appellant might well have been ultimately acquitted had he committed a capital offense. But as we have indicated, this does not constitute a denial of equal protection of the law; the State may treat capital offenders differently without violating the constitutional rights of those charged with lesser crimes. As to the crimes triable by a five-man jury, if appellant's position is that it is easier to convince nine of 12 jurors than to convince all of five, he is simply challenging the judgment of the Louisiana Legislature. That body obviously intended to vary the difficulty of proving guilt with the gravity of the offense and the severity of the punishment. We remain unconvinced by anything appellant has presented that this legislative judgment was defective in any constitutional sense.

IV

Appellant also urges that his nighttime arrest without a warrant was unlawful in the absence of a valid excuse for failing to obtain a warrant and, further, that his subsequent lineup identification was a forbidden fruit of the claimed invasion of his Fourth Amendment rights. The validity of Johnson's arrest, however, is beside the point here, for it is clear that no evidence that might properly be characterized as the fruit of an illegal entry and arrest was used against him at his trial. Prior to the lineup, at which Johnson was represented by counsel, he was brought before a committing magistrate to advise him of his rights and set bail. At the time of the lineup, the detention of the appellant was under the authority of this commitment. Consequently, the lineup was conducted not by "exploitation" of the challenged arrest but "by means sufficiently distinguishable to be purged of the primary taint." *Wong Sun* v. *United States,* 371 U.S. 471, 488 (1963).

The judgment of the Supreme Court of Louisiana is therefore *Affirmed.*

MR. JUSTICE BLACKMUN, concurring.[a]

I join the Court's opinion and judgment in each of these cases. I add only the comment, which should be obvious and should not need saying, that in so doing I do not imply that I regard a State's split-verdict system as a wise one. My vote means only that I cannot conclude that the system is constitutionally offensive. Were I a legislator, I would disfavor it as a matter of policy. Our task here, however, is not to pursue and strike down what happens to impress us as undesirable legislative policy.

I do not hesitate to say, either, that a system employing a 7–5 standard,

a. [This opinion applies also to No. 69-5046, *Apodaca et al.* v. *Oregon, post,* p. 404.]

rather than a 9–3 or 75% minimum, would afford me great difficulty. As MR. JUSTICE WHITE points out, *ante*, at 362, "a substantial majority of the jury" are to be convinced. That is all that is before us in each of these cases.

MR. JUSTICE POWELL, concurring in No. 69-5035 and concurring in the judgment in No. 69-5046.

I concur in the judgment of the Court that convictions based on less-than-unanimous jury verdicts in these cases did not deprive criminal defendants of due process of law under the Fourteenth Amendment. As my reasons for reaching this conclusion in the Oregon case differ from those expressed in the plurality opinion of MR. JUSTICE WHITE, I will state my views separately.

I

69-5035

Duncan v. *Louisiana*, 391 U.S. 145 (1968), stands for the proposition that criminal defendants in state courts are entitled to trial by jury.[7] The source of that right is the Due Process Clause of the Fourteenth Amendment. Due process, as consistently interpreted by this Court, commands that citizens subjected to criminal process in state courts be accorded those rights that are fundamental to a fair trial in the context of our "American scheme of justice." *Id.*, at 149. The right of an accused person to trial by a jury of his peers was a cherished element of the English common law long before the American Revolution. In this country, prior to *Duncan*, every State had adopted a criminal adjudicatory process calling for the extensive use of petit juries. *Id.*, at 150 n. 14; *Turner* v. *Louisiana*, 379 U.S. 466, 471 n. 9 (1965). Because it assures the interposition of an impartial assessment of one's peers between the defendant and his accusers, the right to trial by jury deservedly ranks as a fundamental of our system of jurisprudence. With this principle of due process, I am in full accord.

In *DeStefano* v. *Woods*, 392 U.S. 631 (1968), an Oregon petitioner sought to raise the question, left open in *Duncan*, whether the right to jury trial in a state court also contemplates the right to a unanimous verdict.[8]

Because the Court concluded that *Duncan* was not to have retroactive applicability, it found it unnecessary to decide whether the Fourteenth Amendment requires unanimity. The trial in the case before the Court at that time occurred several years prior to May 20, 1968, the date of decision in *Duncan*. In the Louisiana case now before us, the petitioner also was convicted by a less-than-unanimous verdict before *Duncan* was decided. Accordingly, I read *DeStefano* as foreclosing consideration in this case of the question whether jury trial as guaranteed by the Due Process Clause contemplates a corollary requirement that its judgment be unanimous.

Indeed, in *Johnson v. Louisiana*, appellant concedes that the nonretroactivity of *Duncan* prevents him from raising his due process argument in the classic "fundamental fairness" language adopted there. Instead he claims that he is deprived of due process because a conviction in which only nine of 12 jurors joined is not one premised on a finding of guilt beyond a reasonable doubt, held to be a requisite element of due process in *In re Winship*, 397 U.S. 358, 364 (1970). For the reasons stated in the majority opinion, I do not agree that Louisiana's less-than-unanimous verdict rule undercuts the applicable standard of proof in criminal prosecutions in that State.

Appellant also asks this Court to find a violation of the Equal Protection Clause in Louisiana's constitutional and statutory provisions establishing the contours of the jury trial right in that State. The challenged provisions divide those accused of crimes into three categories depending on the severity of the possible punishment: those charged with offenses for which the punishment might be at hard labor are entitled to a five-juror, unanimous verdict; those charged with offenses for which the punishment will necessarily be at hard labor are entitled to a verdict in which nine of 12 jurors must concur; and those charged with capital offenses are entitled to a 12-juror, unanimous verdict. La. Const., Art. VII, § 41; La. Code Crim. Proc., Art. 782. Such distinctions between classes of defendants do not constitute invidious discrimination against any one of the classes unless the State's classification can be said to lack a reasonable or rational basis. We have been shown no reason to question the rationality of Louisiana's tri-level system. I, therefore, join the Court's opinion in *Johnson v. Louisiana* affirming the decision below.[9]

II

69-5046

In the Oregon case decided today, *Apodaca* v. *Oregon*, the trials occurred after *Duncan* was decided. The question left unanswered in *Duncan* and *DeStefano* is therefore squarely presented. I concur in the plurality opinion in this case insofar as it concludes that a defendant in a state court may constitutionally be convicted by less than a unanimous verdict, but I am not in accord with a major premise upon which that judgment is based. Its premise is that the concept of jury trial, as applicable to the States under the Fourteenth Amendment, must be identical in every detail to the concept required in federal courts by the Sixth Amendment.[10] I do not think that all of the elements of jury trial within the meaning of the Sixth Amendment are necessarily embodied in or incorporated into the Due Process Clause of the Fourteenth Amendment. As Mr. Justice Fortas, concurring in *Duncan* v. *Louisiana*, 391 U.S., at 213, said:

> "Neither logic nor history nor the intent of the draftsmen of the Fourteenth Amendment can possibly be said to require that the Sixth Amendment or its jury trial provision be applied to the States together with the total gloss that this Court's decisions have supplied."

In an unbroken line of cases reaching back into the late 1800's, the Justices of this Court have recognized, virtually without dissent, that unanimity is one of the indispensable features of *federal* jury trial. *Andres* v. *United States*, 333 U.S. 740, 748–749 (1948); *Patton* v. *United States*, 281 U.S. 276, 288–290 (1930); *Hawaii* v. *Mankichi*, 190 U.S. 197, 211–212 (1903) (see also Mr. Justice Harlan's dissenting opinion); *Maxwell* v. *Dow*, 176 U.S. 581, 586 (1900) (see also Mr. Justice Harlan's dissenting opinion); *Thompson* v. *Utah*, 170 U.S. 343, 355 (1898).[11] In these cases, the Court has presumed that unanimous verdicts are essential in federal jury trials, not because unanimity is necessarily fundamental to the function performed by the jury, but because that result is mandated by history.[12] The reasoning that runs throughout this Court's Sixth Amendment precedents is that, in amending the Constitution to guarantee the right to jury trial, the framers desired to preserve the jury safeguard as it was known to them at common law.[13] At the time the Bill of Rights was adopted, unanimity had long been established as one of the attributes of a jury conviction at common law.[14] It therefore seems to me, in accord both with history and precedent, that the Sixth Amendment requires a unanimous jury verdict to convict in a federal criminal trial.

But it is the Fourteenth Amendment, rather than the Sixth, that imposes upon the States the requirement that they provide jury trials to those accused of serious crimes. This Court has said, in cases decided when the intendment of that Amendment was not as clouded by the passage of time, that due process does not require that the States apply the federal jury-trial right with all its gloss. In *Maxwell v. Dow*, 176 U.S., at 605, Mr. Justice Peckham, speaking for eight of the nine members of the Court, so stated:

> "[W]hen providing in their constitution and legislation for the manner in which civil or criminal actions shall be tried, it is in entire conformity with the character of the Federal Government that [the States] should have the right to decide for themselves what shall be the form and character of the procedure in such trials, . . . whether there shall be a jury of twelve or a lesser number, and whether the verdict must be unanimous or not. . . ."

Again, in *Jordan v. Massachusetts*, 225 U.S. 167, 176 (1912), the Court concluded that "[i]n criminal cases due process of law is not denied by a state law which dispenses with . . . the necessity of a jury of twelve, or unanimity in the verdict."

It is true, of course, that the *Maxwell* and *Jordan* Courts went further and concluded that the States might dispense with jury trial altogether. That conclusion, grounded on a more limited view of due process than has been accepted by this Court in recent years,[15] was rejected by the Court in *Duncan*. But I find nothing in the constitutional principle upon which *Duncan* is based, or in other precedents, that requires repudiation of the views expressed in *Maxwell* and *Jordan* with respect to the size of a jury and the unanimity of its verdict. Mr. Justice Fortas, concurring in *Duncan*, commented on the distinction between the requirements of the

Sixth Amendment and those of the Due Process Clause and suggested the appropriate framework for analysis of the issue in this case.

"I see no reason whatever . . . to assume that our decision today should require us to impose federal requirements such as unanimous verdicts or a jury of 12 upon the States. We may well conclude that these and other features of federal jury practice are by no means fundamental—that they are not essential to due process of law—and that they are not obligatory on the States." *Duncan v. Louisiana*, 391 U.S., at 213.

The question, therefore, that should be addressed in this case is whether unanimity is in fact so fundamental to the essentials of jury trial that this particular requirement of the Sixth Amendment is necessarily binding on the States under the Due Process Clause of the Fourteenth Amendment. An affirmative answer, ignoring the strong views previously expressed to the contrary by this Court in *Maxwell* and *Jordan*, would give unwarranted and unwise scope to the incorporation doctrine as it applies to the due process right of state criminal defendants to trial by jury.

The importance that our system attaches to trial by jury derives from the special confidence we repose in a "body of one's peers to determine guilt or innocence as a safeguard against arbitrary law enforcement." *Williams v. Florida*, 399 U.S. 78, 87 (1970). It is this safeguarding function, preferring the commonsense judgment of a jury as a bulwark "against the corrupt or overzealous prosecutor and against the compliant, biased, or eccentric judge,"[16] that lies at the core of our dedication to the principles of jury determination of guilt or innocence.[17] This is the fundamental of jury trial that brings it within the mandate of due process. It seems to me that this fundamental is adequately preserved by the jury-verdict provision of the Oregon Constitution. There is no reason to believe, on the basis of experience in Oregon or elsewhere, that a unanimous decision of 12 jurors is more likely to serve the high purpose of jury trial, or is entitled to greater respect in the community, than the same decision joined in by 10 members of a jury of 12. The standard of due process assured by the Oregon Constitution provides a sufficient guarantee that the government will not be permitted to impose its judgment on an accused without first meeting the full burden of its prosecutorial duty.[18]

Moreover, in holding that the Fourteenth Amendment has incorporated "jot-for-jot and case-for-case"[19] every element of the Sixth Amendment, the Court derogates principles of federalism that are basic to our system. In the name of uniform application of high standards of due process, the Court has embarked upon a course of constitutional interpretation that deprives the States of freedom to experiment with adjudicatory processes different from the federal model. At the same time, the Court's understandable unwillingness to impose requirements that it finds unnecessarily rigid (*e.g.*, *Williams* v. *Florida*, 399 U.S. 78), has culminated in the dilution of federal rights that were, until these decisions, never seriously questioned. The doubly undesirable consequence of this reasoning process, labeled by Mr. Justice Harlan as "constitutional schizophrenia," *id.*, at 136, may well be detrimental both to the state and federal criminal justice systems. Although it is perhaps late in the day for an expression of my views, I would have been in accord with the opinions in similar cases by THE CHIEF JUSTICE and Justices Harlan, STEWART, and Fortas[20] that, at least in defining the elements of the right to jury trial, there is no sound basis for interpreting the Fourteenth Amendment to require blind adherence by the States to all details of the federal Sixth Amendment standards.[21]

While the Civil War Amendments altered substantially the balance of federalism, it strains credulity to believe that they were intended to deprive the States of all freedom to experiment with variations in jury-trial procedure. In an age in which empirical study is increasingly relied upon as a foundation for decisionmaking, one of the more obvious merits of our federal system is the opportunity it affords each State, if its people so choose, to become a "laboratory" and to experiment with a range of trial and procedural alternatives. Although the need for the innovations that grow out of diversity has always been great, imagination unimpeded by unwarranted demands for national uniformity is of special importance at a time when serious doubt exists as to the adequacy of our criminal justice system. The same diversity of local legislative responsiveness that marked the development of economic and social reforms in this country,[22] if not barred by an unduly restrictive application of the Due Process Clause, might well lead to valuable innovations with respect to determining—fairly and more expeditiously—the guilt or innocence of the accused.

Viewing the unanimity controversy as one requiring a fresh look at the question of what is fundamental in jury trial, I see no constitutional infirmity in the provision adopted by the people of Oregon. It is the product of a constitutional amendment, approved by a vote of the people in the State, and appears to be patterned on a provision of the American Law Institute's Code of Criminal Procedure.[23] A similar decision has been echoed more recently in England where the unanimity requirement was abandoned by statutory enactment.[24] Less-than-unanimous verdict provisions also have been viewed with approval by the American Bar Association's Criminal Justice Project.[25] Those who have studied the jury mechanism and recommended deviation from the historic rule of unanimity have found a number of considerations to be significant. Removal of the unanimity requirement could well minimize the potential for hung juries occasioned either by bribery or juror irrationality. Furthermore, the rule that juries must speak with a single voice often leads, not to full agreement among the 12 but to agreement by none and compromise by all, despite the frequent absence of a rational basis for such compromise.[26] Quite apart from whether Justices sitting on this Court would have deemed advisable the adoption of any particular less-than-unanimous jury provision, I think that considerations of this kind reflect a legitimate basis for experimentation and deviation from the federal blueprint.[27]

III

Petitioners in *Apodaca v. Oregon*, in addition to their primary contention that unanimity is a requirement of state jury trials because the Fourteenth Amendment "incorporates" the Sixth, also assert that Oregon's constitutional provision offends the federal constitutional guarantee against the systematic exclusion of any group within the citizenry from participating in the criminal trial process. While the systematic exclusion of identifiable minorities from jury service has long been recognized as a violation of the Equal Protection Clause (see, *e.g., Whitus v. Georgia*, 385 U.S. 545 (1967); *Strauder v. West Virginia*, 100 U.S. 303 (1880)), in more recent years the Court has held that criminal defendants are entitled, as a matter of due process, to a jury drawn from a representative cross section of the community. This is an essential element of a fair and impartial jury trial. See *Williams* v. *Florida*, 399 U.S., at 100; *Alexander* v. *Louisiana*, 405 U.S. 625, 634 (1972) (DOUGLAS J., concurring). Petitioners contend that less-than-unanimous jury verdict provisions undercut that right by implicitly permitting in the jury room that which is prohibited in the jury venire selection process—the exclusion of minority group viewpoints. They argue that unless unanimity is required even of a properly drawn jury, the result—whether conviction or acquittal—may be the unjust product of racism, bigotry, or an emotionally inflamed trial.

Such fears materialize only when the jury's majority, responding to these extraneous pressures, ignores the evidence and the instructions of the court as well as the rational arguments of the minority. The risk, however, that a jury in a particular case will fail to meet its high responsibility is inherent in any system that commits decisions of guilt or innocence to untrained laymen drawn at random from the community. In part, at least, the majority-verdict rule must rely on the same principle that underlies our historic dedication to jury trial: both systems are premised on the conviction that each juror will faithfully perform his assigned duty. MR. JUSTICE DOUGLAS' dissent today appears to rest on the contrary assumption that the members of the jury constituting the majority have no *duty* to consider the minority's viewpoint in the course of deliberation. Characterizing the jury's consideration of minority views as mere "polite and academic conversation," or "courtesy dialogue," he concludes that a jury is under no obligation in Oregon to deliberate at all if 10 jurors vote together at the outset. *Post,* at 389. No such power freely to shut off competing views is implied in the record in this case and it is contrary to basic principles of jury participation in the criminal process. While there may be, of course, reasonable differences of opinion as to the merit of the speculative concerns expressed by these petitioners and reflected in the dissenting opinion, I find nothing in Oregon's experience to justify the apprehension that juries not bound by the unanimity rule will be more likely to ignore their historic responsibility.

Moreover, the States need not rely on the presumption of regularity in a vacuum since each has at its disposal protective devices to diminish significantly the prospect of jury irresponsibility. Even before the jury is sworn, substantial protection against the selection of a representative but wilfully irresponsible jury is assured by the wide availability of peremptory challenges and challenges for cause.[28] The likelihood of miscarriage of justice is further diminished by the judge's use of full jury instructions, detailing the applicable burdens of proof, informing the jurors of their duty to weigh the views of fellow jurors,[29] and reminding them of the solemn responsibility imposed by their oaths. Trial judges also retain the power to direct acquittals in cases in which the evidence of guilt is lacking, or to set aside verdicts once rendered when the evidence is insufficient to support a conviction. Furthermore, in cases in which public emotion runs high or pretrial publicity threatens a fair trial, judges possess broad power to grant changes of venue,[30] and to impose restrictions on the extent of press coverage.[31]

In light of such protections it is unlikely that the Oregon "ten-of-twelve" rule will account for an increase in the number of cases in which injustice will be occasioned by a biased or prejudiced jury. It may be wise to recall MR. JUSTICE WHITE's admonition in *Murphy* v. *Waterfront Comm'n*, 378 U.S. 52, 102 (1964), that the Constitution "protects against real dangers, not remote and speculative possibilities." Since I do not view Oregon's less-than-unanimous jury verdict requirement as violative of the due process guarantee of the Fourteenth Amendment, I concur in the Court's affirmance of these convictions.

MR. JUSTICE DOUGLAS, with whom MR. JUSTICE BRENNAN and MR. JUSTICE MARSHALL concur, dissenting.[b]

Appellant in the Louisiana case and petitioners in the Oregon case were convicted by juries that were less than unanimous. This procedure is authorized by both the Louisiana and Oregon Constitutions. Their claim, rejected by the majority, is that this procedure is a violation of their federal constitutional rights. With due respect to the majority, I dissent from this radical departure from American traditions.

b. [This opinion applies also to No. 69-5046, *Apodaca et al.* v. *Oregon, post,* p. 404.]

I

The Constitution does not mention unanimous juries. Neither does it mention the presumption of innocence, nor does it say that guilt must be proved beyond a reasonable doubt in all criminal cases. Yet it is almost inconceivable that anyone would have questioned whether proof beyond a reasonable doubt was in fact the constitutional standard. And, indeed, when such a case finally arose we had little difficult disposing of the issue. *In re Winship*, 397 U.S. 358, 364.

The Court, speaking through MR. JUSTICE BRENNAN, stated that:

> "[The] use of the reasonable-doubt standard is indispensable to command the respect and confidence of the community in applications of the criminal law. It is critical that the moral force of the criminal law not be diluted by a standard of proof that leaves people in doubt whether innocent men are being condemned. It is also important in our free society that every individual going about his ordinary affairs have confidence that his government cannot adjudge him guilty of a criminal offense without convincing a proper factfinder of his guilt with utmost certainty.

> "Lest there remain any doubt about the constitutional stature of the reasonable-doubt standard, we explicitly hold that the Due Process Clause protects the accused against conviction except upon proof beyond a reasonable doubt of every fact necessary to constitute the crime with which he is charged." *Ibid.*

I had similarly assumed that there was no dispute that the Federal Constitution required a unanimous jury in all criminal cases. After all, it has long been explicit constitutional doctrine that the Seventh Amendment civil jury must be unanimous. See *American Publishing Co.* v. *Fisher*, 166 U.S. 464, where the Court said that "unanimity was one of the peculiar and essential features of trial by jury at the common law. No authorities are needed to sustain this proposition." *Id.*, at 468. Like proof beyond a reasonable doubt, the issue of unanimous juries in criminal cases simply never arose. Yet in cases dealing with juries it had always been assumed that a unanimous jury was required.[32] See *Maxwell* v. *Dow*, 176 U.S. 581, 586; *Patton* v. *United States*, 281 U.S. 276, 288; *Andres* v. *United States*, 333 U.S. 740, 748. Today the bases of those cases are discarded and two centuries of American history are shunted aside.[33]

The result of today's decisions is anomalous: though unanimous jury decisions are not required in state trials, they are constitutionally required in federal prosecutions. How can that be possible when both decisions stem from the Sixth Amendment?

We held unanimously in 1948 that the Bill of Rights requires a unanimous jury verdict:

> "Unanimity in jury verdicts is required where the Sixth and Seventh Amendments apply. In criminal cases this requirement of unanimity extends to all issues—character or degree of the crime, guilt and punishment—which are left to the jury. A verdict embodies in a single finding the conclusions by the jury upon all the questions submitted to it." *Andres* v. *United States*, 333 U.S., at 748.

After today's decisions, a man's property may only be taken away by a unanimous jury vote, yet he can be stripped of his liberty by a lesser standard. How can that result be squared with the law of the land as expressed in the settled and traditional requirements of procedural due process?

Rule 31 (a) of the Federal Rules of Criminal Procedure states, "The verdict shall be unanimous." That Rule was made by this Court with the concurrence of Congress pursuant to 18 U.S. C. § 3771. After today a unanimous verdict will be required in a federal prosecution but not in a state prosecution. Yet the source of the right in each case is the Sixth Amendment. I fail to see how with reason we can maintain those inconsistent dual positions.

There have, of course, been advocates of the view that the duties imposed on the States by reason of the Bill of Rights operating through the Fourteenth Amendment are a watered-down version of those guarantees. But we held to the contrary in *Malloy* v. *Hogan*, 378 U.S. 1, 10–11:

> We have held that the guarantees of the First Amendment, *Gitlow* v. *New York, supra; Cantwell* v. *Connecticut*, 310 U.S. 296; *Louisiana*

ex rel. Gremillion v. *NAACP,* 366 U.S. 293, the prohibition of unreasonable searches and seizures of the Fourth Amendment, *Ker*
v. *California,* 374 U.S. 23, and the right to counsel guaranteed by
the Sixth Amendment, *Gideon* v. *Wainwright, supra,* are all to be
enforced against the States under the Fourteenth Amendment according to the same standards that protect those personal rights
against federal encroachment. In the coerced confession cases,
involving the policies of the privilege itself, there has been no
suggestion that a confession might be considered coerced if used
in a federal but not a state tribunal. The Court thus has rejected
the notion that the Fourteenth Amendment applies to the States
only a 'watered-down, subjective version of the individual guarantees of the Bill of Rights.'"

Malloy, of course, not only applied the Self-Incrimination Clause to the
States but also stands for the proposition, as mentioned, that "the same
standards must determine whether an accused's silence in either a federal or state proceeding is justified." *Id.,* at 11. See also *Murphy* v. *Waterfront Comm'n,* 378 U.S. 52, 79. The equation of federal and state standards
for the Self-Incrimination Clause was expressly reaffirmed in *Griffin* v.
California, 380 U.S. 609, 615; and in *Miranda* v. *Arizona,* 384 U.S. 436, 464.

Similarly, when the Confrontation Clause was finally made obligatory
on the States, Mr. Justice Black for the majority was careful to observe
that its guarantee, "like the right against compelled self-incrimination, is
'to be enforced against the States under the Fourteenth Amendment according to the same standards that protect those personal rights against
federal encroachment.'" *Pointer* v. *Texas,* 380 U.S. 400, 406. Cf. *Dutton* v.
Evans, 400 U.S. 74, 81. Likewise, when we applied the Double Jeopardy
Clause against the States MR. JUSTICE MARSHALL wrote for the Court that
"[o]nce it is decided that a particular Bill of Rights guarantee is 'fundamental to the American scheme of justice,' *Duncan* v. *Louisiana* . . . the
same constitutional standards apply against both the State and Federal
Governments." *Benton* v. *Maryland,* 395 U.S. 784, 795. And, the doctrine
of coextensive coverage was followed in holding the Speedy Trial Clause
applicable to the States. *Klopfer* v. *North Carolina,* 386 U.S. 213, 222.

And, in *Duncan* v. *Louisiana,* 391 U.S. 145, 158 n. 30, in holding the jury trial guarantee binding in state trials, we noted that its prohibitions were to be identical against both the Federal and State Governments. See also *id.*, at 213 (Fortas, J., concurring).

Only once has this Court diverged from the doctrine of coextensive coverage of guarantees brought within the Fourteenth Amendment, and that aberration was later rectified. In *Wolf* v. *Colorado*, 338 U.S. 25, it was held that the Fourth Amendment ban against unreasonable and warrantless searches was enforceable against the States but the Court declined to incorporate the Fourth Amendment exclusionary rule of *Weeks* v. *United States*, 232 U.S. 383. Happily, however, that gap was partially closed in *Elkins* v. *United States*, 364 U.S. 206, and then completely bridged in *Mapp* v. *Ohio*, 367 U.S. 643. In *Mapp* we observed that "[t] his Court has not hesitated to enforce as strictly against the States as it does against the Federal Government the rights of free speech and of a free press, the rights to notice and to a fair, public trial. . . ." We concluded that "the same rule" should apply where the Fourth Amendment was concerned. *Id.*, at 656. And, later, we made clear that "the standard for obtaining a search warrant is . . . 'the same under the Fourth and Fourteenth Amendments,'" *Aguilar* v. *Texas*, 378 U.S. 108, 110; and that the "standard of reasonableness is the same under the Fourth and Fourteenth Amendments." *Ker* v. *California*, 374 U.S. 23, 33.

It is said, however, that the Sixth Amendment, as applied to the States by reason of the Fourteenth, does not mean what it does in federal proceedings, that it has a "due process" gloss on it, and that that gloss gives the States power to experiment with the explicit or implied guarantees in the Bill of Rights.

Mr. Justice Holmes, dissenting in *Truax* v. *Corrigan*, 257 U.S. 312, 344, and Mr. Justice Brandeis, dissenting in *New State Ice Co.* v. *Liebmann*, 285 U.S. 262, 311, thought that the States should be allowed to improvise remedies for social and economic ills. But in that area there are not many "thou shalt nots" in the Constitution and Bill of Rights concerning property rights. The most conspicuous is the Just Compensation Clause of the Fifth Amendment. It has been held applicable with full vigor to the States by reason of the Fourteenth Amendment. *Chicago, B. & Q. R. Co.* v. *Chicago*, 166 U.S. 226.

Do today's decisions mean that States may apply a "watered down" version of the Just Compensation Clause? Or are today's decisions limited to a paring down of civil rights protected by the Bill of Rights and up until now as fully applicable to the States as to the Federal Government?

These civil rights—whether they concern speech, searches and seizures, self-incrimination, criminal prosecutions, bail, or cruel and unusual punishments extend, of course, to everyone, but in cold reality touch mostly the lower castes in our society. I refer, of course, to the blacks, the Chicanos, the one-mule farmers, the agricultural workers, the offbeat students, the victims of the ghetto. Are we giving the States the power to experiment in diluting their civil rights? It has long been thought that the "thou shalt nots" in the Constitution and Bill of Rights protect everyone against governmental intrusion or overreaching. The idea has been obnoxious that there are some who can be relegated to second-class citizenship. But if we construe the Bill of Rights and the Fourteenth Amendment to permit States to "experiment" with the basic rights of people, we open a veritable Pandora's box. For hate and prejudice are versatile forces that can degrade the constitutional scheme.[34]

That, however, is only one of my concerns when we make the Bill of Rights, as applied to the States, a "watered down" version of what that charter guarantees. My chief concern is one often expressed by the late Mr. Justice Black, who was alarmed at the prospect of nine men appointed for life sitting as a super-legislative body to determine whether government has gone too far. The balancing was done when the Constitution and Bill of Rights were written and adopted. For this Court to determine, say, whether one person but not another is entitled to free speech is a power never granted it. But that is the ultimate reach of decisions that let the States, subject to our veto, experiment with rights guaranteed by the Bill of Rights.

I would construe the Sixth Amendment, when applicable to the States, precisely as I would when applied to the Federal Government.

II

The plurality approves a procedure which diminishes the reliability of a jury. First, it eliminates the circumstances in which a minority of jurors (a) could have rationally persuaded the entire jury to acquit, or (b) while unable to persuade the majority to acquit, nonetheless could have convinced them to convict only on a lesser-included offense. Second, it permits prosecutors in Oregon and Louisiana to enjoy a conviction-acquittal ratio substantially greater than that ordinarily returned by unanimous juries.

The diminution of verdict reliability flows from the fact that nonunanimous juries need not debate and deliberate as fully as must unanimous juries. As soon as the requisite majority is attained, further consideration is not required either by Oregon or by Louisiana even though the dissident jurors might, if given the chance, be able to convince the majority. Such persuasion does in fact occasionally occur in States where the unanimous requirement applies: "In roughly one case in ten, the minority eventually succeeds in reversing an initial majority, and these may be cases of special importance."[35] One explanation for this phenomenon is that because jurors are often not permitted to take notes and because they have imperfect memories, the forensic process of forcing jurors to defend their conflicting recollections and conclusions flushes out many nuances which otherwise would go overlooked. This collective effort to piece together the puzzle of historical truth, however, is cut short as soon as the requisite majority is reached in Oregon and Louisiana. Indeed, if a necessary majority is immediately obtained, then no deliberation at all is required in these States. (There is a suggestion that this may have happened in the 10–2 verdict rendered in only 41 minutes in Apodaca's case.) To be sure, in jurisdictions other than these two States, initial majorities normally prevail in the end, but about a tenth of the time the rough-and-tumble of the jury room operates to reverse completely their preliminary perception of guilt or innocence. The Court now extracts from the jury room this automatic check against hasty factfinding by relieving jurors of the duty to hear out fully the dissenters.

It is said that there is no evidence that majority jurors will refuse to listen to dissenters whose votes are unneeded for conviction. Yet human experience teaches that polite and academic conversation is no substitute for the earnest and robust argument necessary to reach unanimity. As mentioned earlier, in Apodaca's case, whatever courtesy dialogue transpired could not have lasted more than 41 minutes. I fail to understand why the Court should lift from the States the burden of justifying so radical a departure from an accepted and applauded tradition and instead demand that these defendants document with empirical evidence what has always been thought to be too obvious for further study.

To be sure, in *Williams v. Florida*, 399 U.S. 78, we held that a State could provide a jury less than 12 in number in a criminal trial. We said: "What few experiments have occurred—usually in the civil area—indicate that there is no discernible difference between the results reached by the two different-sized juries. In short, neither currently available evidence nor theory suggests that the 12-man jury is necessarily more advantageous to the defendant than a jury composed of fewer members." *Id.*, at 101–102.

That rationale of *Williams* can have no application here. *Williams* requires that the change be neither more nor less advantageous to either the State or the defendant. It is said that such a showing is satisfied here since a 3:9 (Louisiana) or 2:10 (Oregon) verdict will result in acquittal. Yet experience shows that the less-than-unanimous jury overwhelmingly favors the States.

Moreover, even where an initial majority wins the dissent over to its side, the ultimate result in unanimous-jury States may nonetheless reflect the reservations of uncertain jurors. I refer to many compromise verdicts on lesser-included offenses and lesser sentences. Thus, even though a minority may not be forceful enough to carry the day, their doubts may nonetheless cause a majority to exercise caution. Obviously, however, in Oregon and Louisiana, dissident jurors will not have the opportunity through full deliberation to temper the opposing faction's degree of certainty of guilt.

The new rule also has an impact on cases in which a unanimous jury would have neither voted to acquit nor to convict, but would have deadlocked. In unanimous-jury States, this occurs about 5.6% of the time. Of these deadlocked juries, Kalven and Zeisel say that 56% contain either one, two, or three dissenters. In these latter cases, the majorities favor the prosecution 44% (of the 56%) but the defendant only 12% (of the 56%).[36] Thus, by eliminating these deadlocks, Louisiana wins 44 cases for every 12 that it loses, obtaining in this band of outcomes a substantially more favorable conviction ratio (3.67 to 1) than the unanimous-jury ratio of slightly less than two guilty verdicts for every acquittal. H. Kalven & H. Zeisel, The American Jury 461, 488 (Table 139) (1966). By eliminating the one-and-two-dissenting-juror cases, Oregon does even better, gaining 4.25 convictions for every acquittal. While the statutes on their face deceptively appear to be neutral, the use of the nonunanimous jury stacks the truth-determining process against the accused. Thus, we take one step more away from the accusatorial system that has been our proud boast.

It is my belief that a unanimous jury is necessary if the great barricade known as proof beyond a reasonable doubt is to be maintained. This is not to equate proof beyond a reasonable doubt with the requirement of a unanimous jury. That would be analytically fallacious since a deadlocked jury does not bar, as double jeopardy, retrial for the same offense. See *Dreyer* v. *Illinois*, 187 U.S. 71. Nevertheless, one is necessary for a proper effectuation of the other. Compare *Mapp* v. *Ohio*, 367 U.S. 643, with *Wolf* v. *Colorado*, 338 U.S. 25.

Suppose a jury begins with a substantial minority but then in the process of deliberation a sufficient number changes to reach the required 9:3 or 10:2 for a verdict. Is not there still a lingering doubt about that verdict? Is it not clear that the safeguard of unanimity operates in this context to make it far more likely that guilt is established beyond a reasonable doubt?

The late Learned Hand said that "as a litigant I should dread a lawsuit beyond almost anything else short of sickness and death."[37] At the criminal level that dread multiplies. Any person faced with the awesome power of government is in great jeopardy, even though innocent. Facts are always elusive and often two-faced. What may appear to one to imply guilt may carry no such overtones to another. Every criminal prosecution crosses treacherous ground, for guilt is common to all men. Yet the guilt of one may be irrelevant to the charge on which he is tried or indicate that if there is to be a penalty, it should be of an extremely light character.

The risk of loss of his liberty and the certainty that if found guilty he will be "stigmatized by the conviction" were factors we emphasized in *Winship* in sustaining the requirement that no man should be condemned where there is reasonable doubt about his guilt. 397 U.S., at 363–364.

We therefore have always held that in criminal cases we would err on the side of letting the guilty go free rather than sending the innocent to jail. We have required proof beyond a reasonable doubt as "concrete substance for the presumption of innocence." *Id.*, at 363.

That procedure has required a degree of patience on the part of the jurors, forcing them to deliberate in order to reach a unanimous verdict. Up until today the price has never seemed too high. Now a "law and order" judicial mood causes these barricades to be lowered.

The requirements of a unanimous jury verdict in criminal cases and proof beyond a reasonable doubt are so embedded in our constitutional law and touch so directly all the citizens and are such important barricades of liberty that if they are to be changed they should be introduced by constitutional amendment.

Today the Court approves a nine-to-three verdict. Would the Court relax the standard of reasonable doubt still further by resorting to eight-to-four verdicts, or even a majority rule? Moreover, in light of today's holdings and that of *Williams* v. *Florida*, in the future would it invalidate three-to-two or even two-to-one convictions?

Is the next step the elimination of the presumption of innocence? Mr. Justice Frankfurter, writing in dissent in *Leland* v. *Oregon*, 343 U.S. 790, 802–803, said:

> "It is not unthinkable that failure to bring the guilty to book for a heinous crime which deeply stirs popular sentiment may lead the legislature of a State, in one of those emotional storms which on occasion sweep over our people, to enact that thereafter an indictment for murder, following attempted rape, should be presumptive proof of guilt and cast upon the defendant the burden of proving beyond a reasonable doubt that he did not do the killing. Can there be any doubt that such a statute would go beyond the freedom of the States, under the Due Process Clause of the Fourteenth Amendment, to fashion their own penal codes and their own procedures for enforcing them? Why is that so? Because from the time that the law which we have inherited has emerged from dark and barbaric times, the conception of justice

which has dominated our criminal law has refused to put an accused at the hazard of punishment if he fails to remove every reasonable doubt of his innocence in the minds of jurors. It is the duty of the Government to establish his guilt beyond a reasonable doubt. This notion—basic in our law and rightly one of the boasts of a free society—is a requirement and a safeguard of due process of law in the historic, procedural content of 'due process.' Accordingly there can be no doubt, I repeat, that a State cannot cast upon an accused the duty of establishing beyond a reasonable doubt that his was not the act which caused the death of another."

The vast restructuring of American law which is entailed in today's decisions is for political not for judicial action. Until the Constitution is rewritten, we have the present one to support and construe. It has served us well. We lifetime appointees, who sit here only by happenstance, are the last who should sit as a Committee of Revision on rights as basic as those involved in the present cases.

Proof beyond a reasonable doubt and unanimity of criminal verdicts and the presumption of innocence are basic features of the accusatorial system. What we do today is not in that tradition but more in the tradition of the inquisition. Until amendments are adopted setting new standards, I would let no man be fined or imprisoned in derogation of what up to today was indisputably the law of the land.

MR. JUSTICE BRENNAN, with whom MR. JUSTICE MARSHALL joins, dissenting.[c]

Readers of today's opinions may be understandably puzzled why convictions by 11–1 and 10–2 jury votes are affirmed in No. 69-5046, when a majority of the Court agrees that the Sixth Amendment requires a unanimous verdict in federal criminal jury trials, and a majority also agrees that the right to jury trial guaranteed by the Sixth Amendment is to be enforced against the States according to the same standards

c. [This opinion applies also to No. 69-5046, *Apodaca* v. *Oregon*, *post*, p. 404.]

that protect that right against federal encroachment. The reason is that while my Brother powell agrees that a unanimous verdict is required in federal criminal trials, he does not agree that the Sixth Amendment right to a jury trial is to be applied in the same way to State and Federal Governments. In that circumstance, it is arguable that the affirmance of the convictions of Apodaca, Madden, and Cooper is not inconsistent with a view that today's decision in No. 69-5046 is a holding that only a unanimous verdict will afford the accused in a state criminal prosecution the jury trial guaranteed him by the Sixth Amendment. In any event, the affirmance must not obscure that the majority of the Court remains of the view that, as in the case of every specific of the Bill of Rights that extends to the States,[d] the Sixth Amendment's jury trial guarantee, however it is to be construed, has identical application against both State and Federal Governments.

I can add only a few words to the opinions of my Brothers DOUGLAS, STEWART, and MARSHALL, which I have joined. Emotions may run high at criminal trials. Although we can fairly demand that jurors be neutral until they have begun to hear evidence, it would surpass our power to command that they remain unmoved by the evidence that unfolds before them. What this means is that jurors will often enter the jury deliberations with strong opinions on the merits of the case. If at that time a sufficient majority is available to reach a verdict, those jurors in the majority will have nothing but their own common sense to restrain them from returning a verdict before they have fairly considered the positions of jurors who would reach a different conclusion. Even giving all reasonable leeway to legislative judgment in such matters, I think it

d. See, for example, First Amendment, *Gitlow* v. *New York*, 268 U.S. 652 (1925); *Cantwell* v. *Connecticut*, 310 U.S. 296 (1940); *Louisiana ex rel. Gremillion* v. *NAACP*, 366 U.S. 293 (1961); Fourth Amendment, *Ker* v. *California*, 374 U.S. 23 (1963); Fifth Amendment's privilege against self-incrimination, *Malloy* v. *Hogan*, 378 U.S. 1 (1964); Fifth Amendment's Double Jeopardy Clause, *Benton* v. *Maryland*, 395 U.S. 784 (1969); Fifth Amendment's Just Compensation Clause, *Chicago, B.&Q.R. Co.* v. *Chicago*, 166 U.S. 226 (1897); Sixth Amendment's Speedy Trial Clause, *Klopfer* v. *North Carolina*, 386 U.S. 213 (1967); Sixth Amendment's guarantee of jury trial, *Duncan* v. *Louisiana*, 391 U.S. 145 (1968); Sixth Amendment's Confrontation Clause, *Pointer* v. *Texas*, 380 U.S. 400 (1965).

simply ignores reality to imagine that most jurors in these circumstances would or even could fairly weigh the arguments opposing their position.

It is in this context that we must view the constitutional requirement that all juries be drawn from an accurate cross section of the community. When verdicts must be unanimous, no member of the jury may be ignored by the others. When less than unanimity is sufficient, consideration of minority views may become nothing more than a matter of majority grace. In my opinion, the right of all groups in this Nation to participate in the criminal process means the right to have their voices heard. A unanimous verdict vindicates that right. Majority verdicts could destroy it.

MR. JUSTICE STEWART, with whom MR. JUSTICE BRENNAN and MR. JUSTICE MARSHALL join, dissenting.

This case was tried before the announcement of our decision in *Duncan* v. *Louisiana*, 391 U.S. 145. Therefore, unlike *Apodaca* v. *Oregon*, decided today, *post*, p. 404, the Sixth Amendment's guarantee of trial by jury is not applicable here. *DeStefano* v. *Woods*, 392 U.S. 631. But I think the Fourteenth Amendment alone clearly requires that if a State purports to accord the right of trial by jury in a criminal case, then only a unanimous jury can return a constitutionally valid verdict.

The guarantee against systematic discrimination in the selection of criminal court juries is a fundamental of the Fourteenth Amendment. That has been the insistent message of this Court in a line of decisions extending over nearly a century. *E.g., Carter* v. *Jury Comm'n*, 396 U.S. 320 (1970); *Whitus* v. *Georgia*, 385 U.S. 545 (1967); *Hernandez* v. *Texas*, 347 U.S. 475 (1954); *Patton* v. *Mississippi*, 332 U.S. 463 (1947); *Norris* v. *Alabama*, 294 U.S. 587 (1935); *Carter* v. *Texas*, 177 U.S. 442 (1900); *Strauder* v. *West Virginia*, 100 U.S. 303 (1880). The clear purpose of these decisions has been to ensure universal participation of the citizenry in the administration of criminal justice. Yet today's judgment approves the elimination of the one rule that can ensure that such participation will be meaningful—the rule requiring the assent of all jurors before a verdict of conviction or acquittal can be returned. Under today's judgment, nine jurors can simply ignore the views of their fellow panel members of a different race or class.[e]

The constitutional guarantee of an impartial system of jury selection in a state criminal trial rests on the Due Process and Equal Protection Clauses of the Fourteenth Amendment. See, *e.g., Whitus* v. *Georgia, supra,* at 549–550; *Carter* v. *Texas, supra,* at 447; *Strauder* v. *West Virginia, supra,* at 310. Only a jury so selected can assure both a fair criminal trial, see *id.,* at 308–309, and public confidence in its result, cf. *Witherspoon* v. *Illinois,* 391 U.S. 510, 519–520; *In re Winship,* 397 U.S. 358, 364. Today's decision grossly undermines those basic assurances. For only a unanimous jury so selected can serve to minimize the potential bigotry of those who might convict on inadequate evidence, or acquit when evidence of guilt was clear. See *Strauder* v. *West Virginia, supra,* at 309. And community confidence in the administration of criminal justice cannot but be corroded under a system in which a defendant who is conspicuously identified with a particular group can be acquitted or convicted by a jury split along group lines. The requirements of unanimity and impartial selection thus complement each other in ensuring the fair performance of the vital functions of a criminal court jury.

It does not denigrate the system of trial by jury to acknowledge that it is imperfect, nor does it ennoble that system to drape upon a jury majority the mantle of presumptive reasonableness in all circumstances. The Court has never before been so impervious to reality in this area. Its recognition of the serious risks of jury misbehavior is a theme unifying a series of constitutional decisions that may be in jeopardy if today's facile presumption of regularity becomes the new point of departure. Why, if juries do not sometimes act out of passion and prejudice, does the Constitution require the availability of a change of venue? Cf. *Groppi* v. *Wisconsin,* 400 U.S. 505; *Irvin* v. *Dowd,* 366 U.S. 717; *Strauder* v. *West Virginia, supra,* at 309. Why, if juries do not sometimes act improperly, does the Constitution require protection from inflammatory press coverage and *ex parte* influence by court officers?

e. And, notwithstanding MR. JUSTICE BLACKMUN's disclaimer, there is nothing in the reasoning of the Court's opinion that would stop it from approving verdicts by 8–4 or even 7–5.

Cf., *e.g.*, *Sheppard* v. *Maxwell*, 384 U.S. 333; *Parker* v. *Gladden*, 385 U.S. 363; *Turner* v. *Louisiana*, 379 U.S. 466. Why, if juries must be presumed to obey all instructions from the bench, does the Constitution require that certain information must not go to the jury no matter how strong a cautionary charge accompanies it? Cf., *e.g.*, *Bruton* v. *United States*, 391 U.S. 123; *Jackson* v. *Denno*, 378 U.S. 368. Why, indeed, should we insist that no man can be constitutionally convicted by a jury from which members of an identifiable group to which he belongs have been systematically excluded? Cf., *e.g.*, *Hernandez* v. *Texas*, 347 U.S. 475.

So deeply engrained is the law's tradition of refusal to engage in after-the-fact review of jury deliberations, however, that these and other safeguards provide no more than limited protection. The requirement that the verdict of the jury be unanimous, surely as important as these other constitutional requisites, preserves the jury's function in linking law with contemporary society. It provides the simple and effective method endorsed by centuries of experience and history to combat the injuries to the fair administration of justice that can be inflicted by community passion and prejudice.

I dissent.

MR. JUSTICE MARSHALL, with whom MR. JUSTICE BRENNAN joins, dissenting.[f]

Today the Court cuts the heart out of two of the most important and inseparable safeguards the Bill of Rights offers a criminal defendant: the right to submit his case to a jury, and the right to proof beyond a reasonable doubt. Together, these safeguards occupy a fundamental place in our constitutional scheme, protecting the individual defendant from the awesome power of the State. After today, the skeleton of these safeguards remains, but the Court strips them of life and of meaning. I cannot refrain from adding my protest to that of my Brothers DOUGLAS, BRENNAN, and STEWART, whom I join.

In *Apodaca* v. *Oregon*, the question is too frighteningly simple to bear

f. [This opinion applies also to No. 69-5046, *Apodaca* v. *Oregon*, *post*, p. 404.]

much discussion. We are asked to decide what is the nature of the "jury" that is guaranteed by the Sixth Amendment. I would have thought that history provided the appropriate guide, and as MR. JUSTICE POWELL has demonstrated so convincingly, history compels the decision that unanimity is an essential feature of that jury. But the majority has embarked on a "functional" analysis of the jury that allows it to strip away, one by one, virtually all the characteristic features of the jury as we know it. Two years ago, over my dissent, the Court discarded as an essential feature the traditional size of the jury. *Williams* v. *Florida*, 399 U.S. 78 (1970). Today the Court discards, at least in state trials, the traditional requirement of unanimity. It seems utterly and ominously clear that so long as the tribunal bears the label "jury," it will meet Sixth Amendment requirements as they are presently viewed by this Court. The Court seems to require only that jurors be laymen, drawn from the community without systematic exclusion of any group, who exercise commonsense judgment.

More distressing still than the Court's treatment of the right to jury trial is the cavalier treatment the Court gives to proof beyond a reasonable doubt. The Court asserts that when a jury votes nine to three for conviction, the doubts of the three do not impeach the verdict of the nine. The argument seems to be that since, under *Williams*, nine jurors are enough to convict, the three dissenters are mere surplusage. But there is all the difference in the world between three jurors who are not there, and three jurors who entertain doubts after hearing all the evidence. In the first case we can never know, and it is senseless to ask, whether the prosecutor might have persuaded additional jurors had they been present. But in the second case we know what has happened: the prosecutor has tried and failed to persuade those jurors of the defendant's guilt. In such circumstances, it does violence to language and to logic to say that the government has proved the defendant's guilt beyond a reasonable doubt.

It is said that this argument is fallacious because a deadlocked jury does not, under our law, bring about an acquittal or bar a retrial. The argument seems to be that if the doubt of a dissenting juror were the "reasonable doubt" that constitutionally bars conviction, then it would necessarily result in an acquittal and bar retrial. But that argument rests on a complete *non sequitur*. The reasonable-doubt rule, properly viewed, simply establishes that, as a prerequisite to obtaining a valid conviction, the prosecutor must overcome all of the jury's reasonable doubts; it does not, of itself, determine what shall happen if he fails to do so. That is a question to be answered with reference to a wholly different constitutional provision, the Fifth Amendment ban on double jeopardy, made applicable to the States through the Due Process Clause of the Fourteenth Amendment in *Benton* v. *Maryland*, 395 U.S. 784 (1969).

Under prevailing notions of double jeopardy, if a jury has tried and failed to reach a unanimous verdict, a new trial may be held. *United States* v. *Perez*, 9 Wheat. 579 (1824). The State is free, consistent with the ban on double jeopardy, to treat the verdict of a nonunanimous jury as a nullity rather than as an acquittal. On retrial, the prosecutor may be given the opportunity to make a stronger case if he can: new evidence may be available, old evidence may have disappeared, and even the same evidence may appear in a different light if, for example, the demeanor of witnesses is different. Because the second trial may vary substantially from the first, the doubts of the dissenting jurors at the first trial do not necessarily impeach the verdict of a new jury on retrial. But that conclusion is wholly consistent with the view that the doubts of dissenting jurors create a constitutional bar to conviction at the trial that produced those doubts. Until today, I had thought that was the law.

I respectfully reject the suggestion of my Brother POWELL that the doubts of minority jurors may be attributable to "irrationality" against which some protection is needed. For if the jury has been selected properly, and every juror is a competent and rational person, then the "irrationality" that enters into the deliberation process is precisely the essence of the right to a jury trial. Each time this Court has approved a change in the familiar characteristics of the jury, we have reaffirmed the principle that its fundamental characteristic is its capacity to render a commonsense, layman's judgment, as a representative body drawn from the community. To fence out a dissenting juror fences out a voice from the community, and undermines the principle on which our whole notion of the jury now rests. My dissenting Brothers have pointed to the danger, under a less-than-unanimous rule, of excluding from the process members of minority groups, whose participation we have elsewhere recognized as a constitutional requirement. It should be emphasized, however, that the fencing-out problem goes beyond the problem of identifiable minority groups. The juror whose dissenting voice is unheard may be a spokesman, not for any minority viewpoint, but simply for himself—and that, in my view, is enough. The doubts of a single juror are in my view evidence that the government has failed to carry its burden of proving guilt beyond a reasonable doubt. I dissent.

406 U.S. 404 (1972)

APODACA ET AL.

V.

OREGON.

No. 69-5046.

Supreme Court of United States.

Argued March 1, 1971.

Reargued January 10, 1972.

Decided May 22, 1972.

CERTIORARI TO THE COURT OF APPEALS OF OREGON.

Richard B. Sobol reargued the cause and filed briefs for petitioners.

Jacob B. Tanzer, Solicitor General of Oregon, reargued the cause for respondent. With him on the brief were *Lee Johnson*, Attorney General, and *Thomas H. Denney*, Assistant Attorney General.

Briefs of *amici curiae* urging reversal were filed by *James J. Doherty* and *Marshall J. Hartman* for the National Legal Aid and Defender Association, and by *Norman Dorsen, Melvin L. Wulf*, and *Paul R. Meyer* for the American Civil Liberties Union.

MR. JUSTICE WHITE announced the judgment of the Court and an opinion in which THE CHIEF JUSTICE, MR. JUSTICE BLACKMUN, and MR. JUSTICE REHNQUIST joined.

Robert Apodaca, Henry Morgan Cooper, Jr., and James Arnold Madden were convicted respectively of assault with a deadly weapon, burglary in a dwelling, and grand larceny before separate Oregon juries, all of which returned less-than-unanimous verdicts. The vote in the cases of Apodaca and Madden was 11–1, while the vote in the case of Cooper was 10–2, the minimum requisite vote under Oregon law for sustaining a conviction.[38] After their convictions had been affirmed by the Oregon Court of Appeals, 1 Ore. App. 483, 462 P. 2d 691 (1969), and review had been denied by the Supreme Court of Oregon, all three sought review in this Court upon a claim that conviction of crime by a less-than-unanimous jury violates the right to trial by jury in criminal cases specified by the Sixth Amendment and made applicable to the States by the Fourteenth. See *Duncan* v. *Louisiana*, 391 U.S. 145 (1968). We granted certiorari to consider this claim, 400 U.S. 901 (1970), which we now find to be without merit.

In *Williams* v. *Florida*, 399 U.S. 78 (1970), we had occasion to consider a related issue: whether the Sixth Amendment's right to trial by jury requires that all juries consist of 12 men. After considering the history of the 12-man requirement and the functions it performs in contemporary society, we concluded that it was not of constitutional stature. We reach the same conclusion today with regard to the requirement of unanimity.

I

Like the requirement that juries consist of 12 men, the requirement of unanimity arose during the Middle Ages[39] and had become an accepted feature of the common-law jury by the 18th century.[40] But, as we observed in *Williams*, "the relevant constitutional history casts considerable doubt on the easy assumption[41] . . . that if a given feature existed in a jury at common law in 1789, then it was necessarily preserved in the Constitution." *Id.*, at 92–93. The most salient fact in the scanty history of the Sixth Amendment, which we reviewed in full in *Williams*, is that, as it was introduced by James Madison in the House of Representatives, the proposed Amendment provided for trial

> "by an impartial jury of freeholders of the vicinage, with the requisite of unanimity for conviction, of the right of challenge, and other accustomed requisites. . . ." 1 Annals of Cong. 435 (1789).

Although it passed the House with little alteration, this proposal ran into considerable opposition in the Senate, particularly with regard to the vicinage requirement of the House version. The draft of the proposed Amendment was returned to the House in considerably altered form, and a conference committee was appointed. That committee refused to accept not only the original House language but also an alternate suggestion by the House conferees that juries be defined as possessing "the accustomed requisites." Letter from James Madison to Edmund Pendleton, Sept. 23, 1789, in 5 Writings of James Madison 424 (G. Hunt ed. 1904). Instead, the Amendment that ultimately emerged from the committee and then from Congress and the States provided only for trial

> "by an impartial jury of the State and district wherein the crime shall have been committed, which district shall have been previously ascertained by law. . . ."

As we observed in *Williams*, one can draw conflicting inferences from this legislative history. One possible inference is that Congress eliminated references to unanimity and to the other "accustomed requisites" of the jury because those requisites were thought already to be implicit in the very concept of jury. A contrary explanation, which we found in *Williams* to be the more plausible, is that the deletion was intended to have some substantive effect. See 399 U.S., at 96–97. Surely one fact that is absolutely clear from this history is that, after a proposal had been made to specify precisely which of the common-law requisites of the jury were to be preserved by the Constitution, the Framers explicitly rejected the proposal and instead left such specification to the future. As in *Williams*, we must accordingly consider what is meant by the concept "jury" and determine whether a feature commonly associated with it is constitutionally required. And, as in *Williams*, our inability to divine "the intent of the Framers" when they eliminated references to the "accustomed requisites" requires that in determining what is meant by a jury we must turn to other than purely historical considerations.

II

Our inquiry must focus upon the function served by the jury in contemporary society. Cf. *Williams v. Florida, supra*, at 99–100. As we said in *Duncan*, the purpose of trial by jury is to prevent oppression by the Government by providing a "safeguard against the corrupt or overzealous prosecutor and against the compliant, biased, or eccentric judge." *Duncan v. Louisiana*, 391 U.S., at 156. "Given this purpose, the essential feature of a jury obviously lies in the interposition between the accused and his accuser of the commonsense judgment of a group of laymen . . ." *Williams v. Florida, supra*, at 100. A requirement of unanimity, however, does not materially contribute to the exercise of this commonsense judgment. As we said in *Williams*, a jury will come to such a judgment as long as it consists of a group of laymen representative of a cross section of the community who have the duty and the opportunity to deliberate, free from outside attempts at intimidation, on the question of a defendant's guilt. In terms of this function we perceive no difference between juries required to act unanimously and those permitted to convict or acquit by votes of 10 to two or 11 to one. Requiring unanimity would obviously produce hung juries in some situations where nonunanimous juries will convict or acquit.[42] But in either case, the interest of the defendant in having the judgment of his peers interposed between himself and the officers of the State who prosecute and judge him is equally well served.

III

Petitioners nevertheless argue that unanimity serves other purposes constitutionally essential to the continued operation of the jury system. Their principal contention is that a Sixth Amendment "jury trial" made mandatory on the States by virtue of the Due Process Clause of the Fourteenth Amendment, *Duncan v. Louisiana, supra*, should be held to require a unanimous jury verdict in order to give substance to the reasonable-doubt standard otherwise mandated by the Due Process Clause. See *In re Winship*, 397 U.S. 358, 363–364 (1970).

We are quite sure, however, that the Sixth Amendment itself has never been held to require proof beyond a reasonable doubt in criminal cases. The reasonable-doubt standard developed separately from both the jury trial and the unanimous verdict. As the Court noted in the *Winship* case, the rule requiring proof of crime beyond a reasonable doubt did not crystalize in this country until after the Constitution was adopted. See *id.*, at 361.[43] And in that case, which held such a burden of proof to be constitutionally required, the Court purported to draw no support from the Sixth Amendment.

Petitioners' argument that the Sixth Amendment requires jury unanimity in order to give effect to the reasonable-doubt standard thus founders on the fact that the Sixth Amendment does not require proof beyond a reasonable doubt at all. The reasonable-doubt argument is rooted, in effect, in due process and has been rejected in *Johnson v. Louisiana, ante,* p. 356.

IV

Petitioners also cite quite accurately a long line of decisions of this Court upholding the principle that the Fourteenth Amendment requires jury panels to reflect a cross section of the community. See, *e.g., Whitus v. Georgia,* 385 U.S. 545 (1967); *Smith v. Texas,* 311 U.S. 128 (1940); *Norris v. Alabama,* 294 U.S. 587 (1935); *Strauder v. West Virginia,* 100 U.S. 303 (1880). They then contend that unanimity is a necessary precondition for effective application of the cross-section requirement, because a rule permitting less than unanimous verdicts will make it possible for convictions to occur without the acquiescence of minority elements within the community.

There are two flaws in this argument. One is petitioners' assumption that every distinct voice in the community has a right to be represented on every jury and a right to prevent conviction of a defendant in any case. All that the Constitution forbids, however, is systematic exclusion of identifiable segments of the community from jury panels and from the juries ultimately drawn from those panels; a defendant may not, for example, challenge the makeup of a jury merely because no members of his race are on the jury, but must prove that his race has been systematically excluded. See *Swain v. Alabama,* 380 U.S. 202, 208–209 (1965); *Cassell v. Texas,* 339 U.S. 282, 286–287 (1950); *Akins v. Texas,* 325 U.S. 398, 403–404 (1945); *Ruthenberg v. United States,* 245 U.S. 480 (1918). No group, in short, has the right to block convictions; it has only the right to participate in the overall legal processes by which criminal guilt and innocence are determined.

We also cannot accept petitioner's second assumption—that minority groups, even when they are represented on a jury, will not adequately represent the viewpoint of those groups simply because they may be outvoted in the final result. They will be present during all deliberations, and their views will be heard. We cannot assume that the majority of the jury will refuse to weigh the evidence and reach a decision upon rational grounds, just as it must now do in order to obtain unanimous verdicts, or that a majority will deprive a man of his liberty on the basis of prejudice when a minority is presenting a reasonable argument in favor of acquittal. We simply find no proof for the notion that a majority will disregard its instructions and cast its votes for guilt or innocence based on prejudice rather than the evidence.

We accordingly affirm the judgment of the Court of Appeals of Oregon. *It is so ordered.*

[For concurring opinion of BLACKMUN, J., see *ante*, p. 365.]
[For opinion of POWELL, J., concurring in judgment, see *ante*, p. 366.]
[For dissenting opinion of DOUGLAS, J., see *ante*, p. 380.]
[For dissenting opinion of BRENNAN, J., see *ante*, p. 395.]
[For dissenting opinion of MARSHALL, J., see *ante*, p. 399.]*

MR. JUSTICE STEWART, with whom MR. JUSTICE BRENNAN and MR. JUSTICE MARSHALL join, dissenting.

In *Duncan v. Louisiana*, 391 U.S. 145, the Court squarely held that the Sixth Amendment right to trial by jury in a federal criminal case is made wholly applicable to state criminal trials by the Fourteenth Amendment. Unless *Duncan* is to be overruled, therefore, the only relevant question here is whether the Sixth Amendment's guarantee of trial by jury embraces a guarantee that the verdict of the jury must be unanimous. The answer to that question is clearly "yes," as my Brother POWELL has cogently demonstrated in that part of his concurring opinion that reviews almost a century of Sixth Amendment adjudication.[g]

Until today, it has been universally understood that a unanimous ver-

---

*Author's note: These opinions can be found in the previous *Johnson* decision earlier in Appendix II.

g. See *ante*, at 369–371 (POWELL, J., concurring in judgment).

dict is an essential element of a Sixth Amendment jury trial. See *Andres v. United States*, 333 U.S. 740, 748; *Patton v. United States*, 281 U.S. 276, 288; *Hawaii v. Mankichi*, 190 U.S. 197, 211–212; *Maxwell v. Dow*, 176 U.S. 581, 586; *Thompson v. Utah*, 170 U.S. 343, 351, 353; cf. 2 J. Story, Commentaries on the Constitution § 1779 n. 2 (5th ed. 1891).

I would follow these settled Sixth Amendment precedents and reverse the judgment before us.

Original Notes to the *Johnson* Decisions

1. Frischertz was seated on the right side of the truck by the door; he was accompanied by two helpers, one of whom drove the truck.

2. On hearing of the motion to suppress, defendant testified:

> "Q. Did they then come in to ask you if you wanted to make any statements?
>
> "A. Yes, sir. About twenty, twenty-five minutes later they came into me and they read off of a piece of paper something to the fact pertaining to the fact that they advised me of my rights, and I told them I didn't want to make any statements; I didn't have anything to say.
>
> "Q. Did you sign such a piece of paper, an arrestee form or anything like that?
>
> "A. Yes, I signed the form that they had, notified me of my rights as an arrestee."

The records contain a form, *Right of an Arrestee or Suspect,* January 20, 1968, 7:10 A.M.; it is signed by Det. John J. Lanza, and the statement is made that Sgt. Larry Vigurie was present. The form contains a check mark by the notation, *Refused to Sign;* this notation appears under the signature of the arrestee or suspect, which in this case is blank.

3. On hearing of the motion to suppress, defendant testified: "Yes, sir; about four and a half, about five hours later on that evening they came back. They came upstairs and brought us back downstairs and they rebooked us with another armed robbery, and about fifteen minutes, later, maybe ten, they rebooked us with another armed robbery."

4. "Since it appears that there is grave potential for prejudice, intentional or not, in the pretrial lineup, which may not be capable of reconstruction at trial, and since presence of counsel itself can often avert prejudice and assure a meaningful confrontation at trial, there can be little doubt that for Wade the post-indictment lineup was a critical stage of the prosecution at which he was 'as much entitled to such aid [of counsel] *** as at the trial itself.' *Powell v. State of Alabama* [supra], 287 U.S. 45 at 57, 53 S.Ct. 55 at 60, 77 L.Ed. 158.

Thus both Wade and his counsel should have been notified of the impending lineup, and counsel's presence should have been a requisite to conduct of the lineup, absent an 'intelligent waiver.' See *Carnley v. Cochran*, 369 U.S. 506, 82 S.Ct. 884, 8 L.Ed.2d 70. ***" *United States v. Wade*, 87 S.Ct. at 1937 (1967).

5. La. Const., Art. VII, § 41, provides:

"Section 41. The Legislature shall provide for the election and drawing of competent and intelligent jurors for the trial of civil and criminal cases; provided, however, that no woman shall be drawn for jury service unless she shall have previously filed with the clerk of the District Court a written declaration of her desire to be subject to such service. All cases in which the punishment may not be at hard labor shall, until otherwise provided by law, be tried by the judge without a jury. Cases, in which the punishment may be at hard labor, shall be tried by a jury of five, all of whom must concur to render a verdict; cases, in which the punishment is necessarily at hard labor, by a jury of twelve, nine of whom must concur to render a verdict; cases in which the punishment may be capital, by a jury of twelve, all of whom must concur to render a verdict."

La. Code Crim. Proc., Art. 782, provides:

"Cases in which the punishment may be capital shall be tried by a jury of twelve jurors, all of whom must concur to render a verdict. Cases in which the punishment is necessarily at hard labor shall be tried by a jury composed of twelve jurors, nine of whom must concur to render a verdict. Cases in which the punishment may be imprisonment at hard labor, shall be tried by a jury composed of five jurors, all of whom must concur to render a verdict. Except as provided in Article 780, trial by jury may not be waived."

6. *Coffin* contains a lengthy discussion on the requirement of proof beyond a reasonable doubt and other similar standards of proof in ancient Hebrew, Greek, and Roman law, as well as in the common law of England. This discussion suggests that the Court of the late 19th century would have held the States bound by the reasonable-doubt standard under the Due Process Clause of the Fourteenth Amendment on the assumption that the standard was essential to a civilized system of criminal procedure. See generally *Duncan v. Louisiana*, 391 U.S. 145, 149–150, n. 14 (1968).

7. That right, of course, is reserved for those crimes that may be deemed "serious." See *id.*, at 159–162; *Bloom v. Illinois*, 391 U.S. 194 (1968); *Baldwin v. New York*, 399 U.S. 66 (1970).

8. This contention was raised in *Carcerano v. Gladden*, which was consolidated and disposed of along with the *DeStefano* opinion.

9. In addition to the jury trial issues in this case, I also join Part IV of the Court's opinion insofar as it concludes that the lineup identification was not the fruit of the prior

warrantless arrest. *Wong Sun* v. *United States,* 371 U.S. 471 (1963). Under the circumstances of this case, I find it unnecessary to reach the question whether appellant's warrantless arrest was constitutionally invalid.

10. Jury trial in federal cases is also assured by Art. III, § 2, of the Constitution: "The Trial of all Crimes . . . shall be by Jury."

11. See also MR. JUSTICE WHITE'S opinion for the Court in *Swain* v. *Alabama,* 380 U.S. 202, 211 (1965), stating, in dictum, that "Alabama adheres to the common-law system of trial by an impartial jury of 12 men who must unanimously agree on a verdict, *the system followed in the federal courts by virtue of the Sixth Amendment.*" (Emphasis supplied.)

The same result has been attained with respect to the right to jury trial in civil cases under the Seventh Amendment. See *American Publishing Co.* v. *Fisher,* 166 U.S. 464, 467–468 (1897); *Springville* v. *Thomas,* 166 U.S. 707 (1897).

12. The process of determining the content of the Sixth Amendment right to jury trial has long been one of careful evaluation of, and strict adherence to the limitations on, that right as it was known in criminal trials at common law. See *Williams* v. *Florida,* 399 U.S. 78, 117, 122–129 (1970) (separate opinion of Harlan, J.).

A recent example of that process of constitutional adjudication may be found in Part II of the Court's opinion in *Duncan* v. *Louisiana,* 391 U.S., at 159–162, in which "petty" offenses were excluded from the rule requiring jury trial because such "offenses were tried without juries both in England and in the Colonies." The Court found "no substantial evidence that the Framers intended to depart from this established common-law practice." *Id.,* at 160. To the same effect, see Mr. Justice Harlan's dissent in *Baldwin* v. *New York* (appearing in *Williams* v. *Florida,* 399 U.S., at 119–121).

Also representative of this historical approach to the Sixth Amendment are the exhaustive majority and dissenting opinions in *Sparf* v. *United States,* 156 U.S. 51 (1895), in which the Court ultimately concluded that federal criminal juries were empowered only to decide questions of "fact." Rather than attempting to determine whether the fact-law distinction was desirable or whether it might be essential to the function performed by juries, the decision was premised on the conclusion that English and Colonial juries had no right to decide questions of law.

The same historical approach accounts for the numerous Supreme Court opinions (see text accompanying n. 5), finding unanimity to be one of the attributes subsumed under the term "jury trial." No reason, other than the conference committee's revision of the House draft of the Sixth Amendment, has been offered to justify departure from this Court's prior precedents. The admitted ambiguity of that piece of legislative history is not sufficient, in my view, to override the unambiguous history of the common-law right. *Williams* v. *Florida,* 399 U.S., at 123 n. 9.

13. See, *e.g.,* R. Perry, Sources of Our Liberties 270, 281–282, 288, 429 (1959); 3 J. Story, Commentaries on the Constitution 652–653 (1st ed. 1833).

14. See, *e.g.,* 4 W. Blackstone, Commentaries *376; W. Forsyth, History of Trial By Jury 238–258 (1852); M. Hale, Analysis of the Law of England 119 (1716).

15. I agree with MR. JUSTICE WHITE's analysis in *Duncan* that the departure from earlier decisions was, in large measure, a product of a change in focus in the Court's approach to due process. No longer are questions regarding the constitutionality of particular criminal procedures resolved by focusing alone on the element in question and ascertaining whether a system of criminal justice might be imagined in which a fair trial could be afforded in the absence of that particular element. Rather, the focus is, as it should be, on the fundamentality of that element viewed in the context of the basic Anglo-American jurisprudential system common to the States. *Duncan* v. *Louisiana, supra,* at 149–150, n. 14. That approach to due process readily accounts both for the conclusion that jury trial is fundamental and that unanimity *is not.* See Part III, *infra.*

16. *Duncan* v. *Louisiana,* 391 U.S., at 156. See also *Baldwin* v. *New York,* 399 U.S., at 72.

17. Indeed, so strongly felt was the jury's role as the protector of "innocence against the consequences of the partiality and undue bias of judges in favor of the prosecution," that, at an earlier point in this country's history, some of the States deemed juries the final arbiters of all questions arising in criminal prosecutions, whether factual or legal. To allow judges to determine the law was considered by some States to pose too great a risk of judicial oppression, favoring the State above the accused. See, *e.g., State* v. *Croteau,* 23 Vt. 14, 21 (1849); Howe, Juries as Judges of Criminal Law, 52 Harv. L. Rev. 582 (1939). That historical preference for jury decisionmaking is still reflected in the criminal procedures of two States. Ind. Const., Art. I, § 19: Md. Const., Art. XV, § 5. See *Brady* v. *Maryland,* 373 U.S. 83 (1963); *Wyley* v. *Warden,* 372 F. 2d 742, 746 (CA4), cert. denied, 389 U.S. 863 (1967); *Beavers* v. *State,* 236 Ind. 549, 141 N. E. 2d 118 (1957).

18. The available empirical research indicates that the jury-trial protection is not substantially affected by less-than-unanimous verdict requirements. H. Kalven and H. Zeisel, in their frequently cited study of American juries (The American Jury [Phoenix ed. 1971]), note that where unanimity is demanded 5.6% of the cases result in hung juries. *Id.,* at 461. Where unanimity is not required, available statistics indicate that juries will still be hung in over 3% of the cases. Thus, it may be estimated roughly that Oregon's practice may result in verdicts in some 2.5% more of the cases—cases in which no verdict would be returned if unanimity were demanded. Given the large number of causes to which this percentage disparity might be attributed, and given the possibility of conviction on retrial, it is impossible to conclude that this percentage represents convictions obtained under standards offensive to due process.

19. *Duncan* v. *Louisiana, supra,* at 181 (Harlan, J., dissenting).

20. *Id.,* at 173–183 (Harlan, J., dissenting); *Bloom* v. *Illinois,* 391 U.S., at 211 (Fortas, J., concurring); *Baldwin* v. *New York,* 399 U.S., at 76–77 (BURGER, C. J., dissenting); *Williams* v. *Florida,* 399 U.S., at 117, 143 (separate opinions of Harlan, J., and STEWART, J.). Cf. MR. JUSTICE DOUGLAS' concurring opinion in *Alexander* v. *Louisiana,* 405 U.S. 625, 637 n. 4 (1972).

21. My unwillingness to accept the "incorporationist" notion that jury trial must be applied with total uniformity does not require that I take issue with every precedent of this Court applying various criminal procedural rights to the States with the same force that

they are applied in federal courts. See Mr. Justice Fortas' opinion in *Bloom* v. *Illinois*, 391 U.S., at 214, which also applied to *Duncan*.

22. See Mr. Justice Brandeis' oft-quoted dissent in *New State Ice Co.* v. *Liebmann*, 285 U.S. 262, 280, 309–311 (1932), in which he details the stultifying potential of the substantive due process doctrine.

23. ALI, Code of Criminal Procedure § 335 (1930).

24. Criminal Justice Act 1967, c. 80, § 13 (Great Britain).

25. American Bar Association, Project on Standards for Criminal Justice, Trial By Jury § 1.1 (Approved Draft 1968) (see also commentary, at 25–28).

26. See, *e.g.*, Kalven & Zeisel, The American Jury: Notes For an English Controversy, 48 Chi. B. Rec. 195 (1967); Samuels, Criminal Justice Act, 31 Mod. L. Rev. 16, 24–27 (1968); Comment, Waiver of Jury Unanimity—Some Doubts About Reasonable Doubt, 21 U. Chi. L. Rev. 438, 444–445 (1954); Comment, Should Jury Verdicts Be Unanimous in Criminal Cases? 47 Ore. L. Rev. 417 (1968).

27. See *State* v. *Gann*, 254 Ore. 549, 463 P. 2d 570 (1969).

Approval of Oregon's 10–2 requirement does not compel acceptance of all other majority-verdict alternatives. Due process and its mandate of basic fairness often require the drawing of difficult lines. See *Francis* v. *Resweber*, 329 U.S. 459, 466, 471 (1947) (Frankfurter, J., concurring). Full recognition of the function performed by jury trials, coupled with due respect for the presumptive validity of state laws based on rational considerations such as those mentioned above, will assist in finding the required balance when the question is presented in a different context.

28. See, *e.g.*, *Swain* v. *Alabama*, 380 U.S. 202, 209–222 (1965).

29. *Allen* v. *United States*, 164 U.S. 492 (1896).

30. See, *e.g.*, *Irvin* v. *Dowd*, 366 U.S. 717 (1961).

31. See, *e.g.*, *Sheppard* v. *Maxwell*, 384 U.S. 333 (1966); *Estes* v. *Texas*, 381 U.S. 532 (1965).

32. See also 2 J. Story, Commentaries on the Constitution 559 n. 2 (5th ed. 1891): "A trial by jury is generally understood to mean *ex vitermini*, a trial by a jury of *twelve* men, impartially selected, who must *unanimously* concur in the guilt of the accused before a legal conviction can be had. Any law, therefore, dispensing with any of these requisites, may be considered unconstitutional." In the 1969 Term we held a jury of six was sufficient, *Williams* v. *Florida*, 399 U.S. 78, but we noted that neither evidence nor theory suggested 12 was more favorable to the accused than six. The same cannot be said for unanimity and impartial selection of jurors. See *infra*, at 388–394.

Story's Commentaries cite no statutory authority for the requirement of unanimity in a criminal jury. That is because such authority has never been thought necessary. The unanimous jury has been so embedded in our legal history that no one would question its constitutional position and thus there was never any need to codify it. Indeed, no criminal case dealing with a unanimous jury has ever been decided by this Court before today, largely because of this unquestioned constitutional assumption. A similar assumption had, of course, been made with respect to the Seventh Amendment civil jury, but that issue did reach the Court. And the Court had no difficulty at all in holding a unanimous jury was a constitutional requirement. *American Publishing Co.* v. *Fisher*, 166 U.S. 464.

33. Of course, the unanimous jury's origin is long before the American Revolution. The first recorded case where there is a requirement of unanimity is *Anonymous Case*, 41 Lib. Assisarum 11 (1367), reprinted in English in R. Pound & T. Plucknett, Readings on the History and System of the Common Law 155–156 (3d ed. 1927).

34. What was said of the impact of *Mapp* v. *Ohio*, 367 U.S. 643, on federalism bears repeating here:

> "*Mapp* . . . established no assumption by this Court of supervisory authority over state courts . . . and, consequently, it implied no total obliteration of state laws relating to arrests and searches in favor of federal law. *Mapp* sounded no death knell for our federalism; rather, it echoed the sentiment of *Elkins* v. *United States*, [364 U.S. 206,] that 'a healthy federalism depends upon the avoidance of needless conflict between state and federal courts' by itself urging that '[f]ederal-state cooperation . . . will be promoted, if only by recognition of their now mutual obligation to respect *the same fundamental criteria* in their approaches." *Ker* v. *California*, 374 U.S. 23, 31.

35. H. Kalven & H. Zeisel, The American Jury 490 (1966). See also The American Jury: Notes For an English Controversy, 48 Chi. B. Rec. 195 (1967).

36. The American Jury, *supra*, n. 3, at 460.

LAST VOTE OF DEADLOCKED JURIES

Vote for Conviction	Percent
1:1	24
10:2	10
9:3	10
8:4	6
7:5	13
6:6	13
5:7	8
4:8	4
3:9	4
2:10	8
1:11	—
	100

Number of Juries in Sample: 48.

37. 3 Lectures on Legal Topics, Association of Bar of the City of New York 105 (1926).

38. Ore. Const., Art. I, § 11, reads in relevant part:

"In all criminal prosecutions, the accused shall have the right to public trial by an impartial jury in the county in which the offense shall have been committed; . . . provided, however, that any accused person, in other than capital cases, and with the consent of the trial judge, may elect to waive trial by jury and consent to be tried by the judge of the court alone, such election to be in writing; provided, however, that in the circuit court ten members of the jury may render a verdict of guilty or not guilty, save and except a verdict of guilty of first degree murder, which shall be found only by a unanimous verdict, and not otherwise. . . ."

39. The origins of the unanimity rule are shrouded in obscurity, although it was only in the latter half of the 14th century that it became settled that a verdict had to be unanimous. See 1 W. Holdsworth, A History of English Law 318 (1956); Thayer, The Jury and its Development, 5 Harv. L. Rev. (pts. 1 and 2) 249, 295, 296 (1892). At least four explanations might be given for the development of unanimity. One theory is that unanimity developed to compensate for the lack of other rules insuring that a defendant received a fair trial. See L. Orfield, Criminal Procedure from Arrest to Appeal 347–351 (1947); Haralson, Unanimous Jury Verdicts in Criminal Cases, 21 Miss. L. J. 185, 191 (1950). A second theory is that unanimity arose out of the practice in the ancient mode of trial by compurgation of adding to the original number of 12 compurgators until one party had 12 compurgators supporting his position; the argument is that when this technique of afforcement was abandoned, the requirement that one side obtain the votes of all 12 jurors remained. See P. Devlin, Trial by Jury 48–49 (1956); Ryan, Less than Unanimous Jury Verdicts in Criminal Trials, 58 J. Crim. L. C. & P. S. 211, 213 (1967). A third possibility is that unanimity developed because early juries, unlike juries today, personally had knowledge of the facts of a case; the medieval mind assumed there could be only one correct view of the facts, and, if either all the jurors or only a minority thereof declared the facts erroneously, they might be punished for perjury. See T. Plucknett, A Concise History of the Common Law 131 (5th ed. 1956); Thayer, *supra*, at 297. Given a view that minority jurors were guilty of criminal perjury, the development of a practice of unanimity would not be surprising. The final explanation is that jury unanimity arose out of the medieval concept of consent. Indeed, "[t]he word consent (*consensus*) carried with it the idea of *concordia* or unanimity. . . ." M. Clarke, Medieval Representation and Consent 251 (1964). Even in 14th-century Parliaments there is evidence that a majority vote was deemed insufficient to bind the community or individual members of the community to a legal decision, see *id.*, at 335–336; Plucknett, The Lancastrian Constitution, in Tudor Studies 161, 169–170 (R. Seton-Watson ed. 1924); a unanimous decision was preferred. It was only in the 15th century that the decisionmaking process in Parliament became avowedly

majoritarian, see 1 K. Pickthorn, Early Tudor Government: Henry VII, p. 93 (1967), as the ideal of unanimity became increasingly difficult to attain. See Clarke, *supra*, at 266–267. For evidence in 18th-century America of a similar concern that decisions binding on the community be taken unanimously, see Zuckerman, The Social Context of Democracy in Massachusetts, 25 Wm. & Mary Q. (3d ser.) 523, 526–527, 540–544 (1968).

40. See 3 W. Blackstone, Commentaries *375–376. Four 18th-century state constitutions provided explicitly for unanimous jury verdicts in criminal cases, see N.C. Const. of 1776, Art. IX; Pa. Const. of 1776, Art. IX; Vt. Const. of 1786, Art XI; Va. Const. of 1776, § 8; while other 18th-century state constitutions provided for trial by jury according to the course of the common law, see Md. Const. of 1776, Art. III, or that trial by jury would remain "inviolate," see Ga. Const. of 1777, Art. LXI; Ky. Const. of 1792, Art. XII, § 6; N.Y. Const. of 1777, Art. XLI; Tenn. Const. of 1796, Art. XI, § 6; be "confirmed," see N.J. Const. of 1776, Art. XXII; or remain "as heretofore." See Del. Const. of 1792, Art. I, § 4; Ky. Const. of 1792, Art. XII, § 6; S.C. Const. of 1790, Art. IX, § 6. See also *Apthorp* v. *Backus*, 1 Kirby 407, 416, 417 (Conn. 1788); *Grinnell* v. *Phillips*, 1 Mass. 530, 542 (1805). Although unanimity had not been the invariable practice in 17th-century America, where majority verdicts were permitted in the Carolinas, Connecticut, and Pennsylvania, see *Williams* v. *Florida*, 399 U.S. 78, 98 n. 45 (1970), the explicit constitutional provisions, particularly of States such as North Carolina and Pennsylvania, the apparent change of practice in Connecticut, and the unquestioning acceptance of the unanimity rule by text writers such as St. George Tucker indicate that unanimity became the accepted rule during the 18th century, as Americans became more familiar with the details of English common law and adopted those details in their own colonial legal systems. See generally Murrin, The Legal Transformation: The Bench and Bar of Eighteenth-Century Massachusetts, in Colonial America: Essays in Politics and Social Development 415 (S. Katz ed. 1971). See also F. Heller, The Sixth Amendment 13–21 (1951).

41. See *Andres* v. *United States*, 333 U.S. 740, 748 (1948); *Maxwell* v. *Dow*, 176 U.S. 581, 586 (1900) (dictum). Cf. *Springville* v. *Thomas*, 166 U.S. 707 (1897); *American Publishing Co.* v. *Fisher*, 166 U.S. 464 (1897).

42. The most complete statistical study of jury behavior has come to the conclusion that when juries are required to be unanimous, "the probability that an acquittal minority will hang the jury is about as great as that a guilty minority will hang it." H. Kalven & H. Zeisel, The American Jury 461 (1966).

43. For the history of the reasonable-doubt requirement, see generally C. McCormick, Evidence § 321 (1954); 9 J. Wigmore, Evidence § 2497 (3d ed. 1940); May, Some Rules of Evidence—Reasonable Doubt in Civil and Criminal Cases, 10 Am. L. Rev. 642, 651–660 (1876). (See 69 U.S. L. Rev. 169, 172 [1935].) According to May and McCormick, the requirement of proof beyond a reasonable doubt first crystallized in the case of *Rex* v. *Finny*, a high treason case tried in Dublin in 1798 and reported in 1 L. MacNally, Rules of Evidence on Pleas of the Crown *4 (1811). Confusion about the rule persisted in the United States in

the early 19th century, where it was applied in civil as well as criminal cases, see, *e.g.*, *Ropps v. Barker*, 21 Mass. (4 Pick.) 239, 242 (1826); it was only in the latter half of the century that the reasonable-doubt standard ceased to be applied in civil cases, see *Ellis v. Buzzell*, 60 Me. 209 (1872), and that American courts began applying it in its modern form in criminal cases. See *Commonwealth v. Webster*, 59 Mass. (5 Cush.) 295, 320 (1850). See generally May, *supra*.

APPENDIX III

Louisiana Case Law

What follows is a chronological list of cases pertaining to nonunanimous jury verdicts appearing in the Louisiana appellate courts from 1899 to the end of the twenty-first century's first decade, with accompanying source citations.

Challenges in the Louisiana Supreme Court Prior to Its 1970 *Johnson* Decision

Louisiana v. Ardoin (Sup.1899) 51 La.Ann. 169; 24 So. 802

Louisiana v. Biagas (Sup.1901) 105 La. 503; 29 So. 971

Louisiana v. Wooten (Sup.1915) 136 La. 560; 67 So. 366

Louisiana v. Trull (Sup.1920) 147 La. 444; 85 So. 70

Louisiana v. Vial (Sup.1923) 153 La. 883; 96 So. 796

Louisiana v. Guillory (Sup.1927) 163 La. 98; 111 So. 612

Louisiana v. Jacques (Sup.1931) 171 La. 994; 132 So. 657

Louisiana v. Flattmann (Sup.1931) 172 La. 620; 135 So. 3

Louisiana v. Doucet (Sup.1933) 177 La. 63; 147 So. 500

Lea v. Orleans Parish School Board (Sup.1955) 228 La. 987; 84 So.2d 610

Louisiana v. Beer (Sup.1968) 252 La. 756; 214 So.2d 133

Louisiana v. Schoonover (Sup.1968) 252 La. 311; 211 So.2d 273, certiorari denied 89 S.Ct. 1199, 394 US 931, 22 L.Ed.2d 460

Louisiana v. White (Sup.1969) 254 La. 389; 223 So.2d 843

Louisiana v. Brumfield (Sup.1969) 254 La. 999; 229 So.2d 76

Louisiana v. Fink (Sup.1970) 255 La. 385; 231 So.2d 360

Louisiana v. Caston (Sup.1970) 256 La. 459; 236 So.2d 800

Challenges Following the Louisiana Supreme
Court's 1970 *Johnson* Decision

Louisiana v. Dillon (Sup.1971) 260 La. 215; 255 So.2d 745

Louisiana v. Jackson (Sup.1971) 259 La. 957; 254 So.2d 259

Louisiana v. Jones (Sup.1971) 257 La. 966; 244 So.2d 849

Louisiana v. Biagas (Sup.1971) 260 La. 69; 255 So.2d 77

Louisiana v. Dell (Sup.1971) 258 La. 1024; 249 So.2d 118

Louisiana v. Anderson (Sup.1972) 261 La. 244; 259 So.2d 310, appeal dismissed, certiorari denied 93 S.Ct. 533, 409 US 1030, 34 L.Ed.2d 481

US ex rel. White v. Henderson (CA5 (La.) 1972) 461 F.2d 657

Louisiana v. Holmes (Sup.1972) 263 La. 685; 269 So.2d 207

Louisiana v. Neal (Sup.1973) 275 So.2d 765

Louisiana v. Blackwell (Sup.1973) 298 So.2d 798, certiorari denied 95 S.Ct. 1401; 420 US 976; 43 L.Ed.2d 656

Louisiana v. Lee (Sup.1973) 275 So.2d 757

Louisiana v. Rollins (Sup.1974) 302 So.2d 288

Louisiana v. Ross (Sup.1975) 320 So.2d 177

Louisiana v. Morgan (Sup.1975) 315 So.2d 632

Louisiana v. Bastida (Sup.1975) 310 So.2d 629

Louisiana v. Williams (Sup.1976) 326 So.2d 815

Louisiana v. Ledet (Sup.1976) 337 So.2d 1126

Louisiana v. Gilmore (Sup.1976) 332 So.2d 789

Louisiana v. Gardner (Sup.1977) 351 So.2d 105

Louisiana v. Hodges (Sup.1977) 349 So.2d 250, certiorari denied 98 S.Ct. 1262; 434 US 1074; 55 L.Ed.2d 779

Louisiana v. Burch (Sup.1978) 365 So.2d 1263

Burch v. Louisiana (1979) 99 S.Ct. 1623; 441 US 130; 60 L.Ed.2d 96

Louisiana v. Green (Sup.1980) 390 So.2d 1253

Louisiana v. Marcantel (Sup.1980) 388 So.2d 383

Louisiana v. Jones (Sup.1980) 381 So.2d 383

Louisiana v. Goodley (Sup.1981) 398 So.2d 1068, dissenting opinion 418 So.2d 650

Louisiana v. Edwards (Sup.1982) 420 So.2d 663

Louisiana v. Simmons (Sup.1982) 414 So.2d 705

Louisiana v. Belgard (Sup.1982) 410 So.2d 720

Louisiana v. Buchanan (App. 1 Cir.1983) 439 So.2d 576

Louisiana v. Sanders (App. 2 Cir.1989) 539 So.2d 114, writ denied 546 So.2d 1212

Louisiana v. Strickland (Sup.1996) 683 So.2d 218, 1994–0025 (La. 11/1/96), rehearing denied

Louisiana v. Shanks (App. 1 Cir.1998) 715 So.2d 157, 1997–1885 (La.App. 1 Cir. 6/29/98)

Louisiana v. Williams (App. 2 Cir.1999) 747 So.2d 1256, 32,631 (La.App. 2 Cir. 12/8/99), writ denied 775 So.2d 441, 2000-0734 (La. 11/27/00), reconsideration denied 783 So.2d 378, 2000-0734 (La. 2/2/01), writ denied 778 So.2d 588, 2000-0358 (La. 1/5/01), writ denied 778 So.2d 588, 2000-0360 (La. 1/5/01)

Louisiana v. Fasola (App. 5 Cir.2005) 901 So.2d 533, 04-902 (La.App. 5 Cir. 3/29/05), writ denied 916 So.2d 1055, 2055-1069 (La. 12/9/05)

Louisiana v. Mizell (App. 1 Cir.2006) 938 So.2d 712, 2005-2516 (La.App. 1 Cir. 6/9/06)

Louisiana v. Lee (App. 1 Cir.2007) 964 So.2d 967, 2005-0456 (La.App. 1 Cir. 5/16/07), writ denied 977 So.2d 896, 2007-1288 (La. 3/7/08), certiorari denied 129 S.Ct. 130, 172 L.Ed.2d 37

Louisiana v. Regis (App. 4 Cir.2009) 25 Sp.3d 183, 2009-0806 (La.App. 4 Cir. 11/12/09), writ denied 38 So.3d 322, 2010-0003 (La. 6/18/10)

Louisiana v. Smith (App. 5 Cir.2009) 20 So.3d 501, 09-100 (La.App. 5 Cir. 8/25/09), writ denied 31 So.3d 357, 2009-2102 (La. 4/5/10)

Louisiana v. Moody (App. 4 Cir.2010) 38 So.3d 451, 2009-1394 (La. App. 4 Cir. 4/21/10)

NOTES

PREFACE

1. *State v. Hankton*, Court of Appeal of Louisiana, Fourth Circuit, 2 August 2013, NO. 2012-KA-0375, 122 So. 3d 1028.

CHAPTER ONE

1. *New Orleans Times-Picayune*, 26 December 1967, 1.

2. Ibid., 28 December 1967, Section 3, 20.

3. "Record from the Criminal District Court, Parish of Orleans, Section 'G,' Number 202-984: Transcript of testimony of March 18, 1968 & May 15, 1968, Testimony of Eugene Frischertz," *Johnson v. Louisiana*, Supreme Court of the United States (October Term, 1970, No. 5161, Appendix), 67. *New Orleans Times-Picayune*, 11 March 1967, Section 3, 23; 13 May 1967, 1; 24 May 1967, 18; 2 August 1967, 16; 12 August 1967, Section 3, 22; 9 September 1967, Section 2, 2; 10 September 1967, 31; 23 September 1967, Section 3, 29.

4. *New Orleans Times-Picayune*, 8 October 1967, 16; 17 January 1968, 6. The truck robbery problem would continue through much of 1968, the police frustrated by the lack of organization and coordination among the robbers. It was a series of copycat crimes that seemed to have no pattern and ultimately petered out on its own, helped in large measure by the work of the Detective Bureau's Robbery Division. For 1968 examples, see *New Orleans Times-Picayune*, 11 January, 19; 7 March, 6; 12 March, 14; 10 September, Section 2, 19; 10 October, Section 7, 15; 13 October, 16; 30 October, Section 5, 13; 1 November, Section 3, 25; 23 November, 15; 1 December, 8; 6 December, Section 2, 14; 20 December, 30; and 31 December 1968, 11.

5. "Record from the Criminal District Court, Parish of Orleans, Section 'G' Number 202-984: Transcript of testimony of March 18, 1968 & May 15, 1968, Testimony of Frank T. Johnson," *Johnson v. Louisiana*, 35–37.

6. "Record from the Criminal District Court, Parish of Orleans, Section 'G' Number 202-984: Transcript of testimony of March 18, 1968 & May 15, 1968, Testimony of Frank T. Johnson," *Johnson v. Louisiana*, 37–39.

7. *State v. Johnson*, 255 La. 314 (1970); "Record from the Criminal District Court, Parish of Orleans, Section 'G' Number 202-984: Motion to quash, filed March 13, 1968," *Johnson v. Louisiana*, 7–9; and "Record from the Criminal District Court, Parish of Orleans, Section

'G' Number 202-984: Transcript of testimony of March 18, 1968 & May 15, 1968, Testimony of Frank T. Johnson," *Johnson v. Louisiana*, 35–37.

8. The full text of the Sixth Amendment reads, "In all criminal prosecutions, the accused shall enjoy the right to a speedy and public trial, by an impartial jury of the State and district wherein the crime shall have been committed, which district shall have been previously ascertained by law, and to be informed of the nature and cause of the accusation; to be confronted with the witnesses against him; to have compulsory process for obtaining witnesses in his favor, and to have the Assistance of Counsel for his defence."

The full text of section one of the Fourteenth Amendment reads, "All persons born or naturalized in the United States, and subject to the jurisdiction thereof, are citizens of the United States and of the State wherein they reside. No State shall make or enforce any law which shall abridge the privileges or immunities of citizens of the United States; nor shall any State deprive any person of life, liberty, or property, without due process of law; nor deny to any person within its jurisdiction the equal protection of the laws" (US Constitution, amend. VI, and amend. XIV, sec. 1).

9. Oklahoma and Montana allowed nonunanimous verdicts in misdemeanor cases. *State v. Johnson*, 255 La. 314 (1970); "Constitution of the State of Louisiana, 1921," *West's Louisiana Statutes Annotated: Treaties and Organic Laws, Early Constitutions, U.S. Constitution and Index* (St. Paul, MN: West Group, 1977), vol. 3: 612, *New Orleans Times-Picayune*, 23 May 1972, 6. *State v. Schoonover*, 252 La. 311 (1968).

10. *Johnson v. Louisiana*, 406 US 356 (1972).

CHAPTER TWO

1. "Territories of Louisiana and Orleans, Act of Congress March 26, 1804, c. 38, 2 U.S. Stat. 283: An Act erecting Louisiana into two territories, and providing for the temporary government thereof," *West's Louisiana Statutes Annotated* (1977), vol. 3: 9; "Territory of Louisiana, Act of Congress March 3, 1805, c. 31, 2 U.S. Stat. 331: An Act further providing for the government of the district of Louisiana," *West's Louisiana Statutes Annotated* (1977), vol. 3: 17–18; and "Constitution of 1812," *West's Louisiana Statutes Annotated* (1977), vol. 3: 36–37.

2. Livingston actually left New York in disgrace, surrendering all of his property after corrupt behavior by one of his clerks during an extended illness. A lucrative New Orleans law practice allowed him to pay back his debt to the government and revive himself in the public's good graces. After six years in the U.S. House of Representatives, from 1823 to 1829, he served as one of Louisiana's senators for two years before becoming Andrew Jackson's secretary of state from 1831 to 1833, where he played a central role in the nullification crisis. The foreign policy experience he received as secretary of state then helped him become the country's minister to France from 1833 to 1835. See William Hatcher, *Edward Livingston: Jeffersonian Republican and Jacksonian Democrat* (Baton Rouge: Louisiana State University Press, 1940).

3. Edward Livingston, *A System of Penal Law, for the State of Louisiana* (1833; Union, NJ:

Lawbook Exchange, 1999), 525–36. See in particular articles 307, 341, 343, 354, 355, 356, 359, 361, 373, 380, 397, and 398.

4. M. M. Robinson, *Digest of the Penal Law of the State of Louisiana, Analytically Arranged* (New Orleans: M. M. Robinson, 1841), 276–94.

5. "Constitution of 1845," *West's Louisiana Statutes Annotated* (1977), vol. 3: 52–53; "Constitution of 1852," *West's Louisiana Statutes Annotated* (1977), vol. 3: 72.

6. The 1868 constitution noted that "the accused shall be entitled to a speedy public trial by an impartial jury of the parish in which the offence was committed, unless the venue be changed." The jury unanimity mandate appeared in Article 527. "Constitution of 1864," *West's Louisiana Statutes Annotated* (1977), vol. 3: 94–95; "Constitution of 1868," *West's Louisiana Statutes Annotated* (1977), vol. 3: 104, 115; and *The Code of Practice of the State of Louisiana* (New Orleans: The Republican, 1870), 74–75.

7. The Constitution of 1879 provided similar leeway as to change of venue as did its predecessors. "Constitution of 1879," *West's Louisiana Statutes Annotated* (1977), vol. 3: 128, 148.

CHAPTER THREE

1. For more on the development of nineteenth-century prison ideology, see David J. Rothman, *The Discovery of the Asylum: Order and Disorder in the New Republic* (Boston: Little, Brown, 1971).

2. Mark T. Carleton, "The Politics of the Convict Lease System in Louisiana: 1868–1901," *Louisiana History* 8 (Winter 1967): 5–10; Burk Foster, "Plantation Days at Angola: Major James and the Origins of Modern Corrections in Louisiana," in *The Wall Is Strong: Corrections in Louisiana,* ed. Burk Foster, Wilbert Rideau, and Douglas Dennis (3rd ed., Lafayette: Center for Louisiana Studies, 1995), 1–5.

3. Carleton, "The Politics of the Convict Lease System in Louisiana: 1868–1901," 9–11; Foster, "Plantation Days at Angola," 1–5; and William Ivy Hair, "Bourbon Democracy," in *The Louisiana Purchase Bicentennial Series in Louisiana History,* vol. 7: *Louisiana Politics and the Paradoxes of Reaction and Reform, 1877–1928,* ed. Matthew J. Scott (Lafayette: University of Louisiana Press, 2000), 131–33.

4. "James (Samuel L.) Letter # 2946, December 10, 1870," Ms. 2946, Louisiana and Lower Mississippi Valley Collections, Hill Memorial Library Special Collections, Louisiana State University, Baton Rouge.

5. Foster, "Plantation Days at Angola," 1–5; Carleton, "The Politics of the Convict Lease System in Louisiana: 1868–1901," 5–25; and Hair, "Bourbon Democracy," 131–33.

6. Hair, "Bourbon Democracy," 132–33.

7. Ibid.; Foster, "Plantation Days at Angola," 1–5; and Mark T. Carleton, *Politics and Punishment: The History of the Louisiana State Penal System* (Baton Rouge: Louisiana State University Press, 1971), 20.

8. Alexander Blanche Papers, W-48 # 3342, folder 1, Hill Memorial Library Special Collections, Louisiana State University, Baton Rouge.

9. Foster, "Plantation Days at Angola," 1–5; Carleton, *Politics and Punishment*, 57, 59. 42.

10. Carleton, *Politics and Punishment*, 42; Foster, "Plantation Days at Angola," 1–5.

11. Foster, "Plantation Days at Angola," 1–5; Carleton, *Politics and Punishment*, 193. For more on convict lease, broadly construed across the South in the period of Redemption and beyond and emphasizing the racial nature of the practice in particular, see Douglas A. Blackmon, *Slavery by Another Name: The Re-Enslavement of Black Americans from the Civil War to World War II* (New York: Anchor, 2009).

CHAPTER FOUR

1. Ann Mays Harlan, "Community House, Parks, Recreation, Pretty Flowers, and Minden Highways: The Minden Male Academy," *Memories of Minden*, www.mindenmemories.org/Parks%20and%20Highways.htm, accessed 23 December 2011.

2. *Official Journal of the Proceedings of the Senate of the State of Louisiana, at the Regular Session, Begun and Held in New Orleans, January 12, 1880* (New Orleans: New Orleans Democrat Office, 1880), iv, v, 13–25, 67–69, 126, 133, 138, 141, 147, 268, 286, 307; and *Official Journal of the Proceedings of the House of Representatives of the State of Louisiana, at the Regular Session, Begun and Held in New Orleans, January 12, 1880* (New Orleans: New Orleans Democrat Office, 1880), 1, 2, 28–29, 201, 216, 222, 266, 279, 328, 350–51.

3. Over the next decade, the legislature would continue to refine its thinking on criminal juries. In 1882, the body passed a law exempting telegraph officers from jury service. Other exemptions followed, New Orleans always being treated as a separate entity from the rest of the state, but its jury laws remaining concurrent with those in far distant parishes. *The Code of Practice of the State of Louisiana*, 75; *Acts Passed by the General Assembly of the State of Louisiana at the Regular Session Begun and Held in the City of New Orleans on the Twelfth Day of January, 1880* (New Orleans: New Orleans Daily Democrat, 1880), 52–53, 140–41; *Acts Passed by the General Assembly of the State of Louisiana, at the Regular Session, Begun and Held at the City of Baton Rouge on the Eighth Day of May, AD 1882* (Baton Rouge: Leon Jastremski, 1882), 54; *Acts Passed by the General Assembly of the State of Louisiana, at the Regular Session, Begun and Held at the City of Baton Rouge, on the Tenth Day of May, AD 1886* (Baton Rouge: Leon Jastremski, 1886), 126; *Acts Passed by the General Assembly of the State of Louisiana, at the Regular Session Begun and Held at the City of Baton Rouge, on the Twelfth Day of May, 1890* (New Orleans: Ernest Marchand, 1890), 21–22, 31l; *Acts Passed by the General Assembly of the State of Louisiana at the Regular Session Begun and Held in the City of Baton Rouge, on the Fourteenth Day of May, 1894* (New Orleans: Ernest Marchand, 1894), 121–24; and *Acts Passed by the General Assembly of the State of Louisiana at the Regular Session, Begun and Held in the City of Baton Rouge on the Eleventh Day of May, 1896* (Baton Rouge: Advocate, 1896), 144–49.

4. Heidenhain was a judge-advocate for Post 1 of the Department of Mississippi and Louisiana of the Grand Army of the Republic in New Orleans. *Official Journal of the Proceedings of the House of Representatives of the State of Louisiana*, 1, 96; Wallace E. Davies, "The

Problem of Race Segregation in the Grand Army of the Republic," *Journal of Southern History* 13 (August 1947): 354–57; Robert Burns Beath, *History of the Grand Army of the Republic* (New Orleans: Willis McDonald & Co., 1888), 642.

5. *Acts Passed by the General Assembly of the State of Louisiana at the Regular Session Begun and Held in the City of New Orleans on the Twelfth Day of January, 1880*, 141–42.

6. Billiu's election would be contested by Democrats in his district, who thought he acted unfairly against fellow Democrat Joseph Acklen. *Official Journal of the Proceedings of the House of Representatives of the State of Louisiana*, 102, 122; "General Notes," *New York Times*, 19 April 1880; "Campaign Notes," *New York Times*, 30 July 1880; "Campaign Notes," *New York Times*, 10 October 1880; and Rebecca J. Scott, "'Stubborn and Disposed to Stand Their Ground': Black Militia, Sugar Workers and the Dynamics of Collective Action in the Louisiana Sugar Bowl, 1863–87," in *From Slavery to Emancipation in the Atlantic World*, ed. Sylvia Frey and Betty Wood (Portland, OR: Frank Cass Publishers, 1999), 112.

7. *Official Journal of the Proceedings of the House of Representatives of the State of Louisiana, at the Regular Session*, 145; "Young, Zachary Taylor," *Dictionary of Louisiana Biography* (Lafayette: Louisiana Historical Association, 2008), www.lahistory.org/site41.php (accessed 8 March 2012).

8. Devereaux wouldn't stay in the House long. In 1881, he was assassinated by another New Orleans detective, Michael Hennesy, after Devereaux charged him with conduct unbecoming an officer after catching Hennesy at a local house of prostitution. Hennesy was acquitted in one of the most notorious trials in nineteenth-century New Orleans. *Official Journal of the Proceedings of the House of Representatives of the State of Louisiana*, 1, 156–57; "Allain, Theophile T.," *Dictionary of Louisiana Biography*; and James Gill, *Lords of Misrule: Mardi Gras and the Politics of Race in New Orleans* (Oxford: University Press of Mississippi, 1997), 139.

9. *Official Journal of the Proceedings of the House of Representatives of the State of Louisiana*, 1, 165–66; A. E. Perkins, "Some Negro Officers and Legislators in Louisiana," *Journal of Negro History* 14 (October 1929): 523–28; and David R. Poynter, *Membership in the Louisiana House of Representatives, 1812–2012* (Baton Rouge: Legislative Research Library, Louisiana House of Representatives, 2011), 285.

10. *Official Journal of the Proceedings of the Senate of the State of Louisiana*, iv, v, 123, 129–30, 134, 164, 172, 177, 344, 346, 358; Perkins, "Some Negro Officers and Legislators in Louisiana," 523; Arthur E. McEnany, *Membership in the Louisiana Senate, 1880–2012* (Baton Rouge: Louisiana State Senate, 2008), n.p.; and "Foster, Murphy James," *Dictionary of Louisiana Biography*.

11. *Acts Passed by the General Assembly of the State of Louisiana at the Regular Session Begun and Held in the City of New Orleans on the Twelfth Day of January, 1880*, 141–42.

12. See, for example, *New Orleans Times-Picayune*, 11 April 1880, 2.

13. Perkins was actually filling the seat of Leland Stanford, who had died during his term in office. The California legislature would allow the former governor to maintain the seat, however, where he would stay until 1913. *Washington Post*, 28 May 1916, 4; *New*

York Times, 28 October 1894, 28; "George Perkins," Governor's Gallery, State Library of California, governors.library.ca.gov/14-Perkins.html (accessed 14 March 2012); and *New Orleans Times-Picayune,* 3 September 1894, 4.

14. Blackmon, *Slavery by Another Name,* 58–83.

15. Alex Lichtenstein, *Twice the Work of Free Labor: The Political Economy of Convict Labor in the New South* (New York: Verso Press, 1996), 41–42, 153–54; Rebecca H. Moulder, "Convicts as Capital: Thomas O'Conner and the Leases of the Tennessee Penitentiary System, 1871–1883," *East Tennessee Historical Society Publications* 48 (1976): 58–59. See also J. C. Powell, *The American Siberia, or Fourteen Years' Experience in a Southern Convict Camp* (Chicago: H. J. Smith & Co., 1891); and Matthew J. Mancini, *One Dies, Get Another: Convict Leasing in the American South, 1866–1928* (Columbia: University of South Carolina Press, 1996).

CHAPTER FIVE

1. "Brief *Amicus Curiae* of the Charles Hamilton Houston Institute for Race and Justice, the National Association of Criminal Defense Lawyers, and the Louisiana Association of Criminal Defense Lawyers," *Bowen v. Oregon,* Supreme Court of the United States (May Term, 2009, No. 08-1117), 9–14; *Official Journal of the Proceedings of the Constitutional Convention of the State of Louisiana* (New Orleans: H. J. Hearsey, 1898), 8–9, 380–81.

2. *Atlanta Constitution,* 12 March 1898, 4; 27 March 1898, 5; 12 April 1898, 1. *Washington Post,* 1 May 1898, 5; *New Orleans Times-Picayune,* 10 April 1898, 2.

3. *Official Journal of the Proceedings of the Constitutional Convention of the State of Louisiana* (1898), 15, 270, 314.

4. *Official Journal of the Proceedings of the Constitutional Convention of the State of Louisiana* (1898), 315; "Sanders, Jared Young," *Dictionary of Louisiana Biography.* See also Mary E. Sanders, "The Political Career of Jared Young Sanders, 1892–1912," M.A. thesis, Louisiana State University, 1955.

5. *Official Journal of the Proceedings of the Constitutional Convention of the State of Louisiana* (1898), 354–55.

6. *Official Journal of the Proceedings of the Constitutional Convention of the State of Louisiana* (1898), 354–55; "Behrman, Martin," and "Ewing, Robert," *Dictionary of Louisiana Biography.*

7. *Washington Post,* 28 May 1916, 4; *New Orleans Times-Picayune,* 23 May 1916, 3.

8. *Official Journal of the Proceedings of the Constitutional Convention of the State of Louisiana* (New Orleans: Ramires-Jones Printing, 1913), 3, 11; "Constitution of 1913," *West's Louisiana Statutes Annotated* (1977), vol. 3: 304; *Official Journal of the Proceedings of the Constitutional Convention of the State of Louisiana* (New Orleans: Ramires-Jones Printing, 1921), 94, 135–36, 166, 735–37, 748–63, 786, 806–10, 841–48, 860–62, 868–81, 901–6, 986–1009, 1023–24; "Constitution of the State of Louisiana, 1921," 612; and St. Clair Adams, "Hints on Reforms in Louisiana Criminal Procedure," *Loyola Law Journal* 2 (November 1920): 7–16.

9. *Acts Passed by the Legislature of the State of Louisiana, 1926* (Baton Rouge: Secretary

of State, 1926), 457; *The Code of Criminal Procedure for the State of Louisiana* (Baton Rouge: Ramires-Jones Printing, 1928), 84–85; and *Louisiana Revised Statutes of 1950*, vol. 2: *Titles 13–21* (Baton Rouge: Secretary of State, 1950), 525–26.

10. *State of Louisiana, Acts of the Legislature*, vol. 2: *Regular Session 1966—Code of Criminal Procedure* (Baton Rouge: Secretary of State, 1966), 410; *West's Louisiana Statutes Annotated: Code of Criminal Procedure, Articles 782 to 830* (St. Paul, MN: West Group, 1998), vol. 2B: 3–15.

CHAPTER SIX

1. Section Nine defined limits on Congress. Among provisions limiting the suspension of habeas corpus and prohibiting taxes on goods exported from state to state, the U.S. Constitution decreed that "No Bill of Attainder or ex post facto Law shall be passed." *State v. Ardoin*, 51 La. Ann. 169 (1899); and U.S. Constitution, art. 1, § 9, subd. 3.

2. After Thompson and his coconspirator stole Heber Wilson's calf, the Utah courts had ruled, he was convicted twice for the crime, both times under the laws of the constitution that existed during the two trials. But the second superseded the first, and it came after Utah's state constitution changed the rules for criminal jury trials. *Thompson v. Utah*, 170 US 343 (1898); and *State v. Ardoin*, 51 La. Ann. 169 (1899).

3. Newton Blanchard began his law practice in Caddo Parish and would remain a Democratic Party stalwart throughout his political career. "Constitution of 1898," *West's Louisiana Statutes Annotated* (1977), vol. 3: 210; "Blanchard, Newton Crain," *Dictionary of Louisiana Biography*; and *State v. Biagas*, 105 La. 503 (1901).

4. In both *Wooten* and *Trull*, unanimity was only one of many grounds of appeal, double jeopardy taking precedence in *Wooten* and definitions of legal marriage in *Trull*. *State v. Wooten*, 136 La. 560 (1915); and *State v. Trull*, 147 La. 444 (1920).

5. The majority of the thirty-one exceptions in the *State v. Vial* appeal dealt with prejudicial witness testimony and prejudicial jurors, one of whom had sworn an affidavit against the accused. *State v. Vial*, 153 La. 883 (1923).

6. *The Code of Criminal Procedure for the State of Louisiana* (1928), 74, 84–85; *State v. Jacques*, 171 La. 904 (1931); Dale E. Bennett, "Louisiana Criminal Procedure—A Critical Appraisal," *Louisiana Law Review* 14 (December 1953): 11; and Dale E. Bennett, "Blind Spots In the Louisiana Code of Criminal Procedure," *Louisiana Bar Journal* 1 (April 1954): 62.

7. *State v. Jacques*, 171 La. 904 (1931).

8. *State v. Flattmann*, 172 La. 620 (1931).

9. *State v. Doucet*, 177 La. 63 (1933).

10. Ralph Slovenko, "The Jury System in Louisiana Criminal Law," *Louisiana Law Review* 17 (June 1957): 655–729.

11. *Duncan* was decided on May 20, *Schoonover* on June 4. *State v. Schoonover*, 252 La. 311 (1968); *Duncan v. Louisiana*, 391 US 145 (1968).

12. *Duncan v. Louisiana*, 391 US 145 (1968).

13. Schoonover's brother, Willie Ernest Schoonover, was also charged, but pled guilty prior to the trial. Other bills of exception dealt with the inherent problems of prosecuting one person for a crime that was necessarily a conspiracy and what role the brother had in the act and the conviction. *State v. Schoonover*, 252 La. 311 (1968); and *Duncan v. Louisiana*, 391 US 145 (1968).

14. George White's appeal also emphasized cruel and unusual punishment. He was convicted of selling three "marijuana cigarettes" and was sentenced to ten years at Angola without the possibility of parole. Though the court didn't address it, the reality was that such harsh sentences only raised the stakes for nonunanimous jury verdicts. *State v. White*, 254 La. 389 (1969).

CHAPTER SEVEN

1. *New Orleans Times-Picayune*, 23 January 1969, 18.

2. "Record from the Criminal District Court, Parish of Orleans, Section 'G' Number 202-984: Transcript of testimony of March 18, 1968 & May 15, 1968, Testimony of Frank T. Johnson," *Johnson v. Louisiana*, 37; "Record from the Criminal District Court, Parish of Orleans, Section 'G' Number 202-984: Motion to quash, filed March 13, 1968," *Johnson v. Louisiana*, 7–9; "Record from the Criminal District Court, Parish of Orleans, Section 'G' Number 202-984: Amendment to motion to suppress the evidence, filed March 20, 1968," *Johnson v. Louisiana*, 10–11; and *State v. Johnson*, 255 La. 314 (1970).

3. Walter B. Hamlin began as a New Orleans lawyer and had served on the Louisiana Supreme Court since 1958. He would become chief justice in 1972, before retiring the following year. *State v. Johnson*, 255 La. 314 (1970); "Hamlin, Walter B.," *Dictionary of Louisiana Biography*.

4. "Record from the Criminal District Court, Parish of Orleans, Section 'G' Number 202-984: Supplemental and Amended Motion in Arrest of Judgment," *Johnson v. Louisiana*, 13; and "Record from the Criminal District Court, Parish of Orleans, Section 'G' Number 202-984: Bill of Exceptions No. 24, filed September 9, 1968," *Johnson v. Louisiana*, 30–32.

5. Billy Carl Brumfield, convicted of manslaughter, also took exception to a denial of the right to counsel and attempts at self-incrimination. *State v. Johnson*, 255 La. 314 (1970); *State v. Brumfield*, 254 La. 999 (1969).

6. *State v. Johnson*, 255 La. 314 (1970).

7. *State v. Fink*, 255 La. 385 (1970); *State v. Caston*, 256 La. 459 (1970).

8. "Conference of March 5, 1971 (Notes of Douglas/Brennan)," *Johnson v. Louisiana*, 406 US 356 (1972), law2.umkc.edu/faculty/projects/ftrials/conlaw/johnsonconf.html (accessed 27 December 2011).

9. William S. Holdsworth, *A History of English Law* (3rd ed., Boston: Little, Brown, and Co., 1922), vol. 1: 317–19; John V. Ryan, "Less Than Unanimous Jury Verdicts in Criminal Trials," *Journal of Criminal Law, Criminology, and Police Science* 58 (June 1967): 211–13; James B. Thayer, "The Jury and Its Development," *Harvard Law Review* 5 (February 1892): 295–97;

William Haralson, "Unanimous Jury Verdicts in Criminal Cases," *Mississippi Law Journal* 21, no. 3 (1950): 185, 191; *Apodaca v. Oregon*, 406 US 404 (1972); Valerie P. Hans and Neil Vidmar, *Judging the Jury* (Cambridge, MA: Perseus Books, 1886), 171–72; and Michael H. Glasser, "Letting the Supermajority Rule: Nonunanimous Jury Verdicts In Criminal Trials," *Florida State University Law Review* 24 (Spring 1997): 663–65.

10. Hans and Vidmar, *Judging the Jury*, 172; John M. Murrin, "The Legal Transformation: The Bench and Bar of Eighteenth-Century Massachusetts," in *Colonial America: Essays in Politics and Social Development*, ed. Stanley N. Katz (Boston: Little, Brown, and Co., 1971), 415; *Apodaca v. Oregon*, 406 US 404 (1972); *Williams v. Florida*, 399 US 78 (1970); Glasser, "Letting the Supermajority Rule," 665; and "Conference of March 5, 1971 (Notes of Douglas/Brennan)," *Johnson v. Louisiana*.

11. Quote from Glasser, "Letting the Supermajority Rule," 665; Hans and Vidmar, *Judging the Jury*, 172; and "Criminal Justice Act 1967," 1967, chap. 80, www.legislation.gov.uk/ukpga/1967/80 (accessed 27 December 2011).

12. "Conference of March 5, 1971 (Notes of Douglas/Brennan)," *Johnson v. Louisiana*; *Duncan v. Louisiana*, 391 US 145 (1968).

13. "Conference of March 5, 1971 (Notes of Douglas/Brennan)," *Johnson v. Louisiana*; *Duncan v. Louisiana*, 391 US 145 (1968). Retroactivity had always been somewhat assumed until *Linkletter v. Walker* (1965), wherein the U.S. Supreme Court decided not to apply the case retroactively so as not to affect thousands of other convictions. John Bernard Corr, "Retroactivity: A Study in Supreme Court Doctrine 'As Applied,'" *North Carolina Law Review* 61 (1982–83): 745; and *Linkletter v. Walker*, 381 US 618 (1965).

14. The one justice not appearing at that first conference was John Marshall Harlan, suffering at the time from spinal cancer. His deteriorating health would lead to his retirement in September and death in December. William Rehnquist would replace him. "Conference of March 5, 1971 (Notes of Douglas/Brennan)," *Johnson v. Louisiana*; "Biography of John Marshall Harlan," John Marshall Harlan Papers, 1884–1972 (bulk 1936–71): Finding Aid MC071, Mudd Manuscript Library, Princeton University, arks.princeton.edu/ark:/88435/44558d293 (accessed 30 December 2011).

15. See Howard Ball, *Of Power and Right: Hugo Black, William O. Douglas, and America's Constitutional Revolution* (New York: Oxford University Press, 1992); and Bryan H. Wildenthal, "The Road to Twining: Reassessing the Disincorporation of the Bill of Rights," *Ohio State Law Journal* 61, no. 4 (2000): 1463.

16. "Conference of March 5, 1971 (Notes of Douglas/Brennan)," *Johnson v. Louisiana*.

17. Robert Apodaca, for whom the case would become known, was convicted of assault with a dangerous weapon after stabbing Ronald Joe Swanson in Salem, Oregon. Harry Morgan Cooper was convicted of burglary after breaking and entering a Eugene house. James Arnold Madden was convicted of grand larceny after stealing $140 from Glen Elwood Haldorson. "Petitioner Robert Apodaca, Indictment, Filed September 17, 1968," *Apodaca v. Oregon*, Supreme Court of the United States (October Term, 1970, No. 5338, On Writ of Certiorari to the Court of Appeals of Oregon), 3; "Petitioner Harry Morgan Cooper,

Jr., Indictment, Filed August 12, 1968," *Apodaca v. Oregon,* 10; and "Petitioner James Arnold Madden, Indictment, Filed September 17, 1968," *Apodaca v. Oregon,* 16.

18. It was Senate Joint Resolution 4 of 1931 that ultimately amended the "Rights of Accused in Criminal Prosecution" of Oregon's original 1859 Bill of Rights. *Constitution of Oregon,* article 1, section 11; *Apodaca v. Oregon,* 406 US 404 (1972); and *New York Times,* 7 July 2009, A10.

19. *Morning Oregonian,* 11 May, 5; 14 May, 3, 8; 19 May, 3, 10; 21 May 1934, 8; *Oregon Daily Journal,* 18 May, 1, 5, 10; 19 May, 1; 20 May, 6; 21 May 1934, 6. Francis Paul Valenti, *The Portland Press, the Ku Klux Klan, and the Oregon Compulsory Education Bill: Editorial Treatment of Klan Themes in the Portland Press in 1922* (Seattle: University of Washington Press, 1993), 68; M. Paul Holsinger, "The Oregon School Bill Controversy 1922–1925," *Pacific Historical Review* 37 (August 1968): 333.

20. *State v. Silverman,* 148 Ore. 296; 36 P.2d 34 (1934); Ellen Eisenberg, "Transplanted to the Rose City: The Creation of East European Jewish Community in Portland, Oregon," *Journal of American Ethnic History* 19 (Spring 2000): 82–97; *Morning Oregonian,* 21 May 1934, 8; *Oregon Daily Journal,* 21 May 1934, 6; "Proclamation from the American Nationalist Party, September 25, 1935," "Portland Jews In Danger of Losing Many Friends, September 11, 1936," and "Surveillance Report on an American Defenders Meeting, August 20, 1937," Mss 2918, George Rennar Collection, Oregon Historical Society. Oregon Historical Society's Ethnic History Collection is available online, content.wsulibs.wsu.edu/cdm/landingpage/collection/wsuvan1 (accessed 4 January 2013).

21. The final vote was 117,446 to 83,430, a difference of 34,016; *Morning Oregonian,* 11 May, 1, 6; 12 May, 1, 12; 14 May, 1, 8; 17 May, 1; 18 May 1934, 1. *Oregon Daily Journal,* 19 May 1934, 1; William Bigelow and Norman Diamond, "Agitate, Educate, Organize: Portland, 1934," *Oregon Historical Quarterly* 89 (Spring 1988): 4–29; "Initiative, Referendum and Recall: 1930–1936," *Oregon Blue Book,* Office of the Secretary of State, bluebook.state.or.us/state/elections/elections15.htm (accessed 2 December 2013).

22. *Apodaca v. Oregon,* 406 US 404 (1972); *New York Times,* 7 July 2009, A10.

23. *Williams v. Florida,* 399 US 78 (1970); *State v. Ardoin,* 51 La. Ann. 169 (1899).

24. Despite this formulation, the U.S. Supreme Court would hold the line at six-member juries. In *Ballew v. Georgia* (1978), the court ruled that unanimous five-member criminal juries were unconstitutional, requiring a minimum of six. *Ballew v. Georgia,* 435 US 223 (1978).

CHAPTER EIGHT

1. *Johnson v. Louisiana,* 406 US 356 (1972).

2. Ibid.

3. Ibid.; and *Williams v. Florida,* 399 US 78 (1970).

4. *Apodaca v. Oregon,* 406 US 404 (1972); *Duncan v. Louisiana,* 391 US 145 (1968); and *Johnson v. Louisiana,* 406 US 356 (1972).

5. Powell had originally asked for another week to consider his opinion. His concurrence, which mirrored his concurrence in *Apodaca*, demonstrated that he had yet to fully recover from his indecision. *Johnson v. Louisiana*, 406 US 356 (1972); *Apodaca v. Oregon*, 406 US 404 (1972).

6. *Johnson v. Louisiana*, 406 US 356 (1972).

7. Douglas's emphasis on the discriminatory nature of nonunanimous criminal jury verdicts would not be the last such complaint. Nonunanimous juries made criminal convictions easier, and criminal convictions took place disproportionately among the lower classes. *Johnson v. Louisiana*, 406 US 356 (1972); *Apodaca v. Oregon*, 406 US 404 (1972).

8. *Johnson v. Louisiana*, 406 US 356 (1972).

9. *New York Times*, 23 May 1972, 1, 28; *Washington Post*, 23 May 1972, A1, A6; *New Orleans Times-Picayune*, 23 May 1972, 6; and *Wall Street Journal*, 23 May 1972, 2. For an example of law review response, all of which tracked along similar lines to a much more limited audience, see J. H. Johnson, "Criminal Law—Jury—Unanimous Jury Verdict Is Not Constitutionally Required in State Criminal Cases," *Wisconsin Law Review* 3 (1978): 926–33.

10. Richard L. Stout, "The Nixon Judges," *Christian Science Monitor*, 22 December 1972, 14.

11. *Swann v. Charlotte-Mecklenburg Board of Education*, 402 US 1 (1971). For more on busing, see Matthew D. Lassiter, *The Silent Majority: Suburban Politics in the Sunbelt South* (Princeton, NJ: Princeton University Press, 2007); Joyce A. Baugh, *The Detroit School Busing Case: Milliken v. Bradley and the Controversy Over Desegregation* (Lawrence: University Press of Kansas, 2011); and Ronald P. Formisano, *Boston Against Busing: Race, Class, and Ethnicity in the 1960s and 1970s* (2nd ed., Chapel Hill: University of North Carolina Press, 2003).

CHAPTER NINE

1. *State v. Dillon*, 260 La. 215 (1971); *State v. Jackson*, 259 La. 957 (1971); *State v. Jones*, 257 La. 966 (1971); *State v. Biagas*, 260 La. 69 (1971); *State v. Dell*, 258 La. 1024 (1971); *State v. Anderson*, 261 La. 244 (1972); *US ex rel. White v. Henderson*, 461 F.2d 657 (CA5 [La.] 1972); and *State v. Holmes*, 263 La. 685 (1972).

2. *State v. Neal*, 275 So.2d 765 (1973); *State v. Lee*, 275 So.2d 757 (1973); *State v. Rollins*, 302 So.2d 288 (1974); and *State v. Blackwell*, 298 So.2d 798; 420 US 976; 43 L.Ed.2d 656 (1973).

3. The six-of-eight misdemeanor jury idea failed because small parishes protested the inconvenience and cost of having to secure eight-person juries for lesser crimes. *Louisiana Constitution of 1974*, article 1, section 17; "Constitution, Article 1, § 14 to 27," *West's Louisiana Statutes Annotated* (St. Paul, MN: Thompson/West, 2006), vol. 1B : 215–18; Lee Hargrave, "Declaration of Rights of Louisiana Constitution of 1974," *Louisiana Law Review* 35 (Fall 1974): 55–57; Bennett, "Louisiana Criminal Procedure—A Critical Appraisal," 27; Bennett, "Blind Spots In the Louisiana Code of Criminal Procedure," 71–72; *Johnson v. Louisiana*, 406 US 356 (1972); and *Williams v. Florida*, 399 US 78 (1970).

4. Crimes necessarily punishable by hard labor and for which parole would not be granted were: abortion; manslaughter; murder; aggravated rape; simple rape; aggravated kidnapping; aggravated arson; aggravated burglary; simple burglary; armed robbery; theft of cattle, horses, mules, sheep, hogs, or goats; incest (if between brother and sister or ascendant and descendant); aggravated crime against nature; aggravated obstruction of a highway of commerce; driving while intoxicated (fourth conviction); aggravated escape; jumping bail; treason; misprision of treason; and criminal anarchy. Hargrave, "Declaration of Rights of Louisiana Constitution of 1974," 56; *Apodaca v. Oregon*, 406 US 404 (1972); Dr. Emmett Asseff Constitutional Convention '72 Papers, #241, Noel Memorial Library Archives and Special Collections, Louisiana State University–Shreveport; *Official Journal of the Proceedings of the Constitutional Convention of 1973 of the State of Louisiana* (Baton Rouge: Secretary of State, 1973), 453–55; and "Committee on Bill of Rights and Elections, August 24, 1973, Staff Memorandum No. 52," *Records of the Louisiana Constitutional Convention of 1973: Committee Documents* (Baton Rouge: Louisiana Constitutional Convention Records Committee, 1974), vol. 10: 128.

5. Glasser, "Letting the Supermajority Rule," 671; Harold J. Rothwax, *Guilty: The Collapse of Criminal Justice* (New York: Random House, 1996), 213.

6. Harry Kalven and Hans Zeisel, *The American Jury* (New York: Little, Brown, 1966), 488; Glasser, "Letting the Supermajority Rule," 672. For more, see Dennis J. Devine et al., "Jury Decision Making: 45 Years of Empirical Research on Deliberating Groups," *Psychology, Public Policy, and Law* 7 (March 2000): 622–727.

7. Glasser, "Letting the Supermajority Rule," 674–75; Reid Hastie, Steven D. Penrod, and Nancy Pennington, *Inside the Jury* (Union, NJ: Lawbook Exchange, 2002), 173. For more critical support of nonunanimous jury verdicts, see Akhil Reed Amar, "Reinventing Juries: Ten Suggested Reforms," *UC Davis Law Review* 28 (Summer 1995): 1169–94; Jere W. Morehead, "A 'Modest' Proposal for Jury Reform: The Elimination of Required Unanimous Jury Verdicts," *University of Kansas Law Review* 46 (June 1998): 933–45; California District Attorneys Association, *Non-Unanimous Jury Verdicts: A Necessary Criminal Justice Reform* (Sacramento: California District Attorneys Association, 1995); and Jeffrey Rosen, "After 'One Angry Woman,'" *University of Chicago Legal Forum* 1998 (The Right to a Fair Trial 1998): 179–95.

8. Kalven and Zeisel, *The American Jury*, 461; Glasser, "Letting the Supermajority Rule," 675; Margo Hunter, "Improving the Jury System: Nonunanimous Verdicts," *Public Law Research Institute*, www.uchastings.edu/public-law/plri/spr96tex/juryuna.html (accessed 2 January 2012); and William S. Neilson and Harold Winter, "The Elimination of Hung Juries: Retrials and Nonunanimous Verdicts," *International Review of Law and Economics* 25, no. 1 (2005): 2–3.

9. Peter J. Coughlan, "In Defense of Unanimous Jury Verdicts: Mistrials, Communication, and Strategic Voting," *American Political Science Review* 94 (June 2000): 375. For more critical support of unanimity, see James Kachmar, "Silencing the Minority: Permitting Nonunanimous Jury Verdicts in Criminal Trials," *Pacific Law Journal* (Fall 1996): 273–310;

Jeremy Osher, "Jury Unanimity in California: Should It Stay or Should It Go?" *Loyola of Los Angeles Law Review* 3 (1996): 1319–70; Michael J. Saks, "What Do Jury Experiments Tell Us About How Juries (Should) Make Decisions?" *Southern California Interdisciplinary Law Journal* 6, no. 1 (1997): 1–53; Douglas G. Smith, "Structural and Functional Aspects of the Jury: Comparative Analysis and Proposals for Reform," *Alabama Law Review* 48 (Winter 1997): 441–581; and Ted Klastorin and Kenneth S. Klein, "Do Diverse Juries Aid or Impede Justice?" *Wisconsin Law Review* 3 (1999): 553–69.

10. *Johnson v. Louisiana*, 406 US 356 (1972); Anthony A. Morano, "Historical Development of the Interrelationship of Unanimous Verdicts and Reasonable Doubt," *Valparaiso University Law Review* 10 (Winter 1976): 223–35.

11. Morano, "Historical Development of the Interrelationship of Unanimous Verdicts and Reasonable Doubt," 224–30.

12. *McDonald v. City of Chicago*, 130 S.Ct. 3020 (2010). See also Kate Riordan, "Ten Angry Men: Unanimous Jury Verdicts In Criminal Trials and Incorporation After *McDonald*," *Journal of Criminal Law and Criminology* 101, no. 4 (2012): 1404, 1406–16.

13. *Billeci v. United States*, 184 F.2d 394 (1950); *In re Winship*, 287 US 358 (1970); and Riordan, "Ten Angry Men," 1425–26.

CHAPTER TEN

1. *State v. Gilmore*, 332 So.2d 789 (1976). See also *State v. Ross*, 320 So.2d 177 (1975); *State v. Morgan*, 315 So.2d 632 (1975); *State v. Bastida*, 310 So.2d 629 (1975); *State v. Williams*, 326 So.2d 815 (1976); *State v. Ledet*, 337 So.2d 1126 (1976); *State v. Gardner*, 351 So.2d 105 (1977); and *State v. Hodges*, 349 So.2d 250 (1977).

2. Brennan, Stewart, and Marshall concurred in part, upholding the reversal of the nonunanimous conviction, but felt that the Louisiana obscenity statute was too broad to generate a constitutional question. The case set a precedent that allowed a similar appeal, *Atkins v. Listi* (1979), to be repealed at the district level. "Brief for the Petitioners, On Writ of Certiorari to the Supreme Court of Louisiana," *Burch v. Louisiana*, Supreme Court of the United States (October Term, 1978, No. 78–90), 3; *Ballew v. Georgia*, 435 US 223 (1978); *Burch v. Louisiana*, 441 US 130 (1979); and *Atkins v. Listi*, 625 F2d 525 (1979). For more see Nathalie M. Walker-Dittman, "Constitutional Criminal Procedure—Six-Member Juries Must Render Unanimous Verdicts in State Criminal Trials for Nonpetty Offenses," *Tulane Law Review* 54 (June 1980): 1178–87; Richard L. Lagarde, "Right to Trial by Jury: New Guidelines for State Criminal Trial Juries," *Louisiana Law Review* 40, no. 3 (1980): 837–46; and James L. Buchwalter, "Construction and Application of Sixth Amendment Right to Trial by Jury—Supreme Court Cases," 6 A.L.R. 2d 213 (2005).

3. *New York Times*, 1 September 1995, A24.

4. For examples, see *State v. Green*, 390 So.2d 1253 (1980); *State v. Marcantel*, 388 So.2d 383 (1980); *State v. Jones*, 381 So.2d 383 (1980); *State v. Goodley*, 398 So.2d 1068 (1981); *State v. Edwards*, 420 So.2d 663 (1982); *State v. Simmons*, 414 So.2d 705 (1982); *State v.*

Belgard, 410 So.2d 720 (1982); *State v. Buchanan*, 439 So.2d 576 (1983); *State v. Sanders*, 539 So.2d 114 (1989); *State v. Strickland*, 683 So.2d 218 (1996); *State v. Shanks*, 715 So.2d 157 (1998); *State v. Williams*, 747 So.2d 1256 (1999); *State v. Fasola*, 901 So.2d 533 (2005); *State v. Mizell*, 938 So.2d 712 (2006); *State v. Regis*, 25 Sp.3d 183 (2009); *State v. Smith*, 20 So.3d 501 (2009); and *State v. Moody*, 38 So.3d 451 (2010).

5. The case of Derrick Todd Lee is ubiquitous in the newspapers of Baton Rouge, New Orleans, and Lafayette throughout 2004, but for more comprehensive treatment of the killings, investigation, trials, and convictions, see Stan Weeber, *In Search of Derrick Todd Lee: The Internet Social Movement That Made a Difference* (New York: University Press of America, 2007); and Susan D. Mustafa, Tony Clayton, and Sue Israel, *Blood Bath* (New York: Pinnacle, 2009).

6. "On Petition for a Writ of Certiorari to the Louisiana Court of Appeal, First Circuit," *Lee v. Louisiana*, Supreme Court of the United States (July Term, 2008, No. 07-1523), 2–3; "Brief of *Amicus Curiae* the Houston Institute for Race and Justice in Support of Petitioner," *Lee v. Louisiana*, Supreme Court of the United States (July Term, 2008, No. 07-1523), 10–15; *State v. Lee*, 964 So.2d 533 (2007); and "Brief *Amicus Curiae* of the Charles Hamilton Houston Institute for Race and Justice, the National Association of Criminal Defense Lawyers, and the Louisiana Association of Criminal Defense Lawyers," *Bowen v. Oregon*, 9–14.

7. Riordan, "Ten Angry Men," 1430–31; Kim Taylor-Thompson, "Empty Votes in Jury Deliberations," *Harvard Law Review* 113 (April 2000): 1292, 1299–1302; and Samuel R. Sommers, "On Racial Diversity and Group Decision Making: Identifying Multiple Effects of Racial Composition on Jury Deliberations," *Journal of Personality and Social Psychology* 90, no. 4 (2006): 606–7.

8. *Bowen v. Oregon*, 130 S.Ct. 52 (2009); *New York Times*, 7 July 2009, A10; and *Barbour v. Louisiana*, 131 S.Ct. 1477 (2011).

9. Riordan, "Ten Angry Men," 1428, referencing "Brief of Amicus Curiae American Bar Association in Support of Petitioner, No. 08-1117," *Bowen v. Oregon*, 130 S.Ct. 52 (2009).

EPILOGUE

1. *Ex parte Plessy*, 45 La. Ann. 80, 11 So. 948 (1893).

2. *Plessy v. Ferguson*, 163 US 537 (1896).

3. Ibid.

4. Adam Fairclough, *Race & Democracy: The Civil Rights Struggle in Louisiana, 1915–1972* (Athens: University of Georgia Press, 1995), 6–8; Victoria R. Dominguez, *White by Definition: Social Classification in Creole Louisiana* (New Brunswick, NJ: Rutgers University Press, 1986), 26–31.

5. George Coppolo and Kevin McCarthy, "Crime Rate and Conviction Rates Broken Down by Race," OLR Research Report, Office of Legislative Research, Connecticut General Assembly, 18 January 2008, www.cga.ct.gov/2008/rpt/2008-R-0008.htm (accessed 10 December 2013). There are myriad works on the relationship between race and incarceration,

but a groundbreaking and accessible recent one is Michelle Alexander's *The New Jim Crow: Mass Incarceration in the Age of Colorblindness* (New York: New Press, 2010). For in-depth accountings of Louisiana's crime and conviction statistics, see the reports generated by the Statistical Analysis Center of the Louisiana Commission on Law Enforcement and Administration of Criminal Justice, www.lcle.la.gov/programs/SAC.asp.

2019 UPDATE

1. In 1883, the Supreme Court ruled parts of the 1875 law constitutional, but not Section 4, which dealt with jury service and remained in tact. Thomas Ward Frampton, "The Jim Crow Jury," *Vanderbilt Law Review* 71 (No. 5 2018): 1594–1595, 1600–1602. Frampton's work, of which I saw an early draft, is the bedrock of the first section of this chapter. His research created my ability to write this section. It is invaluable, and for more on the historical legacy of Louisiana juries, see his article in *Vanderbilt Law Review.*

2. As was described in the Court's ruling in a later case, *Akins v. Texas,* in 1945, "A purpose to discriminate must be present which may be proven by systematic exclusion of eligible jurymen of the proscribed race or by unequal application of the law to such an extent as to show intentional discrimination." Or, even later, as was explained in *Washington v. Davis* in 1976, *Strauder* "established that the exclusion of Negroes from grand and petit juries in criminal proceedings violated the Equal Protection Clause, but the fact that a particular jury or a series of juries does not statistically reflect the racial composition of the community does not in itself make out an invidious discrimination forbidden by the Clause." *Strauder v. West Virginia,* 100 US 303 (1880); *Akins v. Texas,* 325 US 398 (1945); and *Washington v. Davis,* 426 US 229 (1976).

3. *Shreveport Times,* 19 February 1885, 4; and *Baton Rouge Advocate* letter reprinted in *St. Landry Democrat,* 25 January 1885, 1.

4. *New Orleans Daily Picayune,* 1 February 1893, 4.

5. Frampton, "The Jim Crow Jury," 1612–1613; *New Orleans Times-Picayune,* 12 May 1919, 8; National Association for the Advancement of Colored People, *Thirty Years of Lynching in the United States, 1889–1918* (New York: Arno Press, 1969), 71–73, 104–105; and *Papers of the NAACP,* part 7, series A, reel 12, 348–352, 354, 356, 373–380, 383, 393.

6. *St. Martinville Weekly Messengre,* 7 October 1893, 1.

7. *New Orleans Daily Picayune,* 2 March 1895, 3; and Frampton, "The Jim Crow Jury," 1594–1595, 1605–1606.

8. *Murray v. Louisiana,* 163 U.S. 101 (1896); and Frampton, "The Jim Crow Jury," 1595, 1606–1608.

9. *New Orleans Times Democrat,* 9 July 1897, 9; and *New Orleans Daily Picayune,* 9 July 1897, 3; and Frampton, "The Jim Crow Jury," 1608–1609.

10. *New Orleans Times Democrat,* 9 July 1897, 9; Frampton, 17–18.

11. *Congressional Record,* 55th Congress, 2nd sess., vol. 31, pt. 2, 26 January 1898, 1019; Frampton, "The Jim Crow Jury," 1616–1617; and *Baton Rouge Daily Advocate,* 28 January 1898, 2.

12. *New Orleans Times-Picayune* coverage quoted in Frampton, "The Jim Crow Jury," 1617.

13. *Louisiana v. Joshua Lee and Christopher Lee*, no. 500–034, no. 498–666, Criminal District Court for the Parish of Orleans, Transcript of the Motion Hearing, 3 February 2017. See also William Ivy Hair, *Bourbonism and Agrarian Protest: Louisiana Politics, 1877–1900* (Baton Rouge: Louisiana State University Press, 1969); Roger Shugg, *The Origins of the Class Struggle in Louisiana* (Baton Rouge: Louisiana State University Press, 1968); and Donna A. Barnes, *The Louisiana Populist Movement, 1881–1900* (Baton Rouge: Louisiana State University Press, 2011).

14. *Louisiana v. Joshua Lee and Christopher Lee*, no. 500–034, no. 498–666, Criminal District Court for the Parish of Orleans, Transcript of the Motion Hearing, 3 February 2017; and Barnes, *The Louisiana Populist Movement, 1881–1900*, 186–211.

15. Mark T. Carleton, "Fundamental Special Interests: The Constitution of 1974," in *In Search of Fundamental Law: Louisiana's Constitutions, 1812–1974*, ed. Warren M. Billings and Edward F. Haas (Lafayette: Center for Louisiana Studies, 1993), 142.

16. For more on mass incarceration, see Michelle Alexander, *The New Jim Crow: Mass Incarceration in the Age of Colorblindness* (New York: The New Press, 2010). For more on the 1968 election, see Jack Bass, *The Transformation of Southern Politics: Social Change and Political Consequence Since 1945* (Athens: University of Georgia Press, 1995); Dan T. Carter, *From George Wallace to Newt Gingrich: Race in the Conservative Counterrevolution, 1963–1994* (Baton Rouge: Louisiana State University Press, 1999); and Bruce H. Kalk, *The Machiavellian Nominations: Richard Nixon's Southern Strategy and the Struggle for the Supreme Court, 1968–70* (Chapel Hill: University of North Carolina Press, 1992).

17. Adam Fairclough, *Race and Democracy: The Civil Rights Struggle in Louisiana, 1915–1972* (Athens: University of Georgia Press, 1995), 464. For more on Edwards, see Leo Honeycutt, *Edwin Edwards: Governor of Louisiana* (Baton Rouge: Lisburn Press, 2009).

18. *New York Times*, 11 January 1972, 1; 12 January 1972, 27; 13 January 1972, 26; and "Races: Battle in Baton Rouge," *Time*, 24 January 1972, 22.

19. For more on the Tyler saga, see a series of articles by Bob Herbert in the *New York Times*, "A Death In Destrehan," 1 February 2007; "Gary Tyler's Lost Decades," 5 February 2007; and "They Beat Gary So Bad," 8 February 2007.

20. *State v. Brown*, Supreme Court of Louisiana, 21 May 1979, No. 63210, 371 So. 2d 751; and *State v. Washington*, Supreme Court of Louisiana, 25 June 1979, No. 63037, 375 So. 2d 1162.

21. Dr. Emmett Asseff Constitutional Convention '72 Papers, #241, Noel Memorial Library Archives and Special Collections, Louisiana State University–Shreveport; *Official Journal of the Proceedings of the Constitutional Convention of 1973 of the State of Louisiana* (Baton Rouge: Secretary of State, 1973), 453–55; and "Committee on Bill of Rights and Elections, August 24, 1973, Staff Memorandum No. 52," *Records of the Louisiana Constitutional Convention of 1973: Committee Documents* (Baton Rouge: Louisiana Constitutional Convention Records Committee, 1974), vol. 10: 128.

22. Ibid.

23. Ibid.

24. Even before such accounts, Robert J. Smith and Bidish J. Sarma published an account in the *Louisiana Law Review* on the broader racial disparities in the Louisiana criminal justice system, including nonunanimous criminal jury verdicts: "How and Why Race Continues to Influence the Administration of Criminal Justice in Louisiana," *Louisiana Law Review* 72 (2012): 361; Kyle R. Satterfield, "Circumventing *Apodaca:* An Equal Protection Challenge to Nonunanimous Jury Verdicts in Louisiana," *Tulane Law Review* 90 (2016): 693; Angela A. Allen-Bell, "How the Narrative about Louisiana's Non-Unanimous Criminal Jury System Because Person of Interest in the Case against Justice in the Deep South," *Mercer Law Review* 67 (2016): 585; Aliza B. Kaplan and Amy Saack, " Overturning *Apodaca v. Oregon* Should Be Easy: Nonunanimous Jury Verdicts in Criminal Cases Undermine the Credibility of Our Justice System," *Oregon Law Review* 95 (2016): 1.

25. Melinda Deslatte, "Effort to end Louisiana split-jury law gets bipartisan push," Associated Press, 30 July 2018, https://apnews.com/9ff0c873059b43129871b806e1e081b9, accessed 1 August 2018; Deborah Campbell-Tarpley, correspondence with the author; Ed Tarpley, correspondence with the author; and Editorial Board, "When Jurors Are Silenced," *New York Times*, 11 May 2018, A26. See also Bryan Stevenson, *Just Mercy: A Story of Justice and Redemption* (New York: Spiegel and Grau, 2015).

26. This brief summary is just a small sample of the *Advocate*'s exhaustive work. The reporters also found, for example, that at least twelve defendants convicted by a nonunanimous jury were later proven to be innocent. Jeff Adelson, Gordon Russell, and John Simerman, "How an abnormal Louisiana law deprives, discriminates and drives incarceration: Tilting the scales," *New Orleans Advocate*, 1 April 2018, https://www.theadvocate.com/new_orleans/news/courts/article_16fdoece-32b1–11e8-8770–33eca2a325de.html, accessed 1 August 2018; Gordon Russell, "Tilting the Scales: In Louisiana, is it truly a 'jury of one's peers' when race matters?" *New Orleans Advocate*, 1 April 2018, https://www.theadvocate.com/new_orleans/news/courts/article_9176f792–32d3–11e8–889d-0b68e54fb230.html, accessed 1 August 2018; John Simerman, "For prosecutors, Louisiana's split-verdict law produces results," *New Orleans Advocate*, 21 April 2018, https://www.theadvocate.com/new_orleans/news/courts/article_1d1ad7f8–4208–11e8–918e-b700171b2891.html, 1 April 2018; and John Simerman, "Louisiana split juries have convicted several people wrongly, but not enough data to discern a trend," *New Orleans Advocate*, 21 April 2018, https://www.theadvocate.com/new_orleans/news/courts/article_d03c6c68–4201–11e8-b8e7–2be5a32762b2.html, accessed 1 August 2018. For a summary of the *Advocate*'s coverage, see "Tilting the scales series: Everything to know about Louisiana's controversial 10–2 jury law," *New Orleans Advocate*, 1 April 2018, https://www.theadvocate.com/new_orleans/news/courts/article_85b28154–3492–11e8-bfd2–07fee9f093d2.html, accessed 1 August 2018.

27. *Louisiana v. Melvin Cartez Maxie*, 13-CR-072522, Eleventh Judicial District Court, Sabine Parish, Transcript of the Continuation of the Evidentiary Hearing, 9 July 2018.

28. Senate Bill No. 243 by Senators Morrell and Carter, Criminal Procedure, "Constitutional amendment to require unanimous juries for felonies," SLS 18RS-198, Original, 2018

Regular Session; and SB243 by Senator J.P. Morrell, 2018 Regular Session, http://www.
legis.la.gov/legis/BillInfo.aspx?s=18RS&b=SB243&sbi=y, accessed 1 August 2018. Italics
and boldface mine.

29. As the *New Orleans Advocate* demonstrated, however, those jury records were difficult to acquire even before the new statute. House Bill No. 699 by Representative Stagni,
Criminal/Jury Trials: "Removes the requirement that a juror provide a name and signature
for jury polling purposes," HLS 18RS-1077, Original, 2018 Regular Session; House Bill
No. 699 by Representative Stagni, Criminal/Jury Trials: "Provides relative to jury polling
after a verdict is returned," HLS 18RS-1077, Engrossed, 2018 Regular Session; HB 699
by Representative Joe Stagni, 2018 Regular Session, http://www.legis.la.gov/legis/BillInfo.
aspx?s=18RS&b=HB699&sbi=y, accessed 1 August 2018; Gordon Russell, "Bill to keep split
jury votes secret becomes law despite push for jury unanimity in Louisiana," *The Advocate*,
https://www.theadvocate.com/baton_rouge/news/politics/legislature/article_fofd4186–
5a23–11e8-a202–2b7a4b652452.html, accessed 1 August 2018; and Gordon Russell, "Why
are Louisiana jury votes often absent from court record? Tilting the scales," 1 April 2018,
https://www.theadvocate.com/new_orleans/news/courts/article_d9cdff5a-32cd-11e8-a328–
53831061c1ed.html, accessed 1 August 2018.

30. Jessica Rosgaard and Wallis Watkins, "How Louisiana's Unanimous Jury Proposal
Got On the Ballot," WRKF Baton Rouge, http://www.wrkf.org/post/how-louisianas-
unanimous-jury-proposal-got-ballot?fbclid=IwARotnVWmPyepT7arC96°eK-Mb6kDt7PI-
FoIuSXeV2kVToq88VHpLUhRWPwU, accessed 23 November 2018; and John Simerman,
"Louisiana GOP backs constitutional amendment on jury unanimity," *New Orleans Advocate*, 11 June 2018, https://www.theadvocate.com/new_orleans/news/article_192dfbf2–
6dbe-11e8–97f4–2b3ac52019e5.html?fbclid=IwAR1rRav8RBmbSQERIxyxUPEtXUH2yJ4
21pIi1UMsBFaPdqFr5eB2MwRVw4I, accessed 23 November 2018.

31. The final version of the new amendment did include added language specifying that
the standard would be in effect for crimes committed after January 2019, so as not to force
a massive number of retrials throughout the state system. "A case for an offense committed
prior to January 1, 2019, in which the punishment is necessarily confinement at hard labor
shall be tried before a jury of twelve persons, ten of whom must concur to render a verdict.
A case for an offense committed on or after January 1, 2019, in which the punishment is
necessarily confinement at hard labor shall be tried before a jury of twelve persons, all of
whom must concur to render a verdict." HB699 by Representative Joe Stagni, 2018 Regular
Session, http://www.legis.la.gov/legis/BillInfo.aspx?s=18RS&b=HB699&sbi=y, accessed
1 August 2018; SB243 by Senator J. P. Morrell, 2018 Regular Session, http://www.legis.
la.gov/legis/BillInfo.aspx?s=18RS&b=SB243&sbi=y, accessed 1 August 2018; and Act No.
722, Senate Bill No. 243 by Senators Morrell, Barrow, Bishop, Boudreaux, Carter, Claitor,
LaFleur, Long, Luneau, Peterson, Price, and Gary Smith and Representatives Bagneris,
Bishop, Bouie, Brass, Carpenter, Gary Carter, Connick, Cox, Duplessis, Franklin, Gaines,
Glover, Hall, Jimmy Harris, Hunter, Jackson, James, Jefferson, Jenkins, Jordan, Terry
Landry, Lyons, Marcelle, Marino, Gregory Miller, Norton, Pierre, Smith, and Stagni. 2018

Regular Session, Enrolled. The final representative included as an author of the final bill was the original author of the jury -polling legislation that had been signed less than a month prior.

32. Gordon Russell, "Bill to keep split jury votes secret becomes law despite push for jury unanimity in Louisiana," *Baton Rouge Advocate*, https://www.theadvocate.com/baton_rouge/news/politics/legislature/article_fofd4186–5a23–11e8-a202–2b7a4b652452.html, accessed 1 August 2018.

33. Such quotes were reprinted in news outlets throughout the state. For one example, see Melissa Gregory, "Book leads attorney on quest to end non-unanimous juries," *Alexandria Town Talk*, 21 October 2018, https://www.thetowntalk.com/story/news/2018/10/21/book-leads-attorney-quest-end-non-unanimous-verdicts/1696001002/, accessed 16 November 2018.

34. John Simerman, "Over $1M in support, from big-name donors, behind effort to nix Louisiana jury law," *Baton Rouge Advocate*, 11 October 2018, https://www.theadvocate.com/baton_rouge/news/politics/article_a59118a8-ccdd-11e8–9833–07d41f5f038c.html, accessed 16 November 2018; Julia O'Donoghue, "Leading conservative Christian group will work for unanimous juries vote," 27 August 2018, https://www.nola.com/politics/index.ssf/2018/08/louisiana_family_forum_unanimo.html, accessed 16 November 2018; and John Simerman, "Unanimous jury advocates appeal to Louisiana's pro-gun conservatives in new video," *Baton Rouge Advocate*, 30 August 2018, https://www.theadvocate.com/baton_rouge/news/politics/article_528a4e4c-acb0–11e8–95ec-670289866ea5.html, accessed 16 November 2018.

35. Ed Tarpley, correspondence with the author; and Gordon Russell and John Simerman, "Hillar Moore, other Louisiana DAs declare support to change unanimous jury law," *Baton Rouge Advocate*, 17 October 2018, https://www.theadvocate.com/baton_rouge/news/politics/article_d656730c-d20a-11e8–9036-cfd509895b09.html, 16 November 2018.

36. Simerman, "Over $1M in support, from big-name donors, behind effort to nix Louisiana jury law."

37. See the Unanimous Jury Coalition website, https://www.unanimousjury.org/; and Norris Henderson, "Repairing the Tarnished Soul of Louisiana—Yes On Two," *Louisiana Weekly*, 29 October 2018, http://www.louisianaweekly.com/repairing-the-tarnished-soul-of-louisiana-yes-on-two/?fbclid=IwAR2FCNUEeDUvCOUhfi7J2pXN_EmfdrPxeRXpAluCmFWYpw_-Bt_jMYOxS8M, accessed 23 November 2018.

38. Julia O'Donoghue, "Jeff Landry isn't in favor of Louisiana requiring unanimous jury convictions," *New Orleans Times-Picayune*, 6 August 2018, https://www.nola.com/politics/index.ssf/2018/08/jeff_landry_unanimous_juries.html, accessed 16 November 2018.

39. John Simerman and Gordon Russell, "From ACLU to NRA: Campaign for unanimous juries targeted Louisiana voters across the spectrum," *New Orleans Advocate*, 7 November 2018, https://www.theadvocate.com/new_orleans/news/politics/article_50c09b98-e2d9–11e8-b333–87fd78775b22.html?fbclid=IwAR3wNG5uGuDWIfwQKVXT6fv8oJJn1hsBEjB4mbPSDns_XxvEihdogvwgvwU, accessed 16 November 2018; and Conrad

Wilson, "After Louisiana Vote, Oregon Lawmakers Want To Scrap Non-Unanimous Jury Law," *Oregon Public Broadcasting*, 7 November 2018, https://www.opb.org/news/article/non-unanimous-jury-oregon-jim-crow-lousiana-vote/?utm_campaign=Crushin5&utm_source=Twitter&utm_medium=social&fbclid=IwAR2_5yooaJXZpf9UGHT2aqKlynxvomxZdr9266C2ozPrPFcd1Cr1mvk6HL4, accessed 16 November 2018.

40. Matt Sledge and Gordon Russell, "U.S. Supreme Court to reconsider split jury verdicts, prompted by New Orleans case," *New Orleans Advocate*, 18 March 2019, https://www.theadvocate.com/new_orleans/news/courts/article_957f6ade-4995-11e9-8ef2-ffa9189a0004.html?, accessed 2 May 2019; and "The Advocate wins first Pulitzer Prize for series that helped change Louisiana's split-jury law," *Baton Rouge Advocate*, 15 April 2019, https://www.theadvocate.com/baton_rouge/news/article_dba87282-5f28-11e9-92b3-bfbaocfo8ab2.html?, accessed 2 May 2019.

BIBLIOGRAPHY

NEWSPAPERS

Atlanta Constitution.
Christian Science Monitor.
Morning Oregonian.
New Orleans Times-Picayune.
New York Times.
Oregon Daily Journal.
Wall Street Journal.
Washington Post.

CASES

Apodaca v. Oregon, 406 US 404 (1972).
Atkins v. Listi, 625 F2d 525 (1979).
Ballew v. Georgia, 435 US 223 (1978).
Barbour v. Louisiana, 131 S.Ct. 1477 (2011).
Billeci v. United States, 184 F.2d 394 (1950).
Bowen v. Oregon, 130 S.Ct. 52 (2009).
Brown v. Board of Education of Topeka, 347 US 483 (1954).
Burch v. Louisiana, 441 US 130 (1979).
Duncan v. Louisiana, 391 US 145 (1968).
Ex parte Plessy, 45 La. Ann. 80, 11 So. 948 (1893).
Harper v. Virginia Board of Elections 383 US 663 (1966).
In re Winship, 287 US 358 (1970).
Johnson v. Louisiana, 406 US 356 (1972).
Linkletter v. Walker, 381 US 618 (1965).
McDonald v. City of Chicago, 130 S.Ct. 3020 (2010).
Plessy v. Ferguson, 163 US 537 (1896).
State v. Anderson, 261 La. 244 (1972).
State v. Ardoin, 51 La. Ann. 169 (1899).

State v. Bastida, 310 So.2d 629 (1975).

State v. Belgard, 410 So.2d 720 (1982).

State v. Biagas, 105 La. 503 (1901).

State v. Biagas, 260 La. 69 (1971).

State v. Blackwell, 298 So.2d 798; 420 US 976; 43 L.Ed.2d 656 (1973).

State v. Brumfield, 254 La. 999 (1969).

State v. Buchanan, 439 So.2d 576 (1983).

State v. Caston, 256 La. 459 (1970).

State v. Edwards, 420 So.2d 663 (1982).

State v. Dell, 258 La. 1024 (1971).

State v. Dillon, 260 La. 215 (1971).

State v. Doucet, 177 La. 63 (1933).

State v. Fasola, 901 So.2d 533 (2005).

State v. Fink, 255 La. 385 (1970).

State v. Flattmann, 172 La. 620 (1931).

State v. Gardner, 351 So.2d 105 (1977).

State v. Gilmore, 332 So.2d 789 (1976).

State v. Goodley, 398 So.2d 1068 (1981).

State v. Green, 390 So.2d 1253 (1980).

State v. Hodges, 349 So.2d 250 (1977).

State v. Holmes, 263 La. 685 (1972).

State v. Jackson, 259 La. 957 (1971).

State v. Jacques, 171 La. 904 (1931).

State v. Johnson, 255 La. 314 (1970).

State v. Jones, 257 La. 966 (1971).

State v. Jones, 381 So.2d 383 (1980).

State v. Ledet, 337 So.2d 1126 (1976).

State v. Lee, 275 So.2d 757 (1973).

State v. Lee, 964 So.2d 533 (2007).

State v. Marcantel, 388 So.2d 383 (1980).

State v. Mizell, 938 So.2d 712 (2006).

State v. Moody, 38 So.3d 451 (2010).

State v. Morgan, 315 So.2d 632 (1975).

State v. Neal, 275 So.2d 765 (1973).

State v. Regis, 25 Sp.3d 183 (2009).

State v. Rollins, 302 So.2d 288 (1974).

State v. Ross, 320 So.2d 177 (1975).

State v. Sanders, 539 So.2d 114 (1989).

State v. Schoonover, 252 La. 311 (1968).

State v. Shanks, 715 So.2d 157 (1998).

State v. Silverman, 148 Ore. 296; 36 P.2d 34 (1934).

State v. Simmons, 414 So.2d 705 (1982).

State v. Smith, 20 So.3d 501 (2009).

State v. Strickland, 683 So.2d 218 (1996).

State v. Trull, 147 La. 444 (1920).

State v. Vial, 153 La. 883 (1923).

State v. White, 254 La. 389 (1969).

State v. Williams, 326 So.2d 815 (1976).

State v. Williams, 747 So.2d 1256 (1999).

Swann v. Charlotte-Mecklenburg Board of Education, 402 US 1 (1971).

Thompson v. Utah, 170 US 343 (1898).

Trull. State v. Wooten, 136 La. 560 (1915).

US ex rel. White v. Henderson, 461 F.2d 657 (CA5 [La.] 1972).

Williams v. Florida, 399 US 78 (1970).

ADDITIONAL COURT DOCUMENTS

"Brief *Amicus Curiae* of the Charles Hamilton Houston Institute for Race and Justice, the National Association of Criminal Defense Lawyers, and the Louisiana Association of Criminal Defense Lawyers." *Bowen v. Oregon,* Supreme Court of the United States (May Term, 2009, No. 08–1117), 9–14.

"Brief for the Petitioners, On Writ of Certiorari to the Supreme Court of Louisiana." *Burch v. Louisiana,* Supreme Court of the United States (October Term, 1978, No. 78–90), 3.

"Brief of *Amicus Curiae* the Houston Institute for Race and Justice in Support of Petitioner." *Lee v. Louisiana,* Supreme Court of the United States (July Term, 2008, No. 07–1523), 10–15.

"Conference of March 5, 1971 (Notes of Douglas/Brennan)." *Johnson v. Louisiana,* 406 US 35 (1972), law2.umkc.edu/faculty/projects/ftrials/conlaw/johnson-conf.html (accessed 27 December 2011).

"On Petition for a Writ of Certiorari to the Louisiana Court of Appeal, First Circuit." *Lee v. Louisiana,* Supreme Court of the United States (July Term, 2008, No. 07–1523), 2–3.

"Petitioner Harry Morgan Cooper, Jr., Indictment, Filed August 12, 1968." *Apo-*

daca v. Oregon, Supreme Court of the United States (October Term, 1970, No. 5338, On Writ of Certiorari to the Court of Appeals of Oregon), 10.

"Petitioner James Arnold Madden, Indictment, Filed September 17, 1968." *Apodaca v. Oregon,* Supreme Court of the United States (October Term, 1970, No. 5338, On Writ of Certiorari to the Court of Appeals of Oregon), 16.

"Petitioner Robert Apodaca, Indictment, Filed September 17, 1968." *Apodaca v. Oregon,* Supreme Court of the United States (October Term, 1970, No. 5338, On Writ of Certiorari to the Court of Appeals of Oregon), 3.

"Record from the Criminal District Court, Parish of Orleans, Section 'G' Number 202–984: Amendment to motion to suppress the evidence, filed March 20, 1968." *Johnson v. Louisiana,* Supreme Court of the United States (October Term, 1970, No. 5161, Appendix, 10–11.

"Record from the Criminal District Court, Parish of Orleans, Section 'G' Number 202–984: Bill of Exceptions No. 24, filed September 9, 1968." *Johnson v. Louisiana,* Supreme Court of the United States (October Term, 1970, No. 5161, Appendix), 30–32.

"Record from the Criminal District Court, Parish of Orleans, Section 'G' Number 202–984: Motion to quash, filed March 13, 1968." *Johnson v. Louisiana,* Supreme Court of the United States. October Term, 1970, No. 5161, Appendix, 7–9.

"Record from the Criminal District Court, Parish of Orleans, Section 'G' Number 202–984: Supplemental and Amended Motion in Arrest of Judgment." *Johnson v. Louisiana,* Supreme Court of the United States (October Term, 1970, No. 5161, Appendix), 13.

"Record from the Criminal District Court, Parish of Orleans, Section 'G' Number 202–984: Transcript of testimony of March 18, 1968 & May 15, 1968, Testimony of Eugene Frischertz." *Johnson v. Louisiana,* Supreme Court of the United States. October Term, 1970, No. 5161, Appendix, 66–93.

"Record from the Criminal District Court, Parish of Orleans, Section 'G' Number 202–984: Transcript of testimony of March 18, 1968 & May 15, 1968, Testimony of Frank T. Johnson." *Johnson v. Louisiana,* Supreme Court of the United States. October Term, 1970, No. 5161, Appendix, 35–50.

GOVERNMENT DOCUMENTS

Acts Passed by the General Assembly of the State of Louisiana at the Regular Session Begun and Held in the City of New Orleans on the Twelfth Day of January, 1880. New Orleans: New Orleans Daily Democrat, 1880.

Acts Passed by the General Assembly of the State of Louisiana, at the Regular Session, Begun and Held at the City of Baton Rouge on the Eighth Day of May, AD 1882. Baton Rouge: Leon Jastremski, 1882.

Acts Passed by the General Assembly of the State of Louisiana, at the Regular Session, Begun and Held at the City of Baton Rouge, on the Tenth Day of May, AD 1886. Baton Rouge: Leon Jastremski, 1886.

Acts Passed by the General Assembly of the State of Louisiana, at the Regular Session Begun and Held at the City of Baton Rouge, on the Twelfth Day of May, 1890. New Orleans: Ernest Marchand, 1890.

Acts Passed by the General Assembly of the State of Louisiana at the Regular Session Begun and Held in the City of Baton Rouge, on the Fourteenth Day of May, 1894. New Orleans: Ernest Marchand, 1894.

Acts Passed by the General Assembly of the State of Louisiana at the Regular Session, Begun and Held in the City of Baton Rouge on the Eleventh Day of May, 1896. Baton Rouge: Advocate, 1896.

Acts Passed by the Legislature of the State of Louisiana, 1926. Baton Rouge: Secretary of State, 1926.

The Code of Criminal Procedure for the State of Louisiana. Baton Rouge: Ramires-Jones Printing, 1928.

The Code of Practice of the State of Louisiana. New Orleans: The Republican, 1870.

"Committee on Bill of Rights and Elections, August 24, 1973, Staff Memorandum No. 52." *Records of the Louisiana Constitutional Convention of 1973: Committee Documents.* Baton Rouge: Louisiana Constitutional Convention Records Committee, 1974. Vol. 10: 128.

"Constitution, Article 1, § 14 to 27." *West's Louisiana Statutes Annotated.* St. Paul, MN: Thompson/West, 2006. Vol. 1B: 215–18.

Constitution of Oregon.

"Criminal Justice Act 1967." 1967. Chap. 80, www.legislation.gov.uk/ukpga/1967/80.

Louisiana Constitution of 1974.

Louisiana Revised Statutes of 1950. Vol. 2: *Titles 13–21.* Baton Rouge: Secretary of State, 1950, 525–26.

McEnany, Arthur E. *Membership in the Louisiana Senate, 1880–2012.* Baton Rouge: Louisiana State Senate, 2008.

Official Journal of the Proceedings of the Constitutional Convention of the State of Louisiana. New Orleans: H. J. Hearsey, 1898.

Official Journal of the Proceedings of the Constitutional Convention of the State of Louisiana. New Orleans: Ramires-Jones Printing, 1913.

Official Journal of the Proceedings of the Constitutional Convention of the State of Louisiana. New Orleans: Ramires-Jones Printing, 1921.

Official Journal of the Proceedings of the Constitutional Convention of 1973 of the State of Louisiana. Baton Rouge: Secretary of State, 1973.

Official Journal of the Proceedings of the House of Representatives of the State of Louisiana, at the Regular Session, Begun and Held in New Orleans, January 12, 1880. New Orleans: New Orleans Democrat Office, 1880.

Official Journal of the Proceedings of the Senate of the State of Louisiana, at the Regular Session, Begun and Held in New Orleans, January 12, 1880. New Orleans: New Orleans Democrat Office, 1880.

Poynter, David R. *Membership in the Louisiana House of Representatives, 1812–2012.* Baton Rouge: Legislative Research Library, Louisiana House of Representatives, 2011.

Robinson, M. M. *Digest of the Penal Law of the State of Louisiana, Analytically Arranged.* New Orleans: M. M. Robinson, 1841.

State of Louisiana, Acts of the Legislature. Vol. 2: *Regular Session 1966—Code of Criminal Procedure.* Baton Rouge: Secretary of State, 1966.

U.S. Constitution.

West's Louisiana Statutes Annotated: Code of Criminal Procedure, Articles 782 to 830. St. Paul: West Group, 1998. Vol. 2B.

West's Louisiana Statutes Annotated: Treaties and Organic Laws, Early Constitutions, U.S. Constitution and Index. St. Paul, MN: West Group, 1977. Vol. 3.

ARCHIVAL MATERIAL

Alexander Blanche Papers. W-48 # 3342, folder 1, Hill Memorial Library Special Collections, Louisiana State University, Baton Rouge.

Dr. Emmett Asseff Constitutional Convention '72 Papers. #241, Noel Memorial Library Archives and Special Collections, Louisiana State University–Shreveport.

John Marshall Harlan Papers, 1884–1972 (bulk 1936–71). Finding Aid MC071, Mudd Manuscript Library, Princeton University, Princeton, NJ.

"James (Samuel L.) Letter. # 2946, December 10, 1870." Ms. 2946, Louisiana and Lower Mississippi Valley Collections, Hill Memorial Library Special Collections, Louisiana State University, Baton Rouge.

George Rennar Collection. Mss 2918, Oregon Historical Society, Portland, Oregon.

ADDITIONAL PRIMARY SOURCES

Adams, St. Clair. "Hints on Reforms in Louisiana Criminal Procedure." *Loyola Law Journal* 2 (November 1920): 7–16.

Deslatte, Melinda. "Effort to end Louisiana split-jury law gets bipartisan push," Associated Press, 30 July 2018, https://apnews.com/9ff0c873059b43129871b806e1e081b9, accessed 1 August 2018.

Livingston, Edward. *A System of Penal Law, for the State of Louisiana.* 1833. Union, NJ: Lawbook Exchange, 1999.

Powell, J. C. *The American Siberia, or Fourteen Years' Experience in a Southern Convict Camp.* Chicago: H. J. Smith & Co., 1891.

"Races: Battle in Baton Rouge," *Time,* 24 January 1972, 22.

Unanimous Jury Coalition website, https://www.unanimousjury.org/

Wilson, Conrad. "After Louisiana Vote, Oregon Lawmakers Want To Scrap Non-Unanimous Jury Law," Oregon Public Broadcasting, 7 November 2018, https://www.opb.org/news/article/non-unanimous-jury-oregon-jim-crow-lousiana-vote/?utm_campaign=Crushin5&utm_source=Twitter&utm_medium=social&fbclid=IwAR2_5yooaJXZpf9UGHT2aqKlynxvomxZdr9266C2OzPrPFcd1Cr1mvk6HL4, accessed 16 November 2018.

SECONDARY SOURCES

Alexander, Michelle. *The New Jim Crow: Mass Incarceration in the Age of Colorblindness.* New York: The New Press, 2010.

Allen-Bell, Angela A. "How the Narrative about Louisiana's Non-Unanimous Criminal Jury System Because Person of Interest in the Case against Justice in the Deep South," *Mercer Law Review* 67 (Spring 2016): 585–616.

Amar, Akhil Reed. "Reinventing Juries: Ten Suggested Reforms." *UC Davis Law Review* 28 (Summer 1995): 1169–94.

Ball, Howard. *Of Power and Right: Hugo Black, William O. Douglas, and America's Constitutional Revolution.* New York: Oxford University Press, 1992.

Baugh, Joyce A. *The Detroit School Busing Case: Milliken v. Bradley and the Controversy Over Desegregation.* Lawrence: University Press of Kansas, 2011.

Beath, Robert Burns. *History of the Grand Army of the Republic.* New Orleans: Willis McDonald & Co., 1888.

Bennett, Dale E. "Blind Spots In the Louisiana Code of Criminal Procedure." *Louisiana Bar Journal* 1 (April 1954): 62–72.

———. "Louisiana Criminal Procedure—A Critical Appraisal." *Louisiana Law Review* 14 (December 1953): 11–35.

Bigelow, William, and Norman Diamond. "Agitate, Educate, Organize: Portland, 1934." *Oregon Historical Quarterly* 89 (Spring 1988): 4–29.

Blackmon, Douglas A. *Slavery by Another Name: The Re-Enslavement of Black Americans from the Civil War to World War II.* New York: Anchor, 2009.

Buchwalter, James L. "Construction and Application of Sixth Amendment Right to Trial by Jury—Supreme Court Cases." 6 A.L.R. Fed. 2d 213 (2005), 213–78.

California District Attorneys Association. *Non-Unanimous Jury Verdicts: A Necessary Criminal Justice Reform.* Sacramento: California District Attorneys Association, 1995.

Carleton, Mark T. *Politics and Punishment: The History of the Louisiana State Penal System.* Baton Rouge: Louisiana State University Press, 1971.

———. "The Politics of the Convict Lease System in Louisiana: 1868–1901." *Louisiana History* 8 (Winter 1967): 5–25.

Coppolo, George, and Kevin McCarthy. "Crime Rate and Conviction Rates Broken Down by Race." OLR Research Report, Office of Legislative Research, Connecticut General Assembly, 18 January 2008, www.cga.ct.gov/2008/rpt/2008-R-0008.htm (accessed 10 December 2013).

Corr, John Bernard. "Retroactivity: A Study in Supreme Court Doctrine 'As Applied.'" *North Carolina Law Review* 61 (1982–83): 745–97.

Coughlan, Peter J. "In Defense of Unanimous Jury Verdicts: Mistrials, Communication, and Strategic Voting." *American Political Science Review* 94 (June 2000): 375–93.

Davies, Wallace E. "The Problem of Race Segregation in the Grand Army of the Republic." *Journal of Southern History* 13 (August 1947): 354–72.

Devine, Dennis J., Laura D. Clayton, Benjamin B. Dunford, Rasmy Seying, and Jennifer Pryce. "Jury Decision Making: 45 Years of Empirical Research on Deliberating Groups." *Psychology, Public Policy, and Law* 7 (March 2000): 622–727.

Dictionary of Louisiana Biography. Lafayette: Louisiana Historical Association, 2008. www.lahistory.org/site16.php.

Dominguez, Victoria R. *White by Definition: Social Classification in Creole Louisiana.* New Brunswick, NJ: Rutgers University Press, 1986.

Eisenberg, Ellen. "Transplanted to the Rose City: The Creation of East European Jewish Community in Portland, Oregon." *Journal of American Ethnic History* 19 (Spring 2000): 82–97.

Fairclough, Adam. *Race & Democracy: The Civil Rights Struggle in Louisiana, 1915–1972.* Athens: University of Georgia Press, 1995.

Formisano, Ronald P. *Boston Against Busing: Race, Class, and Ethnicity in the 1960s and 1970s.* 2nd ed. Chapel Hill: University of North Carolina Press, 2003.

Foster, Burk. "Plantation Days at Angola: Major James and the Origins of Modern Corrections in Louisiana." In *The Wall Is Strong: Corrections in Louisiana,* ed. Burk Foster, Wilbert Rideau, and Douglas Dennis, 1–5. 3rd ed. Lafayette: Center for Louisiana Studies, 1995.

"George Perkins." The Governor's Gallery, State Library of California. governors. library.ca.gov/14-Perkins.html.

Gill, James. *Lords of Misrule: Mardi Gras and the Politics of Race in New Orleans.* Oxford: University Press of Mississippi, 1997.

Glasser, Michael H. "Letting the Supermajority Rule: Nonunanimous Jury Verdicts In Criminal Trials." *Florida State University Law Review* 24 (Spring 1997): 659–77.

Hair, William Ivy. "Bourbon Democracy." In *The Louisiana Purchase Bicentennial Series in Louisiana History.* Vol. 7: *Louisiana Politics and the Paradoxes of Reaction and Reform, 1877–1928,* ed. Matthew J. Scott, 115–41. Lafayette: University of Louisiana Press, 2000.

Hans, Valerie P., and Neil Vidmar. *Judging the Jury.* Cambridge, MA: Perseus Books, 1886.

Haralson, William. "Unanimous Jury Verdicts in Criminal Cases." *Mississippi Law Journal* 21, no. 3 (1950): 185–91.

Hargrave, Lee. "Declaration of Rights of Louisiana Constitution of 1974." *Louisiana Law Review* 35 (Fall 1974): 1–67.

Harlan, Ann Mays. "Community House, Parks, Recreation, Pretty Flowers, and Minden Highways: The Minden Male Academy." *Memories of Minden,* www .mindenmemories.org/Parks%20and%20Highways.htm (accessed 5 December 2013).

Hastie, Reid, Steven D. Penrod, and Nancy Pennington. *Inside the Jury.* Union, NJ: Lawbook Exchange, 2002.

Hatcher, William. *Edward Livingston: Jeffersonian Republican and Jacksonian Democrat.* Baton Rouge: Louisiana State University Press, 1940.

Holdsworth, William S. *A History of English Law.* 3rd ed. Boston: Little, Brown, and Co., 1922. Vol. 1.

Holsinger, M. Paul. "The Oregon School Bill Controversy 1922–1925." *Pacific Historical Review* 37 (August 1968): 327–41.

Hunter, Margo. "Improving the Jury System: Nonunanimous Verdicts." *Public Law Research Institute*. www.uchastings.edu/public-law/plri/spr96tex/juryuna.html (accessed 2 January 2012).

"Initiative, Referendum and Recall: 1930–1936." *Oregon Blue Book*. Office of the Secretary of State. bluebook.state.or.us/state/elections/elections15.htm (accessed 2 December 2013).

Johnson, J. H. "Criminal Law—Jury—Unanimous Jury Verdict Is Not Constitutionally Required in State Criminal Cases." *Wisconsin Law Review* 3 (1978): 926–33.

Kachmar, James. "Silencing the Minority: Permitting Nonunanimous Jury Verdicts in Criminal Trials." *Pacific Law Journal* (Fall 1996): 273–310.

Kalven, Harry, and Hans Zeisel. *The American Jury*. New York: Little, Brown, 1966.

Kaplan, Aliza B. and Amy Saack. "Overturning *Apodaca v. Oregon* Should Be Easy: Nonunanimous Jury Verdicts in Criminal Cases Undermine the Credibility of Our Justice System," *Oregon Law Review* 95 (No. 1 2016): 1–52.

Klastorin, Ted, and Kenneth S. Klein. "Do Diverse Juries Aid or Impede Justice?" *Wisconsin Law Review* 3 (1999): 553–69.

Lagarde, Richard L. "Right to Trial by Jury: New Guidelines for State Criminal Trial Juries." *Louisiana Law Review* 40, no. 3 (1980): 837–46.

Lassiter, Matthew D. *The Silent Majority: Suburban Politics in the Sunbelt South*. Princeton, NJ: Princeton University Press, 2007.

Lichtenstein, Alex. *Twice the Work of Free Labor: The Political Economy of Convict Labor in the New South*. New York: Verso Press, 1996.

Mancini, Matthew J. *One Dies, Get Another: Convict Leasing in the American South, 1866–1928*. Columbia: University of South Carolina Press, 1996.

Morano, Anthony A. "Historical Development of the Interrelationship of Unanimous Verdicts and Reasonable Doubt." *Valparaiso University Law Review* 10 (Winter 1976): 223–35.

Morehead, Jere W. "A 'Modest' Proposal for Jury Reform: The Elimination of Required Unanimous Jury Verdicts." *University of Kansas Law Review* 46 (June 1998): 933–45.

Moulder, Rebecca H. "Convicts as Capital: Thomas O'Conner and the Leases of the Tennessee Penitentiary System, 1871–1883." *East Tennessee Historical Society Publications* 48 (1976): 58–59.

Murrin, John M. "The Legal Transformation: The Bench and Bar of Eighteenth-Century Massachusetts." In *Colonial America: Essays in Politics and Social Development*, ed. Stanley N. Katz, 540–72. Boston: Little, Brown, and Co., 1971.

Mustafa, Susan D., Tony Clayton, and Sue Israel. *Blood Bath*. New York: Pinnacle, 2009.

Neilson, William S., and Harold Winter. "The Elimination of Hung Juries: Retrials and Nonunanimous Verdicts." *International Review of Law and Economics* 25, no. 1 (2005): 1–19.

Osher, Jeremy. "Jury Unanimity in California: Should It Stay or Should It Go?" *Loyola of Los Angeles Law Review* 3 (1996): 1319–70.

Perkins, A. E. "Some Negro Officers and Legislators in Louisiana." *Journal of Negro History* 14 (October 1929): 523–28.

Riordan, Kate. "Ten Angry Men: Unanimous Jury Verdicts In Criminal Trials and Incorporation After *McDonald*." *Journal of Criminal Law and Criminology* 101, no. 4 (2012): 1403–34.

Rosen, Jeffrey. "After 'One Angry Woman.'" *University of Chicago Legal Forum* 1998 (The Right to a Fair Trial 1998): 179–95.

Rothman, David J. *The Discovery of the Asylum: Order and Disorder in the New Republic.* Boston: Little, Brown, 1971.

Rothwax, Harold J. *Guilty: The Collapse of Criminal Justice.* New York: Random House, 1996.

Ryan, John V. "Less Than Unanimous Jury Verdicts in Criminal Trials." *Journal of Criminal Law, Criminology, and Police Science* 58 (June 1967): 211–17.

Saks, Michael J. "What Do Jury Experiments Tell Us About How Juries (Should) Make Decisions?" *Southern California Interdisciplinary Law Journal* 6, no. 1 (1997): 1–53.

Sanders, Mary E. "The Political Career of Jared Young Sanders, 1892–1912." MA thesis, Louisiana State University, 1955.

Satterfield, Kyle R. "Circumventing *Apodaca:* An Equal Protection Challenge to Nonunanimous Jury Verdicts in Louisiana," *Tulane Law Review* 90 (February 2016): 693–725.

Scott, Rebecca J. "'Stubborn and Disposed to Stand Their Ground': Black Militia, Sugar Workers and the Dynamics of Collective Action in the Louisiana Sugar Bowl, 1863–87." In *From Slavery to Emancipation in the Atlantic World,* ed. Sylvia Frey and Betty Wood, 103–26. Portland, OR: Frank Cass Publishers, 1999.

Slovenko, Ralph. "The Jury System in Louisiana Criminal Law." *Louisiana Law Review* 17 (June 1957): 655–729.

Smith, Douglas G. "Structural and Functional Aspects of the Jury: Comparative Analysis and Proposals for Reform." *Alabama Law Review* 48 (Winter 1997): 441–581.

Smith, Robert J. and Bidish J. Sarma. "How and Why Race Continues to Influence the Administration of Criminal Justice in Louisiana," *Louisiana Law Review* 72 (Winter 2012): 361–407.

Sommers, Samuel R. "On Racial Diversity and Group Decision Making: Identifying Multiple Effects of Racial Composition on Jury Deliberations." *Journal of Personality and Social Psychology* 90, no. 4 (2006): 597–612.

Taylor-Thompson, Kim. "Empty Votes in Jury Deliberations." *Harvard Law Review* 113 (April 2000): 1261–1320.

Thayer, James B. "The Jury and Its Development." *Harvard Law Review* 5 (February 1892): 295–319.

Valenti, Francis Paul. *The Portland Press, the Ku Klux Klan, and the Oregon Compulsory Education Bill: Editorial Treatment of Klan Themes in the Portland Press in 1922*. Seattle: University of Washington Press, 1993.

Walker-Dittman, Nathalie M. "Constitutional Criminal Procedure—Six-Member Juries Must Render Unanimous Verdicts in State Criminal Trials for Non-petty Offenses." *Tulane Law Review* 54 (June 1980): 1178–87.

Weeber, Stan. *In Search of Derrick Todd Lee: The Internet Social Movement That Made a Difference*. New York: University Press of America, 2007.

Wildenthal, Bryan H. "The Road to Twining: Reassessing the Disincorporation of the Bill of Rights." *Ohio State Law Journal* 61, no. 4 (2000): 1458–1537.

INDEX